MW00763108

A PRACTICAL
ENGLISH–CHINESE
LIBRARY OF
TRADITIONAL
CHINESE MEDICINE

PUBLISHING HOUSE OF
SHANGHAI UNIVERSITY OF
TRADITIONAL
CHINESE MEDICINE

EDITOR–IN–CHIEF ZHANG ENQIN

CLINIC OF TRADITIONAL (I) CHINESE MEDICINE

Written by

Zhang Enqin, Zhang Jidong, Liu Zhigang
Jin Weixin, Sun Shushan, Guo Xiaoyue

Translated by

Wang Jizhou, Lian Fang, Dang Yi

Revised by Wei Jiwu, Yu Wenping, Peng Wancheng

Chiefly Translated by Zuo Lianjun, Gao Yan, Zhang Yu
Wang Ziwei

Revised by Li Yulin, Zhang Enqin, Xiao Gong

英汉对照
实用中医文库

主　编　张恩勤

·上册 **中医**
临床各科

编译	张恩勤	张继东	刘治刚
	金维新	孙树山	郭孝月
	王济周	连　方	党　毅
审校	隗继武	于文平	彭万程
主译	左连君	高　艳	张玉玺	王紫薇
审校	李玉麟	张恩勤	肖　琪

上海中医药大学出版社

THE GUIDING COMMITTEE
OF THE LIBRARY

Director Hu Ximing

Deputy Directors Wang Lei Yan Shiyun

Members (in the order of the number of Chinese strokes in the surnames)

Wan Deguang	Wang Yongyan	Lu Chengzhi	Lü Tongjie
Sun Guojie	Liu Chonggang	Liu Mingde	Li Keshao
Su Shisheng	Zhang Zhiyuan	Zhang Canjia	Zhang Minghe
Zhang Qiwen	Zhang Zhenyu	Chen Keji	Chen Weiyang
Zou Ling	Qiu Maoliang	Qiu Dewen	Zhou Fengwu
Zhou Zhongying	Zhou Ciqing	Shang Zhichang	Xiang Ping
Xu Guoqian	Gao Chuantang	Cui Mingxiu	Huang Wenxing
Huang Xiaokai	Huang Jiade		

CHIEF AUTHORS OF THE LIBRARY

Advisors Dong Jianhua Liu Duzhou Deng Tietao

Editor − in − Chief Zhang Enqin

Associate Editors − in − Chief of TCM (in the order of the number of Chinese strokes in the surnames)

Shi Lanhua	Zhang Wengao	Zhang Zhigang	Zhang Jidong
Li Dunqing	Zhao Chunxiu	Dang Yi	Wei Jiwu

Associate Editors − in − Chief of English (in the order of the number of Chinese strokes in the surnames)

Yu Wenping	Wang Zhikui	Li Yulin	Li Yanfu
Xiao Gong	Zhang Minglun	Hou Mingjun	Wen Hongrui

THE EDITING AND TRANSLATING
COMMITTEE OF THE LIBRARY

Director   Zou Jilong

Deputy Directors   (in the order of the number of Chinese strokes in the surnames)

Tian Daihua	Cong Laiting	Sun Xigang	Wu Guanghua
Chen Guangzhen	Jing Jie	Gao Heting	Cao Yixun
Cheng Yichun	Cai Jianqian		

Members   (in the order of the number of Chinese strokes in the surnames)

Yu Shufang	Wang Jun	Wang Min	Wang Qi
Wang Chenying	Wang Baoxiang	Wang Guocai	Wang Ziwei
Yin Hongan	Tai Shuren	Mao Chun	Zuo Lianjun
Shi Renhua	Mi Li	Bi Yongsheng	Chi Yongli
Bao Xianmin	Lü Jianping	Qu Jingfeng	Zhu Xiaoming
Qiao Mingqi	Sun Hua	Sun Xiao	Sun Guangren
Sun Hengshan	Liu Wenjing	Liu Zhongyuan	Liu Rongyuan
Liu Jiayi	Liu Peilu	Jiang Xiuzheng	Mu Junzheng
Shi Xiuqin	Yang Min	Li Yan	Li Wei
Li Changsheng	Li Xuezhen	Li Shaoqing	Li Qingxiu
Zhang Shaohua	Zhang Yuxi	Zhang Qingling	Zhang Zhongtian
Zhang Xuezeng	Zhang Shengxin	Jin Ruhua	Zheng Yi
Zheng Yanchen	Zheng Shouzeng	Zhao Shili	Zhao Laixi
Zhao Lanfeng	Hu Zhaoyun	Jiang Longsheng	Jiang Xueting
Jiang Jingxian	Shao Guanyong	Gao Yan	Gao Yi
Gao Hongren	Gao Yongli	Nie Qingxi	Xia Yunbin
Shang Zhenyong	Liang Shuqun	Yan Ping	Cui Hongjiang
Cui Jipin	Cao Zhiqun	Dong Xinhua	Dong Xuemei
Han Yan	Han Yufang	Xie Guangfa	

Director of the Committee Office   Tai Shuren

《英汉对照实用中医文库》编译委员会

Preface

The books in series, entitled *"A Practical English-Chinese Library of Traditional Chinese Medicine"*, are edited with a view to disseminating the theory and knowledge of traditional Chinese medicine (TCM) across the world, promoting academic exchanges on medical science between China and other countries, and meeting with the ever-increasing international interest in TCM, so as to make it serve the interests of all nations and benefit entire mankind. This library is the first of its kind in China.

The library is composed of 12 books: *Basic Theory of TCM* (in two volumes), *Diagnostics of TCM, The Chinese Materia Medica, Prescriptions of TCM, Clinic of TCM* (in two volumes), *Health Preservation and Rehabilitation, Chinese Acupuncture and Moxibustion, Chinese Massage, Chinese Medicated Diet* and *Chinese Qigong.* The two other English-Chinese books —— *Rare Chinese Materia Medica* and *Highly Efficacious Chinese Patent Medicines* —— chiefly edited by me are also published simultaneously along with this library.

The authors and editors of the series strive to abide by the following principles: maintaining the systematism, integrity, practicability and adaptability in terms of TCM theory; paying full attention to the organic connection between basic theory and clinical treatment, taking in the available results of scientific researches carried out at home and abroad in the field of TCM; and being concise, precise, and easy to understand in the Chinese version, and correct and fluent in the English one. Some of the books mentioned above contain figures and coloured photos. It is our sincere hope that the books will turn out to be good teachers and reliable friends of those abroad who have begun to learn and practise TCM and Chinese, and provide help for those at home who wish to study TCM documents in English.

The component books of this library are written, translated, and edited through joint efforts of professors, associate professors, lecturers and medical research workers from Shandong TCM College and its affiliated hospital, Shandong Medical University and its affiliated hospital, Shandong University, Shandong Teachers Training University, Shandong Medical Academy, Shandong Provincial Anti-epidemic Station, China Academy of TCM, Nanjing TCM College, Shanghai TCM College, Beijing TCM College, etc.

In order to ensure that the present library is of good quality, we have sent its Chinese version for revision to Professor Zhou Fengwu, Professor Li Keshao who was once my tutor when I was a postgraduate student, Professor Xu Guoqian and Professor Zhang Zhenyu at Shandong TCM College, Professor Qiu Maoliang at Nanjing TCM College, and Professor Lu Tongjie, director of the Affiliated Hospital of Shandong TCM College; and the English version for proofreading to Professor Huang Xiaokai of Beijing Medical University, Professor Lu Chengzhi, head of the Foreign Languages Department of Shandong Medical University, Professor Huang Jiade of Shandong University, Mr. Huang Wenxing,

2

professor of pharmacology, Mme. Zou Ling, professor of gynecology and obstetrics, both working in Shandong Medical University, and our foreign friends, Ms. Beth Hocks, Australian teacher of English, Mr. Howard G. Adams, American teacher of English, and some others working in Jinan.

I am deeply indebted to Mr. Li Dichen, Editor-in-Chief of Publishing House of Shanghai TCM College, and his colleagues, Mme. Xu Ping, director of the Editorial Department, and Mr. Yao Yong, responsible editor, for their advice about drawing up an outline for compiling the library to ensure a success of it; to Mr. Chen Keji, professor of China Academy of TCM and advisor on traditional medicine to WHO, Professor Zhang Zhiyuan and Associate Professor Shao Guanyong of Shandong TCM College, Mr. Liu Chonggang, deputy head of the Yellow River Publishing House, for their valuable, instructive suggestions; and to responsible members at various levels, such as Mr. Hu Ximing, Chairman of the World Acupuncture and Moxibustion Association, vice-minister of the Ministry of Public Health and chief of the Administrative Bureau of TCM and Pharmacy of the People's Republic of China, Mr. Zou Jilong, president of Shandong TCM College, Mr. Yan Shiyun, vice-president of Shanghai TCM College, Mr. Gao Heting, president of Beijing TCM College, Mr. Xiang Ping, vice-president of Nanjing TCM College, and Mr. Shang Zhichang, president of Henan TCM College for their warm encouragement and indispensable support as well as their personal participation in compiling and checking the books.

TCM, which dates back to ancient times, has a unique and profound theoretical system. The greater part of its terminology has particular denotations, and is matter-of-factly difficult to understand and translate. Inaccuracies in the library, therefore, are unavoidable. I hope that my friends in the TCM circle will oblige me with timely corrections.

May TCM spread all over the world and everyone under the heaven enjoy a long happy life.

May 20th, 1988 Dr. Zhang Enqin

> Editor-in-Chief of *A Practical English-Chinese Library of Traditional Chinese Medicine,* Director of the Advanced Studies Department of Shandong TCM College

前　言

为扩大中医学在国际上的影响，促进中外医学学术交流，适应国外日趋发展的"中医热"形势，使传统的中医学走向世界，造福人类，我们编写了这套《英汉对照实用中医文库》。在国内，这尚属首部。

该文库包括《中医基础理论》（上、下册）、《中医诊断学》、《中药学》、《方剂学》、《中医临床各科》（上、下册）、《中医养生康复学》、《中国针灸》、《中国推拿》、《中国药膳》和《中国气功》，共十二个分册。与《文库》同时出版的还有其配套书——英汉对照《中国名贵药材》和《中国名优中成药》。

《英汉对照实用中医文库》的编译宗旨是：在理论上，努力保持中医学体系的系统性、完整性，突出实用性和针对性；在内容上，充分注意基础理论与临床治疗的有机联系，汲取国内外已公布的科研成果，以反映当代中医学术水平；在文字上，力求中文简明扼要，通俗易懂，译文准确流畅，并配有图表、彩照。我们竭诚希望《英汉对照实用中医文库》能成为国外读者学习中医、汉语的良师益友，同时也为国内读者学习中医专业英语提供帮助。

负责文库编写、翻译和审校的主要是山东中医学院及其附属医院、山东医科大学及其附属医院、山东大学、山东师范大学、山东省医学科学院、山东省卫生防疫站、中国中医研究院、南京中医学院、上海中医学院和北京中医学院等单位的部分教授、副教授、讲师和科研人员。

为确保文库质量，各分册中文稿还先后承蒙山东中医学院周凤梧教授、李克绍教授、徐国仟教授、张珍玉教授，南京中医学院邱茂良教授，山东中医学院附属医院院长吕同杰教授等审阅；英文稿先后承蒙北京医科大学英语教研室黄孝楷教授，山东医科大学英语教研室主任卢承志教授，山东大学外文系黄嘉德教授，山东医科大学药理教研室黄文兴教授、妇产科教研室邹玲教授以及澳大利亚籍教师 Beth Hocks 女士和美籍教师 Howard G. Adams 先生等审阅。

上海中医学院出版社总编辑李迪臣、编辑部主任徐平和责任编辑姚勇，亲自帮助我们修订编写大纲，指导编译工作；世界卫生组织传统医学顾问、中国中医研究院陈可冀教授，山东中医学院张志远教授、邵冠勇副教授，黄河出版社副社长刘崇刚，也为本文库的编译工作提出了许多宝贵的指导性意见；编译工作还得到了各级领导的支持和帮助，世界针灸学会联合会主席、中华人民共和国卫生部副部长兼国家中医药管理局局长胡熙明先生，山东中医学院院长邹积隆先生，上海中医学院副院长严世芸先生，北京中医学院院长高鹤亭先生，南京中医学院副院长项平先生和河南中医学院院长尚炽昌先生等，亲自参加编审并给予指导，在此一并表示衷心感谢！

由于中医学源远流长，其理论体系独特，不少名词术语深奥难解，译成英文，难度较大。故书中错误、欠妥之处在所难免，敬希国内外同道指正。

愿中医流传世界，求普天下人健康长寿。

主编　张恩勤
1988年5月20日

CONTENTS

目　　录

Clinic of Traditional Chinese Medicine (I)

中医临床各科(上)

Chapter One

COMMON INTERNAL DISEASES

Section 1
Influenza

Influenza, an infectious disease of respiratory tract, is caused by influenza viruses. The viruses may be divided into three types, namely A, B and C. The disease has extremely strong infectivity, transmitted by means of droplets. People are very susceptible to influenza and sometimes pandemics may happen over the world. Although influenza may occur at all seasons, it tends to appear during winter and spring. This disease, in TCM (Traditional Chinese Medicine) is called *"shixing ganmao"* (influenza).

MAIN POINTS OF DIAGNOSIS

1. A large number of patients are affected within a short period with clinical features of fever, headache and myalgia.

2. Clinical features

(1) The onset of the disease is abrupt, with marked general toxemic symptoms such as chill, fever, headache, myalgia, weakness, etc.

(2) Symptoms referable to the respiratory tract such as stuffy nose, rhinorrhea, sore throat and dry cough are usually mild. In some cases, symptoms of the digestive tract such as loss of appetite, nausea, vomiting, abdominal pain and diarrhea may be present.

(3) High fever, chest pain, cough, bloody sputum, dyspnea and even coma may occur in severe cases.

第 一 章

内科常见疾病

第一节　流行性感冒

流行性感冒是由流感病毒所引起的一种呼吸道传染病。其病毒可分为甲、乙、丙三型。本病传染性极强，经飞沫传播，人群普遍易感，甚至造成世界性大流行。一年四季均可发病，但以冬春为多。中医称之为"时行感冒"。

【诊断要点】

1．短时间内在一地区出现大量患者，以发热、头痛、周身肌肉酸痛为特点。

2．临床特点

（1）起病急，有明显全身中毒症状，如畏寒、发热、头痛、周身肌肉酸痛和软弱乏力等。

（2）上呼吸道症状较轻微，如鼻塞、流涕、咽痛、干咳，亦可有食欲不振、恶心、呕吐、腹痛、腹泻等消化道症状。

（3）病情严重者可有高热、胸痛、咳嗽、咳血痰、呼吸困难，甚至昏迷和抽搐。

(4) Physical examination reveals acutely ill complexion and malar flush with congestion of conjunctival and nasopharyngeal mucosa. In patients with influenzal pneumonia or secondary bacterial pneumonia, the respiratory sounds are diminished. Diffuse moist rales may be heard over the lung fields.

3. Laboratory tests show a decreased leukocyte count and the ratio of neutrophils to leukocytes, while the lymphocytes count may be relatively elevated. Mucosal imprint from inferior nasal conchae may show inclusions of influenza virus. This is valuable for the early diagnosis. In serological examinations, hemagglutination inhibition test or complement fixation test can be used for the diagnosis. Viral isolation is helpful in confirming the type of pathogen.

DIFFERENTIATION AND TREATMENT OF COMMON SYNDROMES

1. Wind-cold Syndrome

Main Symptoms and Signs: Severe aversion to cold, slight fever, absence of sweat, headache, aching pain of extremities, stuffy nose with nasal discharge, cough with thin sputum, thin and whitish coating of tongue, floating and tight pulse.

Therapeutic Principle: Relieving exterior syndrome with the drugs pungent in flavor and warm in property, ventilating the lung and expelling pathogenic cold.

Recipe: Modified Antiphlogistic Powder of Schizonepeta and Ledebouriella.

schizonepeta, *Herba Schizonepetae*   10g
ledebouriella root, *Radix Ledebouriellae*   10g
notopterygium root, *Rhizoma Seu Radix Notopterygii*   10g
bupleurum root, *Radix Bupleuri*   10g
peucedanum root, *Radix Peucedani*   10g
perilla leaf, *Folium Perillae*   10g
platycodon root, *Radix Platycodi*   10g
fresh ginger, *Rhizoma Zingiberis Recens*   3 pieces

All the above drugs are to be decocted in water for oral

（4）体检可见患者急性病容、面颊潮红、眼结膜充血、鼻咽部粘膜充血等。流感性肺炎或并发细菌性肺炎者，呼吸音减弱，两肺可闻及弥漫性湿罗音。

3．血化验见白细胞总数和中性粒细胞比例减少，淋巴细胞则相对增多。下鼻甲粘膜印片可查见流感病毒包涵体，对早期诊断有价值。血清学检查可做血凝抑制试验或补体结合试验，以协助诊断。病毒分离对确诊病原体类型有帮助。

【辨证论治】

1．风寒

主证：恶寒重，发热轻，无汗，头痛，四肢酸痛，鼻塞流涕，咳嗽痰稀，舌苔薄白，脉浮紧。

治则：辛温解表，宣肺散寒。

处方：荆防败毒散加减。

荆芥10克，防风10克，羌活10克，柴胡10克，前胡10克，苏

administration.*

Moreover, supplementary drugs should be added with emphasis on certain symptoms: 10 grams of dahurian angelica root (*Radix Angelicae Dahuricae*) and 10 grams of chuanxiong rhizome (*Rhizoma Ligustici Chuanxiong*) are used to treat severe headache; bupleurum root (*Radix Bupleuri*) added to 12 grams and 6 grams of peppermint (*Herba Menthae*) for the case with high fever; 12 grams of notopterygium root (*Rhizoma seu Radix Notepterygii*) and 9 grams of pubescent angelica root (*Radix Angelicae Pubescentis*) or Decoction of Notopterygium for Rheumatism is used instead for exhibiting of more symptoms and signs of exterior dampness; If the case is complicated with exterior syndrome of excess characterized by no sweating, headache and pantalgia, severe aversion to cold, Ephedra Decoction is preferred; If the case is manifested as exterior deficiency with sweating, aversion to wind, slight fever, stuffy nose and retching, Cinnamon Twig Decoction is recommended (All the recipes mentioned above are dealt with in detail in the book, **Prescriptions of TCM** in this Library).

2. Wind-heat Syndrome

Main Symptoms and Signs: Higher fever, slight aversion to cold, headache, sore throat with congestion, expectoration of yellowish sputum, thirst or with epistaxis, reddened tongue with thin and yellowish fur, floating and rapid pulse.

Therapeutic Principle: Relieving exterior syndrome with the drugs pungent in flavor and cool in property, promoting the dispersing function of the lung and clearing up pathogenic heat.

Recipe: Modified Powder of Lonicera and Forsythia.

---

*Generally, a decoction should be taken in two separate doses a day, one in the morning and the other in the evening. The whole course of treatment covers 3—6 successive days, or depends on the patient's condition. This principle is applicable to all the recipes that are mentioned in this book.

叶10克，桔梗10克，生姜3片。水煎服*。

头痛重者，加白芷10克，川芎10克；身热重者，加柴胡至12克，薄荷6克；表湿重者，加羌活至12克，独活9克，或改用羌活胜湿汤；表实无汗，头身疼痛，恶寒重者，改用麻黄汤；表虚有汗，淅淅恶风，翕翕发热，鼻鸣干呕者，改用桂枝汤（以上各方见本文库《方剂学》有关部分）。

2．风热

主证：发热重，微恶寒，头痛，咽喉红痛，咳吐黄痰，口渴，或有鼻衄，舌质红，苔薄黄，脉浮数。

治则：辛凉解表，宣肺清热。

处方：银翘散加减。

---

*汤剂一般为1日1剂，早晚两次分服，连服3～6天为1疗程。亦可根据具体病情而定。以下皆同。

honeysuckle flower, *Flos Lonicerae*   30g
forsythia fruit, *Fructus Forsythiae*   15g
isatis root, *Radix Isatidis*   30g
pueraria root, *Radix Puerariae*   20g
mulberry leaf, *Folium Mori*   10g
chrysanthemum, *Flos Chrysanthemi*   10g
arctium fruit, *Fructus Arctii*   12g
lophatherum, *Herba Lophatheri*   10g
platycodon root, *Radix Platycodi*   10g

All the above drugs are to be decocted in water for oral administration.

In addition, the following ingredients should be included with respect to certain symptoms: 30 grams of gypsum (*Gypsum Fibrosum*) for the patients with high fever; 10 grams of bitter apricot kernel (*Semen Armeniacae Amarum*) and 10 grams of Sichuan fritillary bulb (*Bulbus Fritillariae Cirrhosae*) for patients with severe cough; 10 grams of subprostrate sophora root (*Radix Sophorae Subprostratae*) and 10 grams of scrophularia root (*Radix Scrophulariae*) for patients with severe sore throat; 30 grams of cogongrass rhizome (*Rhizoma Imperatae*) for patients with epistaxis; 12 grams of bupleurum root (*Radix Bupleuri*), 12 grams of scutellaria root (*Radix Scutellariae*) and 10 grams of pinellia tuber (*Rhizoma Pinelliae*) for patients with alternate spells of fever and chill, nausea and vomiting; 15 grams of astragalus root (*Radix Astragali seu Hedysari*) for patients with weak constitution and profuse sweat.

In cases complicated with summer-damp, 10 grams of elscholtzia (*Herba Elscholtziae seu Moslae*) and 20 grams of Six to One Powder (wrapped with cloth in decocting) should be administered; In cases of gastro-intestinal influenza pertaining to the syndrome of exterior cold and interior dampness, marked by fever, aversion to cold, vomiting, diarrhea, feeling of fullness and stuffiness in the chest and hypochondrium, thick and greasy fur of the tongue, Powder of Agastachis for Restoring Health is

银花30克，连翘15克，板蓝根30克，葛根20克，桑叶10克，

菊花10克，牛蒡子12克，竹叶10克，桔梗10克。水煎服。

发热甚者，加生石膏30克；咳嗽重者，加杏仁10克，川贝母

10克；咽痛重者，加山豆根10克，元参10克；鼻衄者，加白茅根

30克；往来寒热、恶心呕吐者，加柴胡12克，黄芩12克，半夏10

克；体虚汗多者，加黄芪15克。

夏令挟湿热者，加香薷10克，六一散20克(布包煎)；胃肠型

流感，证属表寒里湿，表现为发热、恶寒、呕吐、腹泻、胸胁满

preferred (Refer to relevant parts in the book, *Prescriptions of TCM* in this Library).

Section 2
Viral Hepatitis

Viral hepatitis, caused by hepatitis viruses, can be divided into three types: Type A, Type B and Non-A Non-B hepatitis. People are susceptible to the disease. Clinically, the major symptoms are poor appetite, hepatalgia and fatigue. Fever and jaundice may occur. Liver function test shows various degrees of hepatic damage. In TCM, this disease belongs to the categories of "*huang dan*" (jaundice), "*gan yu*" (stagnation of liver-*qi*), "*xie tong*" (hypochondriac pain) and "*zheng ji*" (mass in the abdomen).

MAIN POINTS OF DIAGNOSIS

1. Epidemiologic information: The epidemic condition and a history of close contact with a hepatitis patient, or a history of blood transfusion or receiving blood preparations or immunization injections should be noticed.

2. Clinical features

(1) The onset of the disease is insidious and slow. The patients often complain of fatigue and anorexia. Some have jaundice, but most of them belong to the types of non-icteric or mild hepatitis. Only ten percent of the patients have typical manifestations or jaundice.

(2) Patients with hepatitis A often manifest pyrexia, shorter course and rapid recovery; patients with hepatitis B usually have a chronic course and remain HB virus carriers for a long time. A few of them may progress to cirrhosis. The severity of the clinical features of Non-A Non-B hepatitis is between those of hepatitis A and hepatitis B. And its incubation period can be long or short.

闷、舌苔厚腻者，可改用藿香正气散（见本文库《方剂学》有关部分）。

第二节　病毒性肝炎

病毒性肝炎可分为甲型、乙型和非甲非乙型肝炎三种，均由肝炎病毒引起。人群对本病普遍易感。临床上以食欲减退、肝区疼痛和乏力等为主要表现，亦可有发热、黄疸以及不同程度的肝功能损害。本病属中医"黄疸"、"肝郁"、"胁痛"、"癥积"等范畴。

【诊断要点】

1. 流行病学资料：注意肝炎流行情况，有无同肝炎患者密切接触史，以及是否接受过输血、输注血制品和接种史。

2. 临床特点

（1）起病隐袭而缓慢、乏力、厌食为常见症状，部分患者有黄疸，但多数患者为无黄疸、轻型肝炎。典型或黄疸型仅占1/10。

（2）甲型肝炎多有发热，病程较短，易恢复。乙型肝炎病程多迁延，患者可长期带毒，少数可演变为肝硬化。非甲非乙型肝炎临床表现的严重程度可介于甲、乙两型之间。其潜伏期可有长短两种。

3. Physical signs: The liver becomes enlarged, and tender on palpation and is painful on percussion. There is a mild change of liver texture. A small percentage of cases have splenomegaly. In the patients with icterohepatitis, jaundice may be found in the skin and sclera. Hepatic face, vascular spiders and liver palms may be present in chronic active hepatitis. A few patients suffering from fulminant hepatitis may have skin petechiae, epistaxis and ascites, or even hepatic coma, indicating poor prognosis.

4. Laboratory examination

(1) Liver function: In patients with acute hepatitis, the SGPT is marked elevated up to several hundreds units, even more than one thousand units. In icterohepatitis, the icterus index and the one-minute bilirubin fixed quantity are increased. In severe and chronic active hepatitis, metabolism of protein is disturbed resulting in the change of ratio of serum albumin to globulin. The albumin level lowered but the globulin level elevated, even the ratio may be inverted. Signs of clotting disorder may be present.

(2) The detection of specific antigens and antibodies: It is available to detect the HAAg in filtrate of stools and the anti-HAV of the IgG and IgM class in the serum in the diagnosis of hepatitis A. Three antigen and antibody systems, that is HBsAg, HBcAg and HBeAg with their antibodies, can be detected, which is valuable in the diagnosis and in predicting the severity, infectivity and prognosis of the hepatitis B. Non-A Non-B hepatitis can only be diagnosed by using the exclusive method.

(3) In chronic active hepatitis, tests for cellular immunity, humoral immunity and autoimmunity may be performed to evaluate the host immune mechanisms and severity of the disease so as to give a relevant treatment. Liver biopsy is only indicated for those whose cases defy diagnosis through clinical and laboratory examination.

DIFFERENTIATION AND TREATMENT OF COMMON SYNDROMES

3．体征：肝脏肿大，伴有触痛、叩痛，质地轻度改变，部分患者可有脾肿大。黄疸型肝炎可见皮肤和巩膜黄染。病变进展为慢性活动性肝炎者，可见肝病面容、蜘蛛痣、肝掌；少数患者病情重危，可见皮肤瘀点、鼻血多、腹水等症，甚至出现意识障碍(肝昏迷)，予后较差，称为暴发型肝炎。

4．化验检查

（1）肝功能：急性肝炎多数可见谷丙转氨酶升高，可高达数百单位甚至1千单位以上。黄疸型肝炎患者可见黄疸指数升高和1分钟胆红质定量增加。重症及慢性活动性肝炎蛋白质代谢功能下降，白蛋白下降，球蛋白升高，白球比例下降或倒置。可有凝血功能障碍。

（2）特异性抗原抗体检测：甲型肝炎可测量粪便滤液中甲型肝炎抗原及血清中免疫球蛋白——抗甲型肝炎病毒抗体和免疫球蛋白——抗—甲型肝炎病毒抗体；乙型肝炎可检测三种抗原抗体系统，即表面抗原、核心抗原、E抗原和它们的抗体，对确诊乙肝和估计病情的传染性及予后，均有重要价值；非甲非乙型肝炎主要通过排除法确诊。

（3）慢性活动性肝炎，可检测细胞免疫、体液免疫和自身免疫指标以估价机体免疫功能和病程进展状态，并给予相应治疗。肝脏活体组织检查仅用于临床和化验检查不能确诊者。

【辨证论治】

1. Icterohepatitis

(1) *Yang* Jaundice (Acute Icterohepatitis)

Main Symptoms and Signs: Bright yellow coloration of the skin and sclera, fever, thirst, feeling of fullness and distension in the epigastrium, anorexia, fatigue, hypochondriac distension and pain, restlessness, nausea, scanty dark urine, dry stools, red tongue with yellow and greasy fur, taut and rapid pulse.

Therapeutic Principle: Removing pathogenic heat and dampness.

Recipe: Oriental Wormwood Decoction with additional ingredients.

> oriental wormwood, *Herba Artemisiae Capillaris*　30g
> capejasmine fruit, *Fructus Gardeniae*　10g
> rhubarb root, *Radix et Rhizoma Rhei*　6g (decocted later)
> phellodendron bark, *Cortex Phellodendri*　10g
> honeysuckle flower, *Flos Lonicerae*　30g
> forsythia fruit, *Fructus Forsythiae*　15g
> isatis root, *Radix Isatidis*　30g
> cogongrass rhizome, *Rhizoma Imperatae*　30g

All the above drugs are to be decocted in water for oral administration.

Some other drugs are often employed for certain symptoms. In case of exhibiting more symptoms and signs of pathogenic heat, 30 grams of isatis leaf (*Folium Isatidis*) and 30 grams of dandelion (*Herba Taraxaci*) should be added. And in case of exhibiting more symptoms and signs of pathogenic damp, 10 grams of atractylodes rhizome (*Rhizoma Atractylodis*), 10 grams of magnolia bark (*Cortex Magnoliae Officinalis*) and 10 grams of alismatis rhizome (*Rhizoma Alismatis*) may be added. Nausea and vomiting can be treated with the addition of pinellia tuber (*Rhizoma Pinelliae*) 10g and bamboo shavings (*Caulis Bambusae in Taeniam*) 10g. While abdominal distension and anorexia can be treated with the addition of same dosage of 10 grams of parched hawthorn

1．黄疸型肝炎

（1）阳黄（急性黄疸型肝炎）

主证：身目俱黄，色泽鲜明如橘子色，发热口渴，脘腹闷胀，食欲不振，身困乏力，胁肋胀痛，心烦欲吐，小便短少黄赤，大便干燥，舌质偏红，舌苔黄腻，脉弦数。

治则：清热利湿。

处方：茵陈蒿汤加味。

茵陈30克，栀子10克，大黄6克（后入），黄柏10克，银花30克，连翘15克，板蓝根30克，白茅根30克。水煎服。

热邪偏盛者，加大青叶30克，蒲公英30克；湿邪偏盛者，加苍术10克，厚朴10克，泽泻10克；恶心、呕吐者，加半夏10克，

fruit (*Fructus Crataegi*) parched malt (*Fructus Hordei Germinatus*) and parched medicated leaven (*Massa Fermentata Medicinalis*). To treat the cutaneous pruritus, 15 grams of dittany bark (*Cortex Dictamni Radicis*) and 15 grams of broom cypress fruit (*Fructus Kochiae*) are included.

(2) *Yin* Jaundice (Chronic icterohepatitis)

Main Symptoms and Signs: Dark yellow coloration of the skin and sclera just like smoky colour, poor appetite, feeling of distension in the abdomen, loose stools, general debility, tastelessness in the mouth, whitish thick and greasy fur of the tongue, deep thready and weak pulse.

Therapeutic Principle: Activating the function of the spleen, inducing diuresis and warming *yang*.

Recipe: Modified Decoction of Oriental Wormwood and Bighead Atractylodes and Prepared Aconite.

oriental wormwood, *Herba Artemisiae Capillaris*   30g

bighead atractylodes rhizome, *Rhizoma Atractylodis Macrocephalae*   12g

dangshen, *Radix Codonopsis Pilosulae*   12g

poria, *Poria*   15g

coix seed, *Semen Coicis*   30g

prepared aconite root, *Radix Aconite Praeparata*   6g

tangerine peel, *Pericarpium Citri Reticulatae*   10g

hawthorn fruit, *Fructus Crataegi*   10g

malt, *Fructus Hordei Germinatus*   10g

medicated leaven, *Massa Fermentata Modicinalis*   10g

All the above drugs are to be decocted in water for oral administration.

Apart from the ingredients in the above recipe, 10 grams of dried ginger (*Rhizoma Zingiberis*) should be prescribed for those who complain of aversion to cold and cold limbs; 15 grams of fresh-water turtle shell (*Carapax Trionycis*) and 15 grams of red sage root (*Radix Salviae Miltiorrhizae*) for those with hepatosplenomegaly; and 15 grams of shell of areca nut (*Pericarpium Arecae*) and

竹茹10克；食少腹胀者，加焦三仙各10克；皮肤瘙痒者，加白藓

皮15克，地肤子15克。

（2）阴黄（慢性黄疸型肝炎）

主证：黄色暗晦，如烟熏样，纳少腹胀，大便溏薄，身倦神

疲，口淡无味，舌苔白厚腻，脉沉细弱。

治则：健脾利湿温阳。

处方：茵陈术附汤加减。

茵陈30克，白术12克，党参12克，茯苓15克，苡仁30克，附

子6克，陈皮10克，焦三仙各10克。水煎服。

畏寒肢冷者，加干姜10克；肝脾肿大而硬者，加鳖甲15克，

15 grams of plantain seed (*Semen Plantaginis*) (wrapped in a piece of cloth during decocting) for those with ascite..

2. Anicteric Hepatitis

(1) Dampness and Heat in the Liver and Gallbladder

Main Symptoms and Signs: Chest stuffiness, dysphoria with feverish sensation, pain in the hypochondrium, abdominal distension, lassitude and weakness, anorexia with aversion to greasy food, bitter taste and dry mouth, scanty dark urine, dry stools, reddened tongue with yellow and greasy fur, taut and rapid or smooth and rapid pulse.

Therapeutic Principle: Removing pathogenic heat and dampness.

Recipe: Modified prescriptions of Oriental Wormwood Decoction combined with Decoction of Gentian for Purging Liver-fire.

oriental wormwood, *Herba Artemesiae Capillaris*   30g
capejasmine fruit, *Fructus Gardeniae*   10g
scutellaria root, *Radix Scutellariae*   10g
gentian root, *Radix Gentianae*   10g
isatis root, *Radix Isatidis*   30g
patrinia, *Herba Patriniae*   30g
curcuma root, *Radis Curcumae*   12g
plantain seed, *Semen Plantaginis*   10g (wrapped in a piece of cloth during decocting)
red sage root, *Radix Salviae Miltiorrhizae*   12g
poria, *Poria*   10g
magnolia bark, *Cortex Magnoliae Officinalis*   10g

All the above drugs are to be decocted in water for oral administration.

In addition, 12 grams of Sichuan chinaberry (*Fructus Meliae Toosendan*) and 10 grams of corydalis tuber (*Rhizoma Corydalis*) are added for treating cases with prominent pain in the hypochondrium; 10 grams of amomum fruit (*Fructus Amomi*) and 10 grams of bitter orange (*Fructus Aurantii*) are added for cases with

丹参15克；有腹水者，加大腹皮15克，车前子15克(布包煎)。

2．无黄疸型肝炎

(1)肝胆湿热

主证：胸闷烦热，胁痛腹胀，倦怠无力，纳呆厌油，口苦口

干，小便赤黄，大便干燥，舌质红，苔黄腻，脉弦数或滑数。

治则：清热利湿。

处方：茵陈蒿汤合龙胆泻肝汤加减。

茵陈30克，栀子10克，黄芩10克，龙胆草10克,板蓝根30克，

败酱草30克，郁金12克，车前子10克(布包煎)，丹参12克，茯苓

obvious epigastric distension and stuffiness; 15 grams of hawthorn fruit (*Fructus Crataegi*) and 10 grams of membrane of chicken's gizzard skin (*Endothelium Corneum Gigeriae Calli*) added for cases with poor appetite.

(2) Stagnation of the Liver-*qi* with Deficiency of the Spleen

Main Symptoms and Signs: Dull pain in the right-sided hypochondrium, general debility, anorexia, loose stools, thin and whitish fur of the tongue, deep and taut pulse.

Therapeutic Principle: Relieving the depressed liver-*qi* and reinforcing the function of the spleen.

Recipe: Modified Ease Powder.

bupleurum root, *Radix Bupleuri*　　10g

Chinese angelica root, *Radix Angelicae Sinensis*　　10g

white peony, *Radix Paeoniae Alba*　　10g

dangshen, *Radix Codonopsis Philosulae*　　12g

white atractylodes rhizome, *Rhizoma Atractylodis Macrocephalae*　　10g

poria, *Poria*　　10g

curcuma root, *Radix Curcumae*　　12g

tangerine peel, *Pericarpium Citri Reticulatae*　　10g

red sage root, *Radix Salviae Miltiorrhizae*　　12g

Chinese yam, *Rhizoma Dioscoreae*　　15g

hawthorn fruit, *Fructus Crataegi*　　15g

medicated leaven, *Massa Fermentata Medicinalis*　　12g

prepared licorice root, *Radix Glycyrrhizae Praeparata*　　6g

All the above drugs are to be decocted in water for oral administration.

If the disease is characterized by dryness of the eyes, dizziness, dull pain in the hypochondrium, hot sensation in palms and soles, soreness and weakness in the loins and knees, dry and red tongue coated with a little fur or no fur at all, taut and thready pulse, which is caused by deficiency of the liver-*yin*, nourishing the liver-*yin* should dominates the treatment. The given recipe is Decoction for Nourishing the Liver and Kidney

10克，厚朴10克。水煎服。

胁痛明显者，加川楝子12克，延胡索10克；脘腹胀闷明显者，加砂仁10克，枳壳10克；食欲不振者，加山楂15克，鸡内金（研冲）10克。

（2）肝郁脾虚

主证：右胁隐痛，身困乏力，不思饮食，大便溏薄，舌苔薄白，脉沉弦。

治则：疏肝健脾。

处方：逍遥散加减。

柴胡10克，当归10克，白芍10克，党参12克，白术10克，茯苓10克，郁金12克，陈皮10克，丹参12克，山药15克，山楂15克，陈曲12克，炙甘草6克。水煎服。

若症见两目干涩、头晕目眩、胁肋隐痛、手足心热、腰膝酸软、舌质干红、少苔或无苔、脉弦细者，属肝阴亏虚，治宜滋补

with additional ingredients:

    glehnia root, *Radix Glehniae*   12g

    ophiopogon root, *Radix Ophiopogonis*   12g

    dried rehmannia root, *Radix Rehmanniae*   12g

    wolfberry fruit, *Fructus Lycii*   15g

    Chinese angelica, *Radix Angelicae Sinensis*   10g

    Sichuan chinaberry, *Fructus Meliae Toosendan*   10g

    fresh-water turtle shell, *Carapax Trionycis*   15g

    curcuma root, *Radix Curcumae*   12g

    dendrobium, *Herba Dendrobii*   12g

(3) Stagnation of *Qi* and Blood Stasis

Main Symptoms and Signs: Gloomy complexion, stabbing pain in the right hypochondrium, hepatomegaly or splenomegaly, abdominal distension, anorexia, some telangiectases in the skin of face and neck with vascular spiders, liver palms, dark purple tongue sometimes marked with ecchymoses, taut and uneven pulse.

Therapeutic Principle: Promoting blood circulation, removing blood stasis and softening hard hepatomegaly or splenomegaly.

Recipe: Modified Decoction of Peach Kernel and Safflower with Other Four Ingredients.

    Chinese angelica, *Radix Angelicae Sinensis*   12g

    white peony root, *Radix Paeoniae Alba*   12g

    chuanxiong rhizome, *Rhizoma Ligustici Chuanxiong*   10g

    peach kernel, *Semen Persicae*   10g

    safflower, *Flos Carthami*   10g

    red sage root, *Radix Salviae Miltiorrhizae*   20g

    fresh-water turtle shell, *Carapax Trionycis*   15g

    pangolin scales, *Squama Manitis*   6g

    zedoary, *Rhizoma Zedoariae*   10g

    spatholobus stem, *Caulis Spatholobi*   30g

    cyperus tuber, *Rhizoma Cyperi*   10g

    finger citron, *Fructus Citri Sarcodactylis*   10g

    prepared licorice root, *Radix Glycyrrhizae Praeparata*   10g

肝阴为主，可用一贯煎加味：沙参12克，麦冬12克，生地黄12克，枸杞15克，当归10克，川楝子10克，鳖甲15克，郁金12克，石斛12克。

（3）气滞血瘀

主证：面色晦暗，右胁刺痛，胁下痞块，腹胀食少，面颈赤缕红丝，朱砂掌，舌质紫暗，或有瘀斑，脉弦涩。

治则：活血化瘀，佐以软坚。

处方：桃红四物汤加减。

当归12克，白芍12克，川芎10克，桃仁10克，红花10克，丹参20克，鳖甲15克，穿山甲6克，莪术10克，鸡血藤30克，香附

All the above drugs are to be decocted in water for oral administration.

Apart from the above ingredients, 12 grams of dangshen (*Radix Codonopsis Pilosulae*) and 15 grams of astragalus root (*Radix Astragali seu Hedysari*) are added for those with symptoms of lassitude and weakness.

For all types of clinical manifestations mentioned above, if SGPT is higher than normal, powder of schisandra fruit (*Fructus Schisandrae*) may be taken at the same time, 3 grams are taken each time and 3 times a day; or additional intake of stringy stonecrop powder (*Herba Sedi Sarmentosi*) 50 mg are taken each time and three times a day; or choose any of the appropriate amount of the following ingredients for extra intake: bistort rhizome (*Rhizoma Bistortae*), giant knotweed rhizome (*Rhizoma Polygoni Cuspidati*) and Japanese St. Johns wort (*Herba Hyperici Japonici*).

Section 3
Bacillary Dysentery

Bacillary dysentery is an infectious disease of the intestinal tract caused by Shigella. It commonly occurs in summer and autumn. The sources of infection are patients and bacteria carriers. The disease is transmitted by means of contact with the contaminated food, water and tableware. The major pathological change is the purulent inflammation of the colonic mucosa. Clinically, fever, abdominal pain, diarrhea, tenesmus and bloody purulent stools are major manifestations. In TCM, this disease belongs to the category of "*li ji*" (dysentery).

MAIN POINTS OF DIAGNOSIS

Bacillary dysentery can be divided into acute and chronic types according to the clinical features and courses.

1. Acute bacillary dysentery

(1) In epidemic seasons, the history of eating contaminated

10克，佛手10克，炙甘草10克。水煎服。

倦怠无力者，加党参12克，黄芪15克。

以上各型，若谷丙转氨酶持续高于正常者，可加服五味子粉剂，每次3克，1日3次；或垂盆草粉剂，每次50毫克，1日3次，或酌加紫参、虎杖、田基黄等药。

第三节 细菌性痢疾

细菌性痢疾是由志贺氏菌属所引起的肠道传染病，多见于夏秋季。传染源是病人和带菌者。病菌通过污染食物、水、餐具等而传染。其主要病变为结肠粘膜化脓性炎症。临床上以全身中毒症状、腹痛、腹泻、里急后重和粘液脓血便为主要表现。本病属中医"痢疾"范畴。

【诊断要点】

按其发病特点和病程，可分为急性细菌性痢疾和慢性细菌性痢疾。

1．急性细菌性痢疾

（1）在本病好发季节，不洁饮食史和与病人密切接触史有重

food and close contact with dysentery patients is helpful to diagnosis.

(2) The onset is often abrupt. The patients complain of chill sensation, fever, pantalgia, abdominal cramps and diarrhea. The abdominal pain is mainly around the umbilicus or at the left lower quadrant. The bowel movements may be more than ten times a day. Initially, the stools are soft and yellow in colour, and subsequently are mucopurulent and bloody, accompanied with tenesmus. A few patients, because of old age, general asthenia or having chronic disease, may have trance or coma. The prognosis of patient manifested as severe toxemia or infectious shock is very poor.

(3) Laboratory findings: White blood cell counts are increased with a shift to the left in the differential count. Microscopic examination of the stool reveals a great number of erythrocytes, leukocytes and pus cells and a few macrophages. Stool culture can confirm the diagnosis and identify the causing organisms.

2. Chronic bacillary dysentery

(1) Having a past history of acute bacillary dysentery or a history of chronic persistent course due to the inadequate treatment for acute bacillary dysentery.

(2) Having recurrent or persistent abdominal pain, accompanied with diarrhea or alternation of diarrhea and constipation. Intermittent appearance of mucopurulent and blood-stained stools. Patients of long duration of the disease may appear weak, emaciated and malnourished.

(3) Definite diagnosis can be made when stool culture is positive. Sigmoidoscopy is reserved for the cases difficult to diagnose.

DIFFERENTIATION AND TREATMENT OF COMMON SYNDROMES

1. Dysentery due to Damp-heat Pathogen (Occuring in acute bacillary dysentery)

要参考价值。

（2）起病急，患者可有畏寒、发热、周身痛、腹痛和腹泻。腹痛以脐周和左下腹为主，腹泻可达每天十余次，初为黄色软便，以后为脓血粘液样便，伴里急后重。少部分患者由于年迈、体质虚弱或患有慢性疾病等原因，可出现神志恍惚或昏迷。全身中毒症状严重或并发感染性休克者，予后甚劣。

（3）化验室检查：血象白细胞增高，分类左移；粪便镜检可见成堆红细胞、白细胞及脓细胞，少数巨噬细胞；粪便培养可确诊并区别菌种。

2. 慢性细菌性痢疾

（1）有急性菌痢发作史，或因延误治疗而使病程迁延未愈。

（2）反复发作或持续腹痛不适，伴有腹泻，或腹泻与便秘交替出现，大便间歇地出现粘液和脓血，久病患者体力较差、消瘦及营养不良。

（3）大便培养阳性可以确诊。乙状结肠镜检查用以鉴别确诊困难的病例。

【辨证论治】

1. 湿热痢（多见于急性细菌性痢疾）

Main Symptoms and Signs: Abdominal pain, diarrhea with bloody mucous stool which is moved several times or more than ten times a day with a small amount each time, tenesmus, burning sensation at the anus, scanty deep-coloured urine, or accompanied with chill and fever, yellow and greasy coating of the tongue, slippery and rapid pulse.

Therapeutic Principle: Clearing away heat and eliminating dampness and regulating *qi* to remove stagnancy.

Recipe: Modified Peony Decoction.

white peony root, *Radix Paeoniae Alba*   20g
coptis rhizome, *Rhizoma Coptidis*   10g
scutellaria root, *Radix Scutellariae*   10g
honeysuckle flower, *Flos Lonicerae*   30g
portulaca, *Herba Portulacae*   30g
rhubarb, *Radix et Rhizoma Rhei*   6g
aucklandia root, *Radix Aucklandiae*   6g
areca seed, *Semen Arecae*   10g
bitter orange, *Fructus Aurantii*   10g
licorice root, *Radix Glycyrrhizae*   6g

All the above drugs are to be decocted in water for oral administration.

For the case with the onset of chill and fever, 15 grams of pueraria root (*Rhizoma Puerariae*) is usually added.

2. Fulminant Dysentery (mostly occuring in toxic bacillary dysentery)

Main Symptoms and Signs: Sudden onset, violent attack, purulent and bloody stools, or bloody stools, high fever, restlessness or even coma or convulsion in serious cases, red tongue or deep-red tongue with yellow greasy fur and rapid pulse.

Therapeutic Principle: Removing heat and toxic materials and cooling the blood.

Recipe: Modified Pulsatilla Decoction.

pulsatilla root, *Radix Pulsatillae*   30g

主证：腹痛腹泻，大便日数次或数十次，粪便量少，脓血相杂，里急后重，肛门灼热，小便短赤，或有恶寒发热，苔黄腻，脉滑数。

治则：清热化湿，调气导滞。

处方：芍药汤加减。

白芍20克，黄连10克，黄芩10克，金银花30克，马齿苋30克，大黄6克，木香6克，槟榔10克，枳壳10克，生甘草6克。水煎服。

初起有恶寒发热者，加葛根15克。

2．疫毒痢（多见于中毒性菌痢）

主证：发病急骤，病势较重，大便以脓血为主，或痢下鲜血，高热，烦躁，甚或昏迷、惊厥，舌红或绛，苔黄腻，脉数。

治则：清热解毒，佐以凉血。

处方：白头翁汤加减。

白头翁30克，秦皮15克，黄连10克，黄柏10克，金银花30克，

ash bark, *Cortex Fraxini*   15g

coptis rhizome, *Rhizoma Coptidis*   10g

phellodendron bark, *Cortex Phellodendri*   10g

honeysuckle flower, *Flos Lonicerae*   30g

forsythia fruit, *Fructus Forsythiae*   15g

moutan bark, *Cortex Moutan Radicis*   10g

red peony root, *Radix Paeoniae Rubra*   10g

sanguisorba root, *Radix Sanguisorbae*   15g

pueraria root, *Radix Puerariae*   15g

All the above drugs are to be decocted in water for oral administration.

If there appears coma, convulsion or toxic shock, Bezoar Sedative Bolus, Purple Snowy Powder and the like may be added. Meanwhile, the treatment of TCM should be given in combination with that of Western medicine.

3. Recurrent Dysentery (mostly found in chronic bacillary dysentery)

Main Symptoms and Signs: Chronic dysentery with frequent relapse, and slow recovery, abdominal pain and tenesmus during the attack, dark-coloured mucous stools, fatigue and weakness, pale tongue with greasy fur, deep and weak pluse.

Therapeutic Principle: Invigorating the spleen, replenishing *qi*, removing heat and eliminating dampness.

Recipe: Modified Decoction of Four Noble Drugs.

dangshen, *Radix Codonopsis Pilosulae*   15g

white atractylodes rhizome, *Rhizoma Atractylodis Macrocephalae*   10g

poria, *Poria*   15g

aucklandia root, *Radix Aucklandiae*   15g

tangerine peel, *Pericarpium Citri Reticulatae*   10g

coptis rhizome, *Rhizoma Coptidis*   10g

pulsatilla root, *Radix Pulsatillae*   20g

sanguisorba root, *Radix Sanguisorbae*   15g

prepared licorice root, *Radix Glycyrrhizae Praeparata*   6g

All the above drugs are to be decocted in water for oral

连翘15克，丹皮10克，赤芍10克，地榆 15 克，葛根 15克。水煎服。

若出现昏迷、惊厥或中毒性休克者，可加牛黄清心丸、紫雪丹等，并予以中西医结合治疗。

3．休息痢(多见于慢性细菌性痢疾)

主证：下痢日久不愈，时发时止，发病时腹痛里急，大便带有暗红色粘冻，倦怠无力，舌淡苔腻，脉沉弱。

治则：健脾益气，清热化湿。

处方：四君子汤加减。

党参15克，白术10克，茯苓15克，木香10克，陈皮10克，黄

administration.

If *yin*-blood is injured with symptoms of irritability, thirst, red tongue with little fur, fine and rapid pulse, 15 grams of dried rehmannia root (*Radix Rehmanniae*), 12 grams of white peony root (*Radix Paeoniae Alba*) and 12 grams of black plum (*Fructus Mume*) are to be added.

If the case is ascribed to dysentery of deficiency-cold type with symptoms of watery and purulent stools, abdominal pain with preference for warmth and pressure, cold extremities, loss of appetite, listlessness, pale tongue with whitish fur, deep and fine pulse, it is preferable to employ Modified Decoction for Nourishing the Viscera, including: dangshen (*Radix Codonopsis Pilosulae*) 12g, white atractylodes rhizome (*Rhizoma Atractylodis Macrocephalae*) 10g, baked ginger (*Rhizoma Zingiberis*) 10g, cinnamon bark (*Cortex Cinnamomi*) 6g, nutmeg (*Semen Myristicae*) 10g, chebula fruit (*Fructus Chebulae*) 15g, aucklandia root (*Radix Aucklandiae*) 6g, red halloysite (*Halloysitum Rubrum*) 12g, pomegranate rind (*Pericarpium Granati*) 15g, prepared licorice root (*Radix Glycyrrhizae Praeparata*) 6g. All the above ingredients are to be decocted in water for oral administration.

Section 4
Acquired Immunodeficiency Syndrome (AIDS)

AIDS is a worldwide infectious disease discovered in recent years. Its case-fatality rate is very high. AIDS is known to be viral infection, but the isolation and culture of the virus has not been successful. The Western medicine has had no effective treatment for the disease yet. AIDS is frequently found in homosexuals and drug addicts. It also occurs in infants and children. AIDS is mainly transmitted by means of sexual contacts, infusion, injection and mother-to-infant. This disease, in TCM, probably pertains to the categories of *"wen re bing"* (epidemic febrile diseases), *"xu lao"* (consumptive diseases), etc.

连10克，白头翁20克，地榆15克，炙甘草 6 克。水煎服。

若耗伤阴血，伴见心烦口干、舌红苔少、脉细数者，加生地15克，白芍12克，乌梅12克。

若下痢稀薄，带有白脓，腹痛喜暖喜按，四肢发凉，食少神疲，舌淡苔白，脉沉细者，属虚寒痢，可用养脏汤加减：党参12克，白术10克，炮姜10克，肉桂 6 克，肉豆蔻10克，诃子肉15克，木香 6 克，赤石脂12克，石榴皮15克，炙甘草 6 克。水煎服。

第四节 艾 滋 病

艾滋病是近年来发现的一种在世界范围内传播的疾病，病死率颇高。其病因已知为病毒感染所致，但至今病毒分离培养仍未获成功。目前西医对本病尚无有效疗法。本病多见于同性恋者、吸毒者。婴儿和儿童亦可被感染。主要通过性接触、输血、注射及母婴传播。艾滋病似属中医"温热病"、"虚劳"等范畴。

MAIN POINTS OF DIAGNOSIS

1. Major criteria

(1) A marked loss of weight, up to 10 percent or more than before.

(2) Marked weakness, tiredness and fatigue.

(3) Severe diarrhea persisting for more than one month.

(4) Continuous or intermittent fever lasting for more than one month.

2. Minor criteria

(1) Multiple hemorrhagic and sarcomatoid lesions on the skin.

(2) Candida albicans infection on the oral and pharyngeal mucosae.

(3) Herpetic skin disease or herpes zoster persisting for more than one month.

(4) Generalized pruritus of the skin.

(5) Pulmonary infections (pneumocystic carinii pneumonia being common).

(6) Generalized lymphadenectasis.

(7) Signs of neurologic disorder.

(8) Meningitis showing no obvious response to treatment.

3. Laboratory tests

(1) Immunological tests show a defect and hypofunction in cellular immunity, while in humoral immunity IgG, IgA and IgM are increased. The cause of the immunological changes is not well understood.

(2) Virological examination may find infection of HTLA-III virus.

If three major criteria and one minor criterion are present in a suspected case, serumal immunological tests should be performed to confirm the diagnosis.

DIFFERENTIATION AND TREATMENT OF COMMON SYNDROMES

1. Prodromal Stage

【诊断要点】

1. 主要临床表现

(1)体重明显下降，较原来下降10%以上或更多。

(2)明显虚弱、倦怠和乏力。

(3)严重腹泻持续一个月以上。

(4)持续性或间歇性发热1个月以上。

2. 次要临床表现

(1)皮肤多发性出血性肉瘤样损害。

(2)口腔及咽部白色念珠菌感染。

(3)疱疹性皮肤病或带状疱疹持续1个月以上。

(4)全身皮肤瘙痒症。

(5)肺部感染(常见卡氏肺囊肿肺炎)。

(6)全身淋巴结肿大。

(7)出现神经系统体征。

(8)治疗效果不明显的脑膜炎。

3. 实验室检查

(1)免疫学检查患者多表现为细胞免疫缺陷和功能低下，而体液免疫指标如 IgG、IgA、IgM 则增高，但原因不明。

(2)病毒学检查可发现 HTLA-III 病毒感染。

凡具上述三条主要表现和一条次要表现者，应进一步做血清免疫学测定，从而明确诊断。

【辨证论治】

1. 前驱期

Deficiency of Both *Qi* and *Yin*

Main Symptoms and Signs: Low fever, night sweat, fatigue and weakness, headache, poor appetite, nausea, reddish tongue with little fur, thready and rapid pulse.

Therapeutic Principle: Supplementing *qi* and nourishing *yin*.

Recipe: Modified prescriptions of Pulse-activating Powder combined with Pill of Anemarrhena, Phellodendron and Rehmannia.

pseudostellarua root, *Radix Pseudostellariae*   15g

ophiopogon root, *Radix Ophiopogonis*   12g

schisandra fruit, *Fructus Schisandrae*   10g

dried rehmannia root, *Radix Rehmanniae*   20g

prepared rehmannia root, *Radix Rehmanniae Praeparata*   20g

dogwood fruit, *Fructus Corni*   12g

Chinese yam, *Rhizoma Dioscoreae*   12g

alismatis rhizome, *Rhizoma Alismatis*   6g

moutan bark, *Cortex Moutan Radicis*   12g

poria, *Poria*   10g

anemarrhena rhizome, *Rhizoma Anemarrhenae*   12g

phellodendron bark, *Cortex Phellodendri*   12g

wolfberry fruit, *Fructus Lycii*   12g

glossy privet fruit, *Fructus Ligustri Lucidi*   12g

astragalus root, *Radix Astragali seu Hedysari*   15

sweet wormwood, *Herba Artemisiae*   12g

parched hawthorn fruit, *Fructus Crataegi*   10g

parched germinated barley, *Fructus Hordei Germinatus*   10g

parched medicated leaven, *Massa Fermentata Medicinalis* 10g

All the above drugs are to be decocted in water for oral administration.

2. Stage of Attack

(1) Hyperactivity of Fire due to *Yin* Deficiency

Main Symptoms and Signs: Low fever, lassitude and listlessness, emaciation, cough, dyspnea, shortness of breath, night sweat, sore throat, dry mouth and tongue, red tongue with yellowish fur, deep, thready and rapid pulse.

气阴两虚

主证：低热，盗汗，疲劳无力，头痛，纳呆，恶心，舌质偏红，少苔，脉细数。

治则：益气养阴。

处方：生脉散合知柏地黄丸加减。

太子参15克，麦冬12克，五味子10克，生地20克，熟地20克山萸肉12克，山药12克，泽泻6克，丹皮12克，茯苓10克，知母12克，黄柏12克，枸杞子12克，女贞子12克，黄芪15克，青蒿12克，焦三仙各10克。水煎服。

2．发病期

（1）阴虚火旺

主证：低热，神倦无力，消瘦，咳嗽，气喘，短气，盗汗，咽痛，口干舌燥，舌质红，苔黄，脉沉细数。

Therapeutic Principle: Nourishing *yin* to bring down a fever and aiding in cooling blood and removing toxic material.

Recipe: Modified Great Pearl for Wind Syndrome

dried rehmannia root, *Radix Rehmanniae*, 15—30g

ophiopogon root, *Radix Ophiopogonis*   12g

scrophularia root, *Radix Scrophulariae*   15g

tortoise plastron, *Plastrum Testudinis*   20g

fresh-water turtle shell, *Carapax Trionycis*   15g

donkey-hide gelatin, *Colla Corii Asini*   12g (melted in the finished decoction)

fresh egg yolk   2 pieces

ginseng, *Radix Ginseng*   6g

schisandra fruit, *Fructus Schisandrae*   10g

glossy privet fruit, *Fructus Ligustri Lucidi*   12g

astragalus root, *Radix Astragali seu Hedysari*   15g

moutan bark, *Cortex Moutan Radicis*   12g

sweet wormwood, *Herba Artemisiae*   12g

barbat skullcap, *Herba Scutellariae Barbatae*   15g

All the above drugs, except donkey-hide gelatin which is to be melted and then mixed in the finished decoction, are to be decocted in water for oral administration.

In addition to the above ingredients, 12 grams of airpotato yam (*Rhizoma Dioscoreae Bulbiferae*) and 10 grams of batryticated silkworm (*Bombyx Batrycatus*) should be employed for the case with enlargement of lymph nodes; 12 grams of Chinese yam (*Rhizoma Dioscoreae*), 20 grams of parched coix seed (*Semen Coicis*), 10 grams pinellia tuber (*Rhizoma Pinelliae*), 10 grams of parched germinated barley (*Fructus Hordei Germinatus*), 10 grams of parched hawthorn fruit (*Fructus Crataegi*) and 10 grams of parched medicated leaven (*Massa Fermentata Medicinalis*) for cases with anorexia, nausea and diarrhea; 15 grams of stemona root (*Radix Stemonae*) and 10 grams of Sichuan fritillary bulb (*Bulbus Fritillariae Cirrhosae*) for cases of cough with dyspnea. To deal with ulceration of the mouth, thrush and herpes, 10 grams of coptis root (*Rhizoma Coptidis*) and

治则：滋阴清热，佐以凉血解毒。

处方：大定风珠加减。

生地15～30克，麦冬12克，玄参15克，龟板20克，鳖甲15克，

阿胶12克(烊化)，鸡子黄2枚(生)，人参6克，五味子10克，女

贞子12克，黄芪15克，丹皮12克，青蒿12克，半枝莲15克。水煎

服。

淋巴结肿大者，加黄药子12克，僵蚕10克；纳呆、恶心、腹

泻者，加山药12克，炒苡仁20克，半夏10克，焦三仙各10克；咳

喘者，加百部15克，川贝母10克；有口腔溃疡、鹅口疮、疱疹者，

30 grams of isatis leaf (*Folium Isatidis*) are included in the above recipe, *Xilei* Powder or *Bingpeng* Powder may be chosen for external use.

If the case is manifested as symptoms of exterior syndrome such as fever, chill, pantalgia, the suitable treatment should be to expel pathogenic heat from the muscles and skin. The chosen recipe is Modified Bupleurum and Pueraria Decoction for Dispelling Pathogens from Superficial Muscles, including: bupleurum root (*Radix Bupleuri*) 10g, pueraria root (*Radix Puerariae*) 18g, scutellaria root (*Radix Scutellariae*) 10g, gypsum (*Gypsum Fibrosum*) 30g, isatis root (*Radix Isatidis*) 30g, notopterygium root (*Rhizoma seu Radix Notopterygii*) 6g, honeysuckle flower (*Flos Lonicerae*) 15g, prepared licorice root (*Radix Glycyrrhizae Praeparata*) 6g. All the above drugs are to be decocted in water for oral administration.

(2) Invasion of Heat into *Ying* and Blood Systems

Main Symptoms and Signs: High fever, mucocutaneous hemorrhage, epistaxis, hemoptysis, hematemesis, hematuria, even the presence of coma and deliria, convulsion, dementia or epilepsy in severe cases, deep red tongue, and thready and rapid pulse.

Therapeutic Principle: Clearing up pathogenic heat and toxic material located at the *ying* and blood systems.

Recipe: Modified Antipyretic and Antitoxic Decoction.

powder of rhinoceros horn, *Cornu Rhinocerotis*   3—5g (To be taken after being infused in the finished decoction)

dried rehmannia root, *Radix Rehmanniae*   15—30g

white peony root, *Radix Paeoniae Alba*   12g

moutan bark, *Cortex Moutan Radicis*   12g

scrophularia root, *Radix Scrophulariae*   12g

ophiopogon root, *Radix Ophiopogonis*   12g

arnebia or lithosperm, *Radix Arnebiae seu Lithospermi*   12g

honeysuckle flower, *Flos Lonicerae*   30g

forsythia fruit, *Fructus Forsythiae*   15g

coptis root, *Radix Coptidis*   10g

加黄连10克，大青叶30克。外用锡类散或冰硼散。

若症见发热、恶寒、身痛等表证表现，治宜解肌清热为主，可用柴葛解肌汤加减：柴胡10克，葛根18克，黄芩10克，生石膏30克，板兰根30克，羌活6克，银花15克，炙甘草6克。水煎服。

（2）热陷营血

主证：高热，皮肤粘膜出血，衄血，咯血，吐血，尿血，便血，甚则神昏谵妄，惊厥抽搐，痴呆癫痫，舌质红绛，脉细数。

治则：清营凉血，泻热解毒。

处方：清瘟败毒饮加减。

犀角粉3～5克（冲服），生地15～30克，白芍12克，丹皮12克，玄参12克，麦冬12克，紫草12克，银花30克，连翘15克，黄连10

lophatherum, *Herba Lophatheri* 10g

oldenlandia, *Herba Hedyotis Diffusae* 30g

The above drugs except powder of rhinoceros horn are to be decocted in water for oral administration.

Besides, when the patient has high fever, 30 grams of gypsum (*Gypsum Fibrosum*) and 10 grams of anemarrhena rhizome (*Rhizoma Anemarrhenae*) are included in the recipe; when the patient suffers from convulsion, 3—6 grams of powder of antelope's horn (*Cornu Saigue Tataricae*) and 15—30 grams of uncaria stem with hooks (*Ramulus Uncariae cum Uncis*) are added.

Section 5
Bronchial Asthma

Bronchial asthma is an episodic allergic pulmonary disease. The attack is mostly induced by the inhalation of or contact with allergens, such as pollens, dusts, insects (such as mite), germs, etc. During the attack, patients have severe dyspnea which is due to spasm of bronchial smooth muscles, swelling of the bronchial mucosa, and hypersecretion of the mucus, leading to bronchial obstruction. When the attack can not be relieved for a long time, it is called "status asthmaticus". The disease is often seen in children and teenagers. In TCM, it is attributable to the categories of "*xiao*" (bronchial wheezing) and "*chuan*" (dyspnea).

MAIN POINTS OF DIAGNOSIS

1. Notice whether there is an allergic history of the patient and his family. For patients with histories of allergic rhinitis and urticaria, the disease is easy to be diagnosed.

2. The onset is abrupt, frequently occurring at night. Usually the patients suddenly have a sense of suffocation and of constriction in the chest, and orthopnea. The attack lasts from several minutes to several hours. On auscultation, typical

克，竹叶10克，白花蛇舌草30克。水煎服。

若高热者，加生石膏30克，知母10克；惊厥抽搐者，加羚羊粉3～6克，钩藤15～30克。

第五节　支气管哮喘

支气管哮喘系一发作性肺部过敏性疾病。其发病多因吸入或接触过敏源所致。常见过敏源为植物花粉、灰尘、昆虫（如螨）和病原菌等。发作时多由于支气管平滑肌痉挛、粘膜水肿和分泌液增多而导致气道阻塞，以致出现严重呼吸困难。如哮喘持续长时间不能缓解，称为"哮喘持续状态"。支气管哮喘好发于青少年。本病属中医"哮"、"喘"范畴。

【诊断要点】

1. 注意患者家庭和个人过敏史。既往有过敏性鼻炎、荨麻疹病史者有助于诊断。

2. 起病多突然，以夜间发作者较多，患者往往突然感觉胸闷、呼吸困难，呈端坐呼吸，每次发作持续数分钟至数小时不

wheezes can be heard over the lung fields. Moist rales may be present if pulmonary infection coexists. Termination of the episode is frequently accompanied by a cough with profuse mucoid sputum.

3. The status asthmaticus: In some cases the acute attack may persist for a long time (over 24 hours), or the episode can not be relieved by various drugs. The patients have severe dyspnea, accompanied with profuse sweating, pallor, cyanosis, tachycardia and coldness of limbs. Respiratory failure may occur in critical cases, and death may ensue if timely treatment is not given.

4. Laboratory examinations: The eosinophilic leukocyte count may increase markedly during the attack, up to 5—15 percent or more in differential count. Sputum examination may reveal more eosinopilic leukocytes and rhomboid crystals in the sputum. Serum concentration of IgE may be increased. Skin test for specific antigens is helpful to find the allergic agent, but the provocative allergic test may have potential danger of inducing asthmatic attack. Therefore, it should be performed with caution.

DIFFERENTIATION AND TREATMENT OF COMMON SYNDROMES

1. Asthma of Cold Type

Main Symptoms and Signs: A feeling of fullness and distress in the chest, dyspnea with wheezing sound in the throat, cough with thin sputum, frequent attacks in cold seasons or caused by cold, whitish, moist and glossy fur of the tongue, taut and tight pulse.

Therapeutic Principle: Ventilating the lung and expelling pathogenic cold, eliminating phlegm to relieve asthma.

Recipe: Belamcanda and Ephedra Decoction with additional ingredients.

belamcanda rhizome, *Rhizoma Belamcandae*   10g
ephedra, *Herba Ephedrae*   10g

等。发作结束时常伴咳嗽，咳出大量粘液样痰。发作时肺部可闻及哮鸣音，如合并感染可闻及湿罗音。

3．哮喘持续状态：部分患者哮喘发作持续时间很长（超过24小时），或经多种药物治疗不能缓解，呈严重呼吸困难，伴大汗淋漓、面色苍白、发绀、心率增快、四肢冷，严重者出现呼吸衰竭，如不及时抢救，常危及生命。

4．辅助检查：哮喘发作时，嗜酸性白细胞可增高，达5～15％以上，痰液检查亦可见较多嗜酸性粒细胞和棱形结晶；血清免疫学检查可见 IgE 增加；特异性过敏源检查有助于发现过敏源，但过敏激发试验有引起哮喘发作的潜在危险，应慎用。

【辨证论治】

1．寒哮

主证：胸膈满闷，呼吸急促，喉中痰鸣，咳痰清稀，多发于寒冷季节，或遇寒而发，舌苔白滑，脉弦紧。

治则：宣肺散寒，化痰平喘。

处方：射干麻黄汤加味。

射干10克，麻黄10克，细辛３克，半夏10克，五味子６克，

asarum herb, *Herba Asari*   3g

pinellia tuber, *Rhizoma Pinelliae*   10g

schisandra fruit, *Fructus Schisandrae*   6g

aster root, *Radix Asteris*   12g

coltsfoot flower, *Flos Farfarae*   12g

fresh ginger, *Rhizoma Zingiberis Recens*   10g

Chinese-date, *Fructus Ziziphi Jujubae*   5 pieces

bitter apricot kernel, *Semen Armeniacae Amarum*   10g

perilla fruit, *Fructus Perillae*   10g

All the above drugs are to be decocted in water for oral administration.

Besides, 10 grams of cinnamon twig (*Ramulus Cinnamomi*) is added for the case with chill, 10 grams of lepidium seed (*Semen Lepidii seu Descurainiae*) and 10 grams of earthworm (*Lumbricus*) for the case with severe asthma, which also responds well to the treatment of Minor Decoction of Green Dragon (Refer to the relevent parts in the book *Prescriptions of TCM* in this Library).

2. Asthma of Heat Type

Main Symptoms and Signs: Dyspnea with wheezing, irritable oppressed sensation in the chest even gasping for breath, yellowish mucoid sputum, thirst, frequent occurrence in hot seasons or onset closely associated with heat, reddened tongue with yellow greasy fur, slippery and rapid pulse.

Therapeutic Principle: Removing heat-phlegm and facilitating the flow of the lung-*qi* to relieve asthma.

Recipe: Modified prescriptions of Decoction of Ephedra, Apricot Kernel, Gypsum and Licorice combined with Decoction of Three Kinds of Seed for the Aged.

ephedra, *Herba Ephedrae*   10g

bitter apricot kernel, *Semen Armeniacae Amarum*   10g

gypsum, *Gypsum Fibrosum*   30g

licorice root, *Radix Glycyrrhizae*   6g

perilla fruit, *Fructus Perillae*   10g

紫菀12克，款冬花12克，生姜10克，大枣5枚，杏仁10克，苏子10克。水煎服。

恶寒者，加桂枝10克；喘甚者，加葶苈子10克，地龙10克。

本证用小青龙汤治疗效果亦佳（见本文库《方剂学》有关部分）。

2. 热哮

主证：喘急痰鸣，胸膈烦闷，甚则胸高气粗，痰粘黄稠，口渴，多发于炎热季节，或每因遇热而发，舌质红，苔黄腻，脉滑数。

治则：清热化痰，宣肺平喘。

处方：麻杏石甘汤合三子养亲汤加减。

麻黄10克，杏仁10克，生石膏30克，甘草6克，苏子10克。

lepidium seed, *Semen Lepidii seu Descurainiae*   10g

earthworm, *Lumbricus*   12g

mulberry bark, *Cortex Mori Radicis*   12g

trichosanthes seed, *Semen Trichosanthis*   18g

Sichuan fritillary bulb, *Bulbus Fritillariae Cirrhosae*   10g

All the above drugs are to be decocted in water for oral administration.

In case of profuse perspiration, ephedra (*Herba Ephedrae*) is removed from the above recipe, on the other hand, 30 grams of honeysuckle flower (*Flos Lonicerae*) is added if fever is present; 18 grams of powder of clam shell (*Concha Meratricis seu Cyclinae*), 15 grams of glehnia root (*Radix Glehniae*) are employed for patients who cough with thick yellowish sputum; 6 grams of eagle wood (*Lignum Aquilariae Resinatum*) and 10 grams of magnolia bark (*Cortex Magnoliae Officinalis*) for patients with dyspnea and adverse flow of *qi*.

3. Asthma of Deficiency Type

Main Symptoms and Signs: Chronic and recurrent attacks for a long time, constant minor and persistent asthma at ordinary times. The sound of cough being low and weak, palpitation and shortness of breath, spontaneous perspiration and aversion to wind, general debility, pale tongue with little fur, deep thready and weak pulse.

Therapeutic Principle: Tonifying the lung and spleen, improving inspiration to relieve asthma.

Recipe: Powder of Ginseng and Gecko with additional ingredients.

ginseng, *Radix Ginseng*   10g

gecko, *Gecko*   3g   (ground and taken after being infused in the finished decoction)

walnut kernel, *Semen Juglandis*   15g

ophiopogon root, *Radix Ophiopogonis*   10g

schisandra fruit, *Fructus Schisandrae*   10g

astragalus root, *Radix Astragali seu Hedysari*   12g

葶苈子10克，地龙12克，桑白皮12克，瓜蒌仁18克，川贝母10克。

水煎服。

汗多者，去麻黄；身热者，加银花30克；痰粘黄稠者，加海蛤壳粉18克，沙参15克；喘急气逆者，加沉香6克，厚朴10克。

3. 虚哮

主证：哮喘反复发作日久，平时常有轻度持续性喘息，咳声低弱，心悸气短，自汗畏风，形神疲惫，舌质淡，苔少，脉沉细弱。

治则：补肺健脾，纳气定喘。

处方：人参蛤蚧散加味。

人参10克，蛤蚧粉3克（冲服），胡桃肉15克，麦冬10克，五味子10克，黄芪12克，冬虫夏草12克，百合15克，茯苓12克，橘

cordyceps, *Cordyceps*   12g
lily bulb, *Bulbus Lilii*   15g
poria, *Poria*   12g
red tangerine peel, *Exocarpium Citri Reticulatae*   12g
prepared licorice root, *Radix Glycyrrhizae Praeparata*   6g

All the above drugs except gecko are to be decocted in water for oral administration.

Section 6
Chronic Bronchitis

The disease is a chronic inflammation of bronchi due to infection, physical and chemical irritations and allergic agents. The majority of the patients are of over middle age. It is characterized by chronic course and recurrent episodes. In some chronic cases, the disease may progress to chronic obstructive emphysema and chronic pulmonary heart disease. In TCM, this disease is related to the categories of *"ke sou"* (cough), *"tan yin"* (phlegm retension), *"xiao chuan"* (asthma) and so on.

MAIN POINTS OF DIAGNOSIS

1. Long-term cough, sputum production and dyspnea which attack repeatedly and fluctuate are worse in autumn and winter. There may be fever, exacerbation of cough and mucopurulent sputum production, and dyspnea is more marked if acute concurrent infection is present.

2. Chronic bronchitis usually persists for many years. It can be classified into 3 stages, acute episodic stage, chronic persistent stage and clinically remissive stage. The last stage may last for a period of time and an attack may be induced by infections or catching a cold. Based on the clinical manifestations, the disease can be divided into simple chronic bronchitis and chronic asthmatic bronchitis. In the former, cough and sputum production are predominant. In the latter, in addition to the above symptoms, there are dyspnea and wheezing, indicat-

红12克，炙甘草6克。水煎服。

第六节　慢性支气管炎

慢性支气管炎是由于支气管感染、物理和化学因素刺激或过敏所致的慢性支气管炎症。患者以中年以上居多。临床上以病情迁延、反复发作为其特点，久病者常引起慢性阻塞性肺气肿和慢性肺心病。本病属中医"咳嗽"、"痰饮"、"哮"、"喘"等范畴。

【诊断要点】

1. 长期反复发作的咳嗽、咳痰和喘息，病情时轻时重，秋冬季节发作频繁。合并急性感染者可有发热、咳嗽加剧、咳脓性和粘性痰，喘息症状明显加重。

2. 慢性支气管炎常迁延多年不愈。其病程临床上可分为急性发作阶段、慢性迁延阶段和临床缓解阶段。后者可持续一段时间，又可因感染或受凉等因素而诱发。根据临床发病特点，又可分为单纯性慢性支气管炎和慢性喘息性支气管炎。前者以咳嗽、咳痰为主要表现；后者在前者基础上增加喘息症状，并常闻及哮

ing that the spasm of the smooth muscles of bronchi and bronchioli is an important pathogenetic factor.

3. On auscultation, moist rales can usually be heard. Wheezes can be heard in patients with asthmatic bronchitis. In patients with chronic bronchitis of long duration, a complicating obstructive emphysema is commonly present. In such cases, the respiratory sounds are diminished, heart sounds become faint, intercostal spaces are widened, the thorax is barrel-shaped, and there is hyperresonance on percussion.

4. On radiographic examination the lung-markings are increased in the lower lung fields. Pulmonary functional tests show no change in the early stage, but in the late stage residual volume is increased, maximal ventilatory equivalent and time vital capacity are decreased.

DIFFERENTIATION AND TREATMENT OF COMMON SYNDROMES

1. Interior Retension of Phlegm with Exopathic Cold

Main Symptoms and Signs: Cough with whitish thin sputum, dyspnea, or accompanied with chills and headache, whitish and moist fur of the tongue, string-like and tight or floating and tight pulse.

Therapeutic Principle: Relieving exterior syndome and warming the interior organs, ventilating the lung to resolve phlegm retention.

Recipe: Modified Minor Decoction of Green Dragon.

ephedra, *Herba Ephedrae*   6g

cinnamon twig, *Ramulus Cinnamomi*   6g

schisandra fruit, *Fructus Schisandrae*   6g

white peony root, *Radix Paeoniae Alba*   10g

asarum herb, *Herba Asari* 3g

pinella tuber, *Rhizoma Pinelliae*   10g

dried ginger, *Rhizoma Zingiberis*   6g

coltsfoot flower, *Flos Farfarae*   12g

licorice root, *Radix Glycyrrhizae*   6g

鸣音，提示支气管和细支气管平滑肌痉挛是发病的重要因素。

3．肺部听诊常闻及湿性罗音，喘息性支气管炎常闻及哮鸣音。久病者常合并阻塞性肺气肿，此时呼吸音减弱，心音遥远，肋间隙变宽，胸廓呈桶状，叩诊呈过清音。

4．胸部X线检查两肺纹理增多，以下肺野较明显。肺功能检查早期无改变，晚期出现残气量增加，最大通气量和时间肺活量减低。

【辨证论治】

1．外寒内饮

主证：咳嗽气喘，痰白而稀，或兼有恶寒头痛，舌苔白润，脉弦紧或浮紧。

治则：解表温里，宣肺化饮。

处方：小青龙汤加减。

麻黄6克，桂枝6克，五味子6克，白芍10克，细辛3克，

All the above drugs are to be decocted in water for oral administration.

The disorder is marked with absence of exterior syndrome, manifested as cough with profuse sputum which is whitish and mucous, feeling of fullness and distress in the chest, anorexia, abdominal distension, all these suggest that the accumulation of phlegm-dampness is in the lung. The principle of treatment should be aimed at eliminating dampness and removing phlegm. The above recipe can be modified for treatment with the exception of ephedra, cinnamon twig and white peony root, and with the addition of 12 grams of red tangerine peel (*Exocarpium Citri Reticulatae*), 15 grams of poria (*Poria*), 10 grams of perilla fruit (*Fructus Perillae*), 10 grams of magnolia bark (*Cortex Magnoliae Officinalis*) and 10 grams of atractylodes rhizome (*Rhizoma Atractylodis*).

2. Stagnation of Phlegm-heat

Main Symptoms and Signs: Bad cough with thick yellowish sputum, thirst, dry throat, yellow-coloured urine, constipation, reddened tongue with yellow fur, slippery and rapid or taut and rapid pulse.

Therapeutic Principle: Removing pathogenic heat and resolving phlegm.

Recipe: Modified prescriptions of Lung-heat Expelling Powder combined with Decoction for Clearing Away Lung-heat and Disolving Phlegm.

  mulberry bark, *Cortex Mori Radicis*   12g
  wolfberry bark, *Cortex Lucii Radicis*   12g
  scutellaria root, *Radix Scutellariae*   12g
  anemarrhena rhizome, *Rhizoma Anemarrhenae*   12g
  Sichuan fritillary bulb, *Bulbus Fritilariae Cirrhosae*   10g
  bitter apricot kernel, *Semen Armeniacae Amarum*   10g
  stemona root, *Radix Stemonae*   15g
  trichosanthes seed, *Semen Trichosanthis*   18g
  honey fried loquat leaf, *Folium Eriobotryae Praeparata*   15g

半夏10克，干姜6克，款冬花12克，甘草6克。水煎服。

若无表证，咳嗽痰多，痰白而粘，胸胁满闷，纳差腹胀者，属痰湿犯肺。治宜燥湿祛痰，可予上方去麻黄、桂枝、芍药，加橘红12克，茯苓15克，苏子10克，厚朴10克，苍术10克。

2. 痰热蕴结

主证：咳嗽较剧，咯痰黄稠，口渴咽干，尿黄便秘，舌质红，苔黄，脉滑数或弦数。

治则：清热化痰。

处方：泻白散合清金化痰汤加减。

桑白皮12克，地骨皮12克，黄芩12克，知母12克，川贝10克，

platycodon root, *Radix Platycodi*   10g

All the above drugs are to be decocted in water for oral administration.

Besides, 20 grams of gypsum (*Gypsum Fibrosum*) are added for the case with high fever; 15 grams of clam shell powder (*Concha Meretricis seu Cyclinae*) for the case with profuse sputum which is difficult to cough out; 20 grams of lily bulb (*Bulbus Lilii*) and 20 grams of dried rehmannia root (*Radix Rehmanniae*) for treating the case of *yin* deficiency of both the lung and kidney marked by nonproductive cough or little sputum, hot sensation in the palms and soles, night sweat, reddened tongue with little fur, fine and rapid pulse.

3. Deficiency of Both the Lung and Spleen

Main Symptoms and Signs: Weak cough, spontaneous perspiration, shortness of breath, tendency to catch cold, exacerbation of cough in contact with wind-cold, or anorexia and loose stools, thin whitish fur of tongue, and deep fine pulse.

Therapeutic Principle: Nourishing the lung by reinforcing the function of the spleen.

Recipe: Modified Decoction for Tonifying the Lung.

dangshen, *Radix Codonopsis Pilosulae*   10g

astragalus root, *Radix Astragali seu Hedysari*   10g

schisandra fruit, *Fructus Schisandrae*   10g

aster root, *Radix Asteris*   12g

coltsfoot flower, *Flos Farfarae*   12g

white atractylodes rhizome, *Rhizoma Atractylodis Macrocephalae*   10g

poria, *Poria*   12g

honey-fried licorice root, *Radix Glycyrrhizae Praeparata*   6g

All the above drugs are to be decocted in water for oral administration.

杏仁10克，百部15克，瓜蒌仁18克，炙杷叶15克，桔梗10克。水煎服。

热甚者，加生石膏20克；痰多难咯者，加海蛤壳粉15克；干咳痰少、手足心热、盗汗、舌红少苔、脉细数者，属肺肾阴虚，可加百合20克，生地20克。

3. 肺脾两虚

主证：咳嗽无力，自汗气短，易患感冒，每遇风寒咳嗽加重，或有纳差便溏，苔薄白，脉沉细。

治则：健脾补肺。

处方：补肺汤加减。

党参10克，黄芪10克，五味子10克，紫菀12克，款冬花12克，白术10克，茯苓12克，炙甘草6克。水煎服。

Section 7
Pulmonary Abscess

Pulmonary abscess, a suppurative infection of the lung, is caused by a variety of pathogenic bacteria, most of which are anaerobe. The pathogens mostly invade the lung by aspiration. In a small percentage of patients the abscess arises from hematogenous infections. Since antibiotics are widely used in clinical practice, the incidence of the disease has become lower and lower. In TCM, the disease is called *"feiyong"* (abscess of lung).

MAIN POINTS OF DIAGNOSIS

1. Medical history and onset of the disease: Pulmonary abscess due to aspiration is frequently caused by vomit resulting from coma, drunken state and esophageal and pylonic obstruction, or by oral inflammation and pharyngolaryngeal operation. The pathogenic bacteria, carried into the lung through respiratory movements, multiply there. Hematogenous pulmonary abscess is often secondary to pyemia due to the pyogenic infections of the skin and deep tissues, osteomyelitis, etc.

2. Clinical manifestations: The onset is abrupt with initial symptoms of chills, fever, chest pain, cough, hemoptysis and the production of a large amount of purulent sputum. The sputum is viscid and fetid. At the initial stage physical examination may show no obvious changes on the lung. When there is consolidation resulting from inflammation, there may be dullness on percussion. If there is a cavity formation, an amphoric sound may be elicited on percussion.

3. In blood examination leukocyte count is markedly increased up to $20—30 \times 10^9/L$, increased neutrophil with a shift to left. In hemato genous pulmonary abscess blood culture may be positive and pathogenic bacteria can be identified. Bloody sputum culture and antimicrobial sensitive test should be done,

第七节　肺脓肿

肺脓肿可由各种病原菌引起，其中以厌氧菌所致者较多，系肺部化脓性病变。病原菌侵入肺部的途径，多数为吸入所致，少部分来自血源性感染。自抗菌素广泛应用于临床以来，本病已逐渐少见。中医称之为"肺痈"。

【诊断要点】

1. 病史和发病：吸入性肺脓肿多因昏迷、醉酒、胃和食道梗阻所致呕吐、口腔炎症和咽喉部手术等，使细菌随呼吸进入肺内繁殖所致；血源性肺脓肿多继发于皮肤和深部组织化脓性感染、骨髓炎等，细菌侵入血流发生脓毒血症而引起。

2. 临床表现：起病急骤，患者多有畏寒、发热、胸痛、咳嗽、咯血以及咳大量脓性痰，痰常粘稠，味臭。体检时初期肺部体征不明显。当肺组织由于炎症而实变时，叩诊可呈实音；出现空洞时，叩诊呈空盒音。

3. 血化验白细胞明显增高，可达 $20\sim30\times10^9/L$，中性增高伴核左移。血源性肺脓肿血培养可发现致病菌。血痰培养结合药

which are helpful for selecting effective antibiotics. Chest X-ray examination is useful for discovering early lesions. Aspiration pulmonary abscess is mostly located in the posterior segment of the right upper lobe and apical segment of the right lower lobe. At the initial stage there is a large area of consolidation. When abscess or abscess cavity is formed, fluid level within it can be seen. In hematogenous pulmonary abscess, many small dense shadows or globular shadows or thinwall cavities in both left and right middle and lower lobes may be present. Computerized tomography is helpful in making correct diagnosis and in identifying the degree of involvement of the bronchi.

DIFFERENTIATION AND TREATMENT OF COMMON SYNDROMES

1. The Primary Stage

Main Symptoms and Signs: Chills, fever, cough, chest pain, small amount of mucous sputum, disturbance of breath, thin and yellowish coating of the tongue, floating and rapid pulse.

Therapeutic Principle: Clearing away and dispelling lung-heat and removing toxic substances from the lung.

Recipe: Modified Powder of Lonicera and Forsythia.

honeysuckle flower, *Flos Lonicerae*   30g
forsythia fruit, *Fructus Forsythiae*   15g
isatis leaf, *Folium Isatidis*   15g
scutellaria root, *Radix Scutellariae*   12g
dandelion herb, *Herba Taraxaci*   30g
peppermint, *Herba Menthae*   10g
houttuynia, *Herba Houttuyniae*   30g
Sichuan fritillary bulb, *Bulbus Fritillariae Cirrhosae*   10g
platycodon root, *Radix Platycodi*   10g

All the above drugs are to be decocted in water for oral administration.

Notice should be taken of the cases complicated with chest pain, for which 20 grams of trichosanthes fruit (*Fructus Trichosanthis*) and 12 grams of curcuma root (**Radix Curcumae**) may

敏试验，对选择有效抗菌素很有帮助。胸部X线检查有助早期发现病变。吸入性肺脓肿多见于右上叶后段和下叶尖段，早期呈大片致密影，脓肿形成或空洞形成后，其内可见液平面，血源性肺脓肿在两中下肺可见多数小块状或球形阴影或薄壁空洞。X线断层摄影有助于正确诊断，并可了解支气管受累情况。

【辨证论治】

1. 初期

主证：恶寒发热，咳嗽胸痛，痰粘量少，呼吸不利，舌苔薄黄，脉浮数。

治则：清肺散邪，佐以解毒。

处方：银翘散加减。

银花30克，连翘15克，大青叶15克，黄芩12克，蒲公英30克，薄荷10克，鱼腥草30克，川贝母10克，桔梗10克。水煎服。

胸痛者，加全瓜蒌20克，郁金12克。

be added.

2. The Abscess-forming Stage

Main Symptoms and Signs: Fever, cough with dyspnea, chest fullness, chest pain, productive cough, polypnea, dry mouth without thirst, reddened tongue with yellow greasy fur, and smooth rapid pulse.

Therapeutic Principle: Removing pathogenic heat and toxic materials.

Recipe: Modified Reed Rhizome Decoction Worth a Thousand Gold.

reed chizome, *Rhizoma Phragmitis*   30g
coix seed, *Semen Coicis*   30g
waxgourd seed, *Semen Benincasae*   24g
peach kernel, *Semen Persicae*   10g
honeysuckle flower, *Flos Lonicerae*   30g
forsythia fruit, *Fructus Forsythiae*   15g
scutellaria root, *Radix Scutellariae*   12g
houttuynia, *Herba Houttuyniae*   30g
trichosanthes fruit, *Fructus Trichosanthis*   20g
platycodon root, *Radix Platycodi*   10g
licorice root, *Radix Glycyrrhizae*   6g

All the above drugs are to be decocted in water for oral administration.

Apart from the above ingredients, 30 grams of gypsum (*Gypsum Fibrosum*) and 10 grams of anemarrhena rhizome (*Rhizoma Anemarrhenae*) are to be dosed for the patients with high fever and thirst; 30 grams of dandelion herb (*Herba Taraxaci*), 15 grams of herb of Tokyo violet (*Herba Violae*) and 10 grams of capejasmine fruit (*Fructus Gardeniae*) for the case with persisting high fever; 20 grams of dried rehmannia root (*Radix Rehmanniae*) and 12 grams of hyacinth bletilla (*Rhizoma Bletillae*) for treating profuse hemoptysis; 12 grams of mulberry bark (*Cortex Mori Radicis*) and 10 grams of lepidium seed (*Semen Lepidii seu Descurainiae*) for overcoming profuse sputum and dyspnea with chest distension.

2．成痈期

主证：发热，咳嗽喘满，胸闷疼痛，咳吐粘痰，呼吸迫促，口燥不渴，舌质红，苔黄腻，脉滑数。

治则：清热解毒。

处方：千金苇茎汤加减。

苇茎30克，生苡仁30克，冬瓜子24克，桃仁10克，银花30克，连翘15克，黄芩12克，鱼腥草30克，全瓜蒌20克，桔梗10克，生甘草6克。水煎服。

高热口渴者，加生石膏30克，知母10克；持续高热者，加蒲公英30克，地丁15克，栀子10克；咯血甚者，加生地20克，白芨12克；痰多喘满者，加桑白皮12克，葶苈子10克。

3. The Abscess-bursting Stage

Main Symptoms and Signs: Coughing out a large quantity of fetid and purulent sputum, sometimes mixed with blood, chest pain, stuffiness and distension in the chest, slow lysis of fever, red tongue with yellow and greasy fur, deep and forceful or slippery and rapid pulse.

Therapeutic Principle: Draining pus and removing the poisonous substanses.

Recipe: Decoction of Platycodon Root with additional ingredients.

platycodon root, *Radix Platycodi*   15g
coix seed, *Semen Coicis*   20g
houttuynia, *Herba Houttuyniae*   30g
patrinia, *Herba Patriniae*   30g
fibraurae stem, *Caulis Sargentodoxae*   30g
waxgourd seed, *Semen Benincasae*   30g
fritillary bulb, *Bulbus Fritillariae Thunbergii*   15g
honeysuckle flower, *Flos Lonicerae*   30g
licorice root, *Radix Glycyrrhizae*   6g

All the above drugs are to be decocted in water for oral administration.

If the case in the restoration stage is accompanied with impaired *qi* and *yin* manifested as low fever, weakness, cough with little sputum, and expectorating persistently purulent blood, spontaneous perspiration and night sweat, red tongue with little fur, fine and rapid pulse, it is suitable to aim the treatment at nourishing *qi* and *yin* and clearing away the remaining poisonous substances. The chosen recipe is Modified prescriptions of Decoction of Glehnia and Ophiopogon and Pulse-activating Powder. The compositions are: glehnia root (*Radix Glehniae*) 15g, ophiopogon root (*Radix Ophiopogonis*) 15g, pseudostellaria root (*Radix Pseudostellariae*) 12g, astragalus root (*Radix Astragali seu Hedysari*) 12g, waxgourd seed (*Semen Benincasae* 20g, platycodon root (*Radix Platycodi*) 12g, hyacinth bletilla (*Rhizoma Bletillae*)

3. 溃脓期

主证：咳吐大量腥臭脓痰，或痰中带血，胸痛，胸中闷胀，

身热渐退，舌质红，苔黄腻，脉沉实或滑数。

治则：排脓解毒。

处方：桔梗汤加味。

桔梗15克，生苡仁20克，鱼腥草30克，败酱草30克，红藤30

克，冬瓜子30克，浙贝15克，银花30克，生甘草6克。水煎服。

若在恢复期气阴耗损，低热无力，咳嗽痰少，但咳吐脓血，

久延不净，自汗盗汗，舌红少苔，脉细数。治宜补养气阴，兼清

余毒。可用沙参麦冬汤合生脉散加减：沙参15克，麦冬15克，太

子参12克，黄芪12克，冬瓜子20克，桔梗12克，白芨12克，生地

12g, dried rehmannia root (*Radix Rehmanniae*) 15g, honeysuckle flower (*Flos Lonicerae*) 15g, prepared licorice root (*Radix Glycyrrhizae Praeparata*) 6g.

Section 8
Rheumatic Fever

Rheumatic fever is an allergic disease which occurs as a delayed sequel to group A hemolytic streptococcal infection. It involves in connective tissues of the heart, joints, skin and vessels. It appears most commonly in school-age children, and between the ages of 20—30. Repeated recurrences of rheumatic fever may cause valvular damage and eventually a chronic rheumatic valvular disease. In TCM, this disease belongs to the categories of "*bi zheng*" (arthralgia-syndrome) and "*xin bi*" (obstruction of the heart-*qi*).

MAIN POINTS OF DIAGNOSIS

According to the revised Jones criteria for the diagnosis of rheumatic fever, if there is an evidence of group A streptococcal infection 1—4 weeks previous to the rheumatic attack and if cases manifest 2 major criteria or one major criterion and 2 minor criteria listed below, the diagnosis of rheumatic fever can be established.

1. Major criteria

(1) Carditis: This includes endocarditis, myocarditis and pericarditis, manifested as tachycardia, cardiac enlargement, attenuation of the first heart sound and the presence of a systolic and diastolic murmurs (Coomb's murmur) at the apex area of heart. Pericardial friction rub may be present. Electrocardiogram may show various kinds of arrhythmia, among which various degrees of conduction block are of the greatest significance.

(2) Migratory polyarthritis: The large joints of the extremities are most frequently affected. The affected joints are

15克，银花15克，炙甘草6克。

第八节　风湿热

风湿热是由A族溶血性链球菌感染后引起的一种变态反应性疾病。病变可累及心脏、关节、皮肤和血管等部位的结缔组织。临床上以学龄儿童和20～30岁青年为多见。本病反复发病可导致心脏瓣膜损害，最终引起慢性风湿性瓣膜病。本病属中医"痹证"、"心痹"等范畴。

【诊断要点】

根据修正的Jones诊断标准，发病前1～4周有A族溶血性链球菌的感染证据，凡符合下述条件中两项主要条件或一项主要条件伴二项次要条件，均可诊为风湿热。

1. 主要条件

（1）心脏炎：包括心内膜炎、心肌炎和心包炎。表现为心动过速、心脏增大、第一心音减弱、心脏收缩期和舒张期杂音或出现心包摩擦音。心电图检查可发现各种心律失常，其中以不同程度的心脏传导阻滞意义为最大。

（2）多发性、游走性关节炎：多累及较大关节，伴局部红肿

red, swollen, hot and tender. The acute arthritis subsides without sequel.

(3) Erythema annulare.

(4) Subcutaneous nodules.

(5) Chorea.

2. Minor criteria

(1) Fever: Fever is mild or moderate accompanied with hidrosis, weakness and weight loss.

(2) Elevated erythrocyte sedimentation rate, positive C-reactive protein or increased white cell count.

3. The evidence of recent streptococcal infection

(1) There was angina, acute tonsillitis and others 1—4 weeks prior to the onset of rheumatic fever. Or the throat swab culture is positive for group A hemolytic streptococci.

(2) Elevation of antistreptolysin (ASO) titer > 500 units, elevation of antistreptokinase (ASK) > 80 units or elevation of antihyaluronidase titer (AHT) > 128 units. Other nonspecific serum components may also have changes.

DIFFERENTIATION AND TREATMENT OF COMMON SYNDROMES

1. Wind-dampness-heat Syndrome

Main Symptoms and Signs: Redness, swelling, heat sensation and pain of the joints which is too painful to be touched but relieved by cold, inability to move, restlessness and discomfort in the chest, sometimes accompanied with fever and thirst, red tongue with dry and yellow fur, slippery and rapid pulse.

Therapeutic Principle: Dispelling pathogenic heat, removing obstruction in the channels and dispelling pathogenic wind and dampness.

Recipe: Modified White Tiger Decoction Added with Cinnamon Twig.

gypsum, *Gypsum Gibrosum*   30g

anemarrhena rhizome, *Rhizoma Anemarrhenae*   12g

polished round-grained nonglutinous rice   12g

热痛，愈后无后遗症。

（3）环形红斑。

（4）皮下结节。

（5）舞蹈病。

2．次要条件

（1）发热：多为轻度或中度发热，并伴有多汗、乏力、体重减轻。

（2）血沉增快、C—反应蛋白阳性或白细胞增高。

3．新近链球菌感染证据

（1）发病前1～4周有咽峡炎、急性扁桃体炎等，或咽拭子培养A族溶血性链球菌阳性。

（2）抗链球菌溶血素O效价增高（>500单位）或抗链球菌激酶>80单位或抗透明质酸酶>128单位，以及其他非特异性血清成份改变。

【辨证论治】

1．风湿热证

主证：关节疼痛，局部灼热红肿，痛不可及，得冷则舒，不能活动，烦闷不适，或有发热口渴，舌质红，苔黄燥，脉滑数。

治则：清热通络，佐以疏风除湿。

处方：白虎加桂枝汤加减。

石膏30克，知母12克，粳米12克，甘草6克，桂枝6克，薏

licorice root, *Radix Glycyrrhizae*   6g

cinnamon twig, *Ramulus Cinnamomi*   6g

coix seed, *Semen Coicis*   30g

honeysuckle stem, *Caulis Lonicerae*   30g

mulberry twigs, *Ramulus Mori*   30g

phellodendron bark, *Cortex Phellodendri*   10g

red peony root, *Radix Paeoniae Rubra*   10g

large-leaf gentian root, *Radix Gentianae Macrophyllae*   15g

All the above drugs are to be decocted in water for oral administration.

When the case is accompanied with erythema annulare and subcutaneous nodule, the above recipe should include the following ingredients: red sage root (*Radix Salviae Miltiorrhizae*) 15g, safflower (*Flos Carthami*) 10g and arnebia root (*Radix Arnebiae seu Lithospermi*) 10g.

2. Wind-cold-dampness Syndrome

Main Symptoms and Signs: Persistent arthralgia of the extremities aggravated by cold and relieved by warmth, pale tongue with whitish thin and greasy fur, floating and slow pulse. If the pain is migratory, involving more joints, it is mainly due to pathogenic wind. If the pain is comparatively aggravated and localized accompanied with a feeling of cold in the affected region, it is chiefly due to pathogenic cold; if the involved joints is marked by heavy sensation, numbness or swelling, it is mainly due to pathogenic dampness.

Therapeutic Principle: Dispersing pathogenic wind, cold and dampness.

Recipe: Modified Decoction for Treating Rheumatic or Rheumatoid Arthritis.

notopterygium root, *Rhizoma seu Radix Notopterygii*   10g

pubescent angelica root, *Radix Angelicae Pubescentis*   10g

cinnamon twig, *Ramulus Cinnamomi*   10g

large-leaf gentian root, *Radix Gentianae Mocrophyllae*   12g

Chinese angelica, *Radix Angelicae Sinensis*   10g

苡仁30克，忍冬藤30克，桑枝30克，黄柏10克，赤芍10克，秦艽15克。水煎服。

若伴有环形红斑、皮下结节，加丹参15克，红花10克，紫草10克。

2. 风寒湿证

主证：肢体关节疼痛，遇寒更甚，得暖则减，病久不愈，舌质淡，苔薄白或腻，脉濡迟。若疼痛游走不定，涉及多个关节者，为风邪偏盛；若疼痛较剧，痛有定处，局部有冷感者，为寒邪偏盛；若痛处重着、麻木或肿胀者，为湿邪偏盛。

治则：祛风散寒除湿。

处方：蠲痹汤加减。

羌活10克，独活10克，桂枝10克，秦艽12克，当归10克，川

chuanxiong rhizome, *Rhizoma Ligustici Chuanxiong*   10g

futokadsura stem, *Caulis Piperis Futokadsurae*   30g

spatholobus stem, *Caulis Spatholobi*   30g

mulberry twigs, *Ramulus Mori*   30g

All the above drugs are to be decocted in water for oral administration.

In cases mainly due to pathogenic wind, 12 grams of clematis root (*Radix Clematidis*) and 10 grams of ledebouriella root (*Radix Ledebouriellae*) should be added; In cases chiefly due to pathogenic cold, 3 grams of prepared Sichuan aconite root (*Radix Aconiti Praeparata*), 3 grams of prepared wild aconite root (*Radix Aconiti Kusnezoffii Praeparata*) and 6 grams of licorice root (*Radix Glycyrrhizae*) may be employed. As for cases mainly due to pathogenic dampness, 30 grams of coix seed (*Semen Coicis*) and 12 grams of atractylodes rhizome (*Rhizoma Atractylodis*) are to be added. When the disorder is accompanied with chorea, 12 grams of white peony root (*Radix Paeoniae Alba*), 12 grams of achyranthes root (*Radix Achyranthis Bidentatae*), 10 grams of gastrodia tuber (*Rhizoma Gastradiae*) and 20 grams of uncaria stem with hooks (*Ramulus Uncariae cum Uncis*) are to be included. When the case becomes chronic marked by repeated attacks and aggravated arthralgia, it is advisable to overcome it with the addition of 10 grams of frankincense (*Resina Olibani*), 10 grams of myrrh (*Myrrha*), 12 grams of earthworm (*Lumbricus*) and 6 grams of scorpion (*Scorpio*). When there are symptoms of deficiency and weakness of both *qi* and blood as well as deficiency of the liver and kidney caused by delayed recovery, the above recipe should also include 15 grams of astragalus root (*Radix Astragali seu Hedysari*), 12 grams of dangshen (*Radix Codonopsis Pilosulae*), 12 grams of eucommia bark (*Cortex Eucommiae*) and 15 grams of loranthus mulberry mistletoe (*Ramulus Loranthi*).

3. Deficiency of *Qi* and *Yin*

Main Symptoms and Signs: Palpitation, shortness of breath, chest stuffiness or chest pain, insomnia, arthralgia with slight

芎10克，海风藤30克，鸡血藤30克，桑枝30克。水煎服。

若风邪偏盛者，加威灵仙12克，防风10克；寒邪偏盛者，加

制川乌3克，制草乌3克，甘草6克；湿邪偏盛者，加薏苡仁30

克，苍术12克。若伴有舞蹈症者，加白芍12克，牛膝12克，天麻

10克，钩藤20克。若病情迁延，反复发作，关节疼痛加剧，可加

乳香10克，没药10克，地龙12克，全蝎6克。若病久气血虚弱，

肝肾亏损者，加黄芪15克，党参12克，杜仲12克，桑寄生15克。

3．气阴两虚

主证：心悸，气短，胸闷或胸痛，不寐，关节疼痛微肿，舌

swelling, red tongue with whitish thin fur, thready and rapid pulse.

Therapeutic Principle: Tonifying *qi* and nourishing *yin*, removing pathogenic dampness and obstruction in the channels.

Recipe: Pulse-activating Powder with additional ingredients.

dangshen, *Radix Codonopsis Pilosulae*   15g

ophiopogon root, *Radix Ophiopogonis*   10g

schisandra fruit, *Fructus Schisandrae*   10g

large-leaf gentian root, *Radix Gentianae Macrophyllae*   10g

Chinese angelica, *Radix Angelicae Sinensis*   10g

red sage root, *Radix Salviae Miltiorrhizae*   15g

coix seed, *Semen Coicis*   15g

arborvitae seed, *Semen Biotae*   10g

tetrandra root, *Radix Stephaniae Tetrandrae*   12g

chaenomeles fruit, *Fructus Chaenomelis*   10g

All the above drugs are to be decocted in water for oral administration.

Section 9
Coronary Heart Disease

Coronary heart disease is the abbreviation of coronary atherosclerotic heart disease. The incidence is high in all the countries especially in the developed countries. Recently, the incidence in China is increasing. The risk factors for coronary heart disease are hypertension, hyperlipemia, diabetes mellitus and cigarette-smoking. According to the diagnostic criteria made by WHO, coronary heart disease can be divided into: (1) primary sudden cardiac arrest; (2) angina pectoris: (3) myocardiac infarction; (4) heart failure due to coronary heart disease and (5) arrhythmia. In this section, only angina pectoris and myocardiac infarction are described. This disease, in

质红，苔薄白，脉细数。

治则：益气养阴，利湿通络。

处方：生脉散加味。

党参15克，麦冬10克，五味子10克，秦艽10克，当归10克，

丹参15克，薏苡仁15克，柏子仁10克，防己12克，木瓜10克。水

煎服。

第九节　冠心病

冠心病是冠状动脉粥样硬化性心脏病的简称，世界各国特别

是发达国家患病率甚高，我国近年来亦有上升趋势。本病的易患

因素为高血压、高血脂、糖尿病和吸烟等。按世界卫生组织的诊

断标准，冠心病的分类诊断为：（1）原发心脏骤停；（2）心绞痛；

（3）心肌梗塞；（4）冠心病心力衰竭；（5）心律失常。本节重点

TCM, pertains to the categories of *"xiong bi"* (obstruction of *qi* in the chest), *"xiong tong"* (chest pain), *"zhen xin tong"* (myocardiac infarction) and *"iue xin tong"* (precordial pain with cold limbs).

Angina Pectoris

Angina pectoris is caused by trancient myocardial ischemia due to decreased coronary flow, manifested as episodic retrosternal pain, smothering and choking, etc.

MAIN POINTS OF DIAGNOSIS

1. Overworked angina: A transient attack of chest pain is induced by exertion, heavy meals, exposure to cold, or emotion. The typical manifestations are sudden attacks of retrosternal constricting oppressive pain or gripping pain. The pain commonly radiates to the left shoulder and left arm, accompanied with cold sweat. The pain lasts 1—5 minutes and can be relieved by resting or by placing a nitroglycerin tablet under the tongue. Overworked angina can be divided into incipient type, stable type and increscent type. In incipient type the duration of the illness is within one month. In stable type, the state of illness can be stable for a long time. The episodes have a definite regularity. In increscent type both the incidence and the severity of the attack increase, indicating the unstableness of the disease.

2. Spontaneous angina: The episodes are not related to exertion. The attack may occur in the recumbent position or during sleep, accompanied with restlessness, fright and hypertension. The symptoms persist longer and become more severe which could not be relieved by nitroglycerin.

Variant angina is a special type of angina pectoris. It is considered that the attacks are related to the spasm of the major one of coronary arteries. Its symptoms are similar to those of spontaneous angina. Many attacks may occur cyclically in a day. During the episodes ECG shows ST-segment elevation.

阐述心绞痛和心肌梗塞，属中医"胸痹"、"胸痛"、"真心痛"、"厥心痛"等范畴。

心绞痛

由于冠状动脉供血不足，心肌暂时性缺血引起发作性胸骨后疼痛或胸闷憋气等症状，称为心绞痛。

【诊断要点】

1. 劳累型心绞痛：由活动、饱餐、寒冷和情绪激动等因素，诱发短暂性胸痛发作，其典型表现为突然发作的胸骨后压榨性闷痛或绞痛，疼痛多放射到左肩、左臂，可伴出冷汗。疼痛多历时 1～5 分钟，休息或服用硝酸甘油即可缓解。劳累性心绞痛又分为初发性、稳定性和增剧性心绞痛。初发性心绞痛指病程在一个月以内；稳定性心绞痛的病情可长期稳定，其发作常有一定规律；增剧性心绞痛是指发作频度和严重程度均有增加，提示病情不稳定。

2. 自发性心绞痛：发作时与劳累无关，可在卧位或睡眠中发作，伴烦躁、惊恐不安及血压升高，症状持续较久，程度亦较重，不易被硝酸甘油所缓解。

变异性心绞痛是一种特殊心绞痛，其发作据认为与冠状动脉主支痉挛有关。其症状和自发性心绞痛相似，常一天内周期性发作多次，发作时心电图 ST 段升高。

In incipient angina, increscent angina, spontaneous angina and variant angina, the state of illness changes rapidly and transforms in a short period. This is a transitional state. Therefore, they are also called unstable angina and patients need to be admitted for treatment.

3. Electrocardiographic examination is convenient for the diagnosis of angina pectoris. During the attack of angina, most cases show various degrees of transient ST segment depression and inversion or flatness of T wave or accompanied with different types of arrhythmia. In the cases of variant angina and some spontaneous angina, ST segment elevation may be present, suggesting transmural ischemia at corresponding walls of ventricle. To exercise electrocardiogram stress test can help physicians in confirming the diagnosis of untypical cases.

4. Coronary arteriography is an invasive procedure by which the disease status and left ventricle function of more than 90% of the patients with coronary heart disease can be determined. Echocardiogram examination can give us some parameters for reference but its value in the diagnosis of coronary heart disease is limited. Radionuclide scanning is very helpful in diagnosing ischemic heart disease and evaluating heart function.

Myocardiac Infarction

Myocardiac infarction is the myocardial necrosis resulting from persistent and severe myocardial ischemia due to occlusion of a coronary artery and interruption of myocardial blood supply. Myocardiac infarction can be complicated by arrhythmia, heart failure, and cardiogenic shock. In severe cases or in patients who are not treated in time, death usually ensues.

MAIN POINTS OF DIAGNOSIS

1. Premonitory symptoms of myocardiac infarction: Some patients may have premonitory symptoms for a period of time prior to the onset of myocardiac infarction. The patients may have frequent episodes of angina pectoris which last longer

初发性、增剧性、自发性和变异性心绞痛病情变化较快，往往短时间内出现病情转化，是一种过渡情况，统称为不稳定性心绞痛，需住院治疗。

3. 心电图检查对于诊断冠心病心绞痛安全而方便，多数患者心冠痛发作时有一过程性S—T段下移和T波低平或倒置，或伴随有各种形式心律失常；变异性心绞痛和某些自发性心绞痛患者发作时可出现ST段上移，提示透壁心肌缺血。病情不典型患者可做心电图负荷试验，以帮助诊断。

4. 冠状动脉造影虽为有创检查，但能确诊90%以上冠心病患者的病变情况和左室功能；超声心电图检查对冠心病心绞痛诊断有一定限度，但可以提示一些有用指标作参考；心脏核素扫描对于诊断缺血性心脏病和判定心脏功能都很有帮助。

心肌梗塞

心肌梗塞是由于冠状动脉闭塞，心肌供血中断，导致心肌持久而严重的缺血所引起心肌坏死。心肌梗塞可出现心律失常、心力衰竭和心源性休克等并发症，重者或救治不及时常导致死亡。

【诊断要点】

1. 心肌梗塞先兆：部分患者在发病前一段时间表现为心绞痛发作频繁，持续时间长，疼痛程度重，或伴恶心、呕吐及心律

and more severe or are accompanied with nausea, vomiting and arrhythmia. The episodes can not be relieved by placing nitroglycerin tablet under the tongue. But many patients have not premonitory symptoms prior to the episode.

2. Clinical manifestations of myocardiac infarction: Retrosternal or precordial persistent pain occurs suddenly with a sensation of oppression. The pain may radiate to the neck and left shoulder. The patients commonly have profuse sweating, anxiety, pallor, thready pulse and lowering of blood pressure. In some of senile patients, the pain may not be obvious but confusional state, shock and heart failure are commonly seen.

3. In acute myocardiac infarction the electrocardiogram shows specific changes. In acute stage all the leads relevant to the site of infarction show arcuate elevation of ST segments, inversion of T waves and appearance of pathologic Q waves. Subsequently, as the disease turns better, the electrocardiogram undergoes a stereotyped changes.

4. Serum enzyme studies are very valuable for the diagnosis of acute myocardiac infarction. Their accuracies are high. Creatinine phosphokinase (CPK) and the MB isoenzyme are very valuable for diagnosing early myocardiac infarction. Serum glutamic oxalacetic transaminase (SGOT), lactic dehydrogenase (LDH) and isoenzymes are of value in the diagnosis of myocardiac infarction. In addition, the examinations of leukocyte count, blood sugar and serum myoglobin are also helpful for the diagnosis and the prognosis of the disease.

DIFFERENTIATION AND TREATMENT OF COMMON SYNDROMES

1. Obstruction of the Chest-*yang*

Main Symptoms and Signs: Oppressed feeling in the chest, paroxysmal chest pain with palpitation and shortness of breath often brought out by the attack of cold, white greasy fur of the tongue, and taut pulse.

Therapeutic Principle: Warming up and benefiting the

失常，含服硝酸甘油不能缓解。但不少患者发作前并无任何先兆症状。

2．心肌梗塞表现：胸骨后或心前区突然出现持续性疼痛，伴有压迫感，可放射到颈部和左肩，患者常出现多汗、焦虑、面色苍白、脉细和血压下降。部分老年患者疼痛不明显，但可出现意识障碍，休克和心衰亦常见。

3．急性心肌梗塞心电图有特异性改变。急性期在病变室壁所对应导联有 ST 段弓背上抬呈单项曲线，伴 T 波倒置和出现病理性 Q 波，以后伴随病情恢复，心电图可出现有规律的演变。

4．血清酶检查对急性心肌梗塞诊断意义很大，准确性亦高。肌酸磷酸激酶和同功酶 MB 对诊断早期心梗价值最大；谷—草转氨酶和乳酸脱氢酶及同功酶亦有相当价值。此外，白细胞、血糖和血清肌红蛋白检查对心肌梗塞诊断和预后都有一定价值。

【辨证论治】

1．胸阳痹阻

主证：胸闷憋气，阵发性胸痛，心悸气短，常于受寒后诱发，苔白腻，脉弦。

治则：温助胸阳，宣通心脉。

chest-*yang* to remove obstruction of blood flow in the heart-vessels.

Recipe: Decoction of Trichosanthes, Macrostem and Pinellia with additional ingredients:

trichosanthes fruit, *Fructus Trichosanthis*   20g

macrostem onion, *Bulbus Allii Macrostemi*   12g

pinellia tuber, *Rhizoma Pinelliae*   10g

cinnamon twig, *Ramulus Cinnamomi*   10g

red sage root, *Radix Salviae Miltiorrhizae*   30g

cat tail pollen, *Pollen Typhae*   10g

trogopterus dung, *Faeces Trogopterorum*   10g

All the above drugs are to be decocted in water for oral administration.

2. Blood Stasis in the Heart-vessels

Main Symptoms and Signs: Twinge in the chest radiating to the shoulder and back, stuffy sensation in the chest and shortness of breath, deep purple tongue with ecchymoses, taut or uneven pulse.

Therapeutic Principle: Promoting the flow of *qi* and blood, removing blood stasis and activating the heart-vessels.

Recipe: Modified prescriptions of Red Sage Drink and Decoction of Four Ingredients with Peach Kernel and Safflower.

red sage root, *Radix Salviae Miltiorrhizae*   30g

sandalwood, *Lignum Santali*   3g

amomum fruit, *Fructus Amomi*   10g

green tangerine orange peel, *Pericarpium Citri Reticulatae Viride*   5g

lindera root, *Radix Linderae*   5g

Chinese angelica, *Radix Angelicae Sinensis*   10g

chuanxiong rhizome, *Rhizoma Ligustici Chuanxiong*   10g

red peony root, *Radix Paeoniae Rubra*   10g

safflower, *Flos Carthami*   9g

peach kernel, *Semen Persicae*   10g

dalbergia wood, *Lignum Dalbergiae Odoriferae*   10g

处方：瓜蒌薤白半夏汤加味。

全瓜蒌20克，薤白12克，半夏10克，桂枝10克，丹参30克，

蒲黄10克，五灵脂10克。水煎服。

2. 心脉瘀阻

主证：心胸刺痛，痛引肩背，胸闷气短，舌质暗紫，有瘀点

或瘀斑，脉弦或涩。

治则：行气活血，化瘀通络。

处方：丹参饮合桃红四物汤加减。

丹参30克，檀香 3 克，砂仁10克，青皮 5 克，乌药 5 克，当

归10克，川芎10克，赤芍10克，红花 9 克，桃仁10克，降香10克。

All the above drugs are to be decocted in water for oral administration.

Clinically, blood stasis often coexists with and stagnation of *qi*. If stagnation of *qi* is dominative, more drugs for regulating *qi* are supposed to be administered. 12 grams of Sichuan chinaberry (*Fructus Meliae Toosendan*) and 10 grams of nutgrass flatsedge rhizome (*Rhizoma Cyperi*) are recommended. Whereas, if blood stasis is dominative, more drugs for activating blood circulation to remove blood stasis should be prescribed, such as cat tail pollen (*Pollen Typhae*) 10g, and trogopterus dung (*Faeces Trogopterorum*) 10g or frankincense (*Resina Olibanum*) 10g and myrrh (*Myrrha*) 10g.

If precordial pain is accompanied with choking sensation in the chest and it is closely related to emotional changes which are characterized by unhappiness, eructation, malaise in the bilateral hypochondriac regions and taut pulse, it is advisable to aim the treatment at relieving the depressed liver, regulating the circulation of *qi* and promoting blood circulation to remove blood stasis. Recipe for the above syndrome is Powder for Treating Cold Limbs with additional ingredients, namely: bupleurum root (*Radix Bupleuri*) 10g, immature bitter orange (*Fructus Aurantii Immaturus*) 10g, white peony root (*Radix Paeoniae Alba*) 10g, licorice root (*Radix Glycyrrhizae*) 6g, chuanxiong rhizome (*Rhizoma Ligustici Chuanxiong*) 10g, dalbergia wood (*Lignum Dalbergiae Odoriferae*) 10g, nutgrass flatsedge rhizome (*Rhizoma Cyperi*) 10g, red sage root (*Radix Salviae Miltiorrhizae*) 15g, curcuma root (*Radix Curcumae*) 12g. All the above drugs are to be decocted in water for oral administration.

As for patients suffering from stagnation of phlegm in the body marked by pain and oppressed feeling in the chest, obesity, heavy sensation of body and fatigue, palpitation and shortness of breath, white greasy fur of the tongue, taut and smooth pulse, the treatment should be directed at regulating the spleen and eliminating dampness with aromatics. Decoction for Clearing

水煎服。

临床上血瘀常与气滞并存。气滞偏重者，应加重理气药，可加川楝子12克，香附10克；血瘀偏重者，应加重活血化瘀药，可加蒲黄10克，五灵脂10克，或乳香10克，没药10克。

若心痛伴有胸闷，且与情绪变化关系密切，并兼见郁闷不乐、嗳气、两胁不适、脉弦等症，治宜舒肝理气，活血化瘀。方用四逆散加味：柴胡10克，枳实10克，白芍10克，甘草6克，川芎10克，降香10克，香附10克，丹参15克，郁金12克。水煎服。

若胸闷胸痛，形体肥胖，身重乏力，心悸气短，舌苔白腻，脉弦滑，属痰浊内阻。治宜理脾化痰，芳香化浊。方用温胆汤加

Away Gallbladder-heat with additional ingredients is the chosen recipe: tangerine peel (*Pericarpium Citri Reticulatae*) 10g, pinellia tuber (*Rhizoma Pinelliae*) 10g, poria (*Poria*) 10g, bamboo shavings (*Caulis Bambusae in Taenis*) 10g, bitter orange (*Fructus Aurantii*) 10g, trichosanthes fruit (*Fructus Trichosanthis*) 20g, round cardamon seed (*Semen Amomi Cardamomi*) 10g, red sage root (*Radix Salviae Miltiorrhizae*) 15g, curcuma root (*Radix Curcumae*) 12g. All the above drugs are to be decocted in water for oral administration.

3. Deficiency of Both *Qi* and *Yin*

Main Symptoms and Signs: Indistinct pain in the precordial region, lassitude, palpitation, shortness of breath, spontaneous perspiration, dry mouth, red tongue with little fur, taut and weak pulse.

Therapeutic Principle: Replenishing *qi*, nourishing *yin* and promoting blood circulation.

Recipe: Pulse-activating Powder with additional ingredients.

astragalus root, *Radix Astragali seu Hedysari*   15g
dangshen, *Radix Codonopsis Pilosulae*   12g
opiopogon root, *Radix Ophiopogonis*   10g
schisandra fruit, *Fructus Schisandrae*   10g
Chinese angelica root, *Radix Angelicae Sinensis*   12g
red sage root, *Radix Salviae Miltiorrhizae*   20g
fragrant solomonseal rhizome, *Rhizoma Polygonati Odorati* 12g

All the above drugs are to be decocted in water for oral administration.

In addition, in case of excess of *yang* due to deficiency of *yin* marked by dizziness, tinnitus, restlessness and irritation, 10 grams of wolfberry fruit (*Fructus Lycii*) and 10 grams of chrysanthemum flower (*Flos Chrysanthemi*) may be added. If there appear palpitation and insomnia, 10 grams of wild jujube seed (*Semen Ziziphi Spinosae*) and 30 grams of fleece-flower stem (*Caulis Polygoni Multiflori*) may be added.

味：陈皮10克，半夏10克，茯苓10克，竹茹10克，枳壳10克，全

瓜蒌20克，白豆蔻10克，丹参15克，郁金12克。水煎服。

3. 气阴两虚

主证：心痛隐隐，身困乏力，心悸气短，自汗，口干少津，

舌红少苔，脉弦细无力。

治则：益气养阴，佐以活血。

处方：生脉散加味。

黄芪15克，党参12克，麦冬10克，五味子10克，当归12克，

丹参20克，玉竹12克。水煎服。

若阴虚阳亢，症见头晕耳鸣、心烦易怒者，加枸杞子10克，

菊花10克；心悸、失眠者，加酸枣仁10克，夜交藤30克。

In case of worsening of deficiency of *yang* marked by profuse sweat, cold limbs, pale complexion and even syncope, the treatment should be focused on supplementing *qi* and *yang* to restore the vital function from collapse. The chosen recipe is Decoction of Ginseng, Prepared Aconite, Dragon's Bone and Oyster with additional ingredients. The compositions are: ginseng (*Radix Ginseng*) 10g, prepared aconite root (*Radix Aconiti Praeparata*) 10g, dragon's bone (*Os Draconis Fossilia*) 30g, oyster (*Concha Ostreae*) 30g, astragalus root (*Radix Astragali seu Hedysari*) 15g, ophiopogon root (*Radix Ophiopogonis*) 10g, cinnamon bark (*Cortex Cinnamomi*) 10g, prepared licorice root (*Radix Glycyrrhizae Preaparata*) 6g. The above drugs are to be decocted together in water for oral administration. Western medicine should also be administered to coordinate the treatment.

Section 10
Essential Hypertension

Hypertension may be divided into two kinds — essential hypertension and secondary hypertension. This section only deals with essential hypertension. Its major symptoms are vertigo, headache and others, so in traditional Chinese medicine it is included in the categories of "*xuan yun*" (vertigo) and "*tou tong*" (headache).

MAIN POINTS OF DIAGNOSIS

1. Common symptoms are dizziness, headache, fullness of head, restlessness, temperamental tendency, insomnia, palpitation, numbness of extremities.

2. Hypertension is defined as a pressure greater than 18.7 / 12.0 kPa. The elevation of diastolic pressure is of more significance for clinical diagnosis.

3. In severe cases or cases of long duration, the heart, brain, and kidney may be compromised with the presentation of

若阳虚欲脱，症见汗出肢冷，面色苍白，甚至昏厥，治宜益气扶阳，固脱救逆。方用参附龙牡汤加味：人参10克，附子10克，龙骨30克，牡蛎30克，黄芪15克，麦冬10克，肉桂10克，炙甘草6克。水煎服。并配合西药治疗。

第十节　原发性高血压

高血压可分为原发性高血压和继发性高血压两种。本节仅讨论原发性高血压，临床主要表现为眩晕、头痛等，故属中医"眩晕"、"头痛"等范畴。

【诊断要点】

1．常见症状有头晕、头痛、头胀、烦躁易怒、失眠、心悸、四肢麻木等。

2．血压通常在 18.7/12.0 kPa 以上，以舒张压增高的临床诊断意义较大。

3．病情较重和病程较久者常并发心、脑、肾等脏器疾患，

relevant clinical manifestations.

4. In some patients blood pressure may be markedly elevated abruptly under certain precipitating factors accompanied with severe headache, dizziness, nausea and vomiting, which is called hypertensive crisis. If disturbance of consciousness, convulsion, transient hemiplegia or aphasia are present, that is called hypertensive encephalopathy.

5. In addition to blood and urine routine examinations and chest roentgenography, fundus examination is very helpful in evaluating the state of disease process.

DIFFERENTIATION AND TREATMENT OF COMMON SYNDROMES

1. Hyperactivity of Liver-*yang*

Main Symptoms and Signs: Dizziness, headache, head distension, vexation, temperamental tendency, flushed eyes, bitter taste, red tongue with thin yellow fur, taut and forceful pulse.

Therapeutic Principle: Calming the liver and subduing hyperactivity of liver-*yang*.

Recipe: Modified Decoction of Gastrodia and Uncaria.

gastrodia tuber, *Rhizoma Gastrodiae*   9g

hooked uncaria, *Ramulus Uncariae cum Uncis*   15–30g

chrysanthemum flower, *Flos Chysanthemi*   9g

scutellaria root, *Radix Scutellariae*   9g

abalone shell, *Concha Haliotidis*   30g

achyranthes root, *Radix Achyranthis Bidentatae*   12g

prunella spike, *Spica Prunellae*   15g

dragon's bone, *Os Draconis*   30g

raw oyster shell, *Concha Ostreae*   30g

eucommia bark, *Cortex Eucommiae*   12g

loranthus mulberry mistletoe, *Ramulus Loranthi*   15–30g

All the above drugs are to be decocted in water for oral administration.

In addition to the above ingredients, 6–10 grams of rhub-

并出现相应的各种临床表现。

4．部分患者在某些因素诱发下，血压突然明显升高，并伴有剧烈的头痛、头晕、恶心、呕吐等症状，称为高血压危象；如出现意识障碍、抽搐或暂时偏瘫、失语等症状，称为高血压脑病。

5．实验室检查除常规验血、尿和胸部 X 线检查外，眼底检查对确诊病情很有帮助。

【辨证论治】

1．肝阳上亢

主证：头晕，头痛，头胀，烦躁易怒，目赤口苦，舌质红，苔薄黄，脉弦有力。

治则：平肝潜阳。

处方：天麻钩藤饮加减。

天麻 9 克，钩藤15～30克，菊花 9 克，黄芩 9 克，生石决明30克，牛膝12克，夏枯草15克，生龙牡各30克，杜仲12克，桑寄生15～30克。水煎服。

若大便秘结者，加大黄 6 ～ 9 克；眩晕甚者，加珍珠母15～

arb (*Radix et Rhizoma Rhei*) should be added for cases of con- stipation; 15–30 grams of pearl shell (*Concha Margaritifera Usta*) should be included for severe vertigo; for those with dry mouth and tongue, 15 grams of dried rehmannia root (*Radix Rehmannia*) and 9 grams of scrophularia root (*Radix Scrophulariae*) supplement- ed; 9–15 grams of earthworm (*Lumbricus*) and 9–12 grams of siegesbeckia herb (*Herba Siegesbeckiae*) added for treating the case with numbness of the limbs. If the patient shows symp- toms or signs indicating hypertensive crisis or hypertensive encephalopathy, Tranquilizing Liver-wind Decoction can be chosen in stead of the above recipe (See **Prescriptions of TCM** in this Library). Simultaneously, western medicine should be used to coordinate the treatment.

2. Deficiency of the Liver-*yin* and Kidney-*yin*

Main Symptoms and Signs: Headache, vertigo, tinnitus, dryness of eyes, vexation, palpitation, insomnia, poor memory, feverish sensation in the palms and soles, aching and lassitude of the loins and legs, dry mouth, red tongue with a little or no fur, fine and string-like pulse.

Therapeutic Principle: Nourishing *yin* and suppressing hy- peractive *yang*.

Recipe: Modified Decoction of Fleece-flower For Lon- gevity.

fleece-flower root, *Radix Polygoni Multiflori*   15g
dried rehmannia root, *Radix Rehmanniae*   12g
wolfberry fruit, *Fructus Lycii*   12g
tortoise-plastron glue, *Golla Plastri Testudinis*   15g
eucommia bark, *Cortex Eucommiae*   9g
loranthus mulberry mistletoe, *Ramulus Loranthi*   15g
achyranthes root, *Radix Achyranthis Bidentatae*   15g
magnetite, *Magnetitum*, 15—30g
parched wild jujuba seed, *Semen Ziziphi Sprinosae*   12g
chrysanthemum flower, *Flos Chrysanthemi*   9g
All the above drugs are to be decocted in water for oral

30克；口干舌燥者，加生地15克，元参9克；肢体麻木者，加地

龙9～15克，豨莶草9～12。如出现高血压危象或高血压脑病症

状时，可改用镇肝熄风汤（见本文库《方剂学》有关部分），并配合

西药治疗。

2. 肝肾阴虚

主证：头痛眩晕，耳鸣目涩，心悸心烦，失眠健忘，手足心

热，腰腿酸软，口干，舌质红，少苔或无苔，脉弦细。

治则：滋阴潜阳。

处方：首乌延寿丹加减。

何首乌15克，生地12克，枸杞12克，龟板胶15克，杜仲9克，

桑寄生15克，怀牛膝15克，磁石15～30克，炒枣仁12克，菊花9

administration.

Besides, in case of oppressive sensation in the chest or precordial pain, 15–30 grams of red sage root (*Radix Salviae Miltiorrihizae*) and 15–30 grams of trichosanthes fruit (*Fructus Trichosanthis*) should be added.

3. Deficiency of Both *Yin* and *Yang*

Main Symptoms and Signs: Dizziness, tinnitus, amnesia, palpitation, lassitude, soreness of the loins and knees. Inclination to *yang* dificiency gives rise to cold extremities, pale tongue and deep thready pulse, while inclination to *yin* deficiency brings about dysphoria with feverish sensation in the chest, palms and soles, red tongue and fine rapid pulse.

Therapeutic Principle: Nourishing *yin* and restoring *yang*.

Recipe: Modified Decoction of Curculigo and Epimedium.

curculigo rhizome, *Rhizoma Curculiginis*   9–15g
epimedium, *Herba Epimedii*   9–15g
morinda root, *Radix Morindae Officinalis*   9g
Chinese angelica root, *Radix Angelicae Sinensis*   9g
phellodendron bark, *Cortex Phellodendri*   9g
anemarrhema rhizome, *Rhizoma Anemarrhenae*   9g
eucommia bark, *Cortex Eucommiae*   12g
achyranthes root, *Radix Achyranthis Bidentatae*   12g

All the above drugs are to be decocted in water for oral administration.

The recipe is also effective for climacteric hypertension in women.

Section 11
Sick Sinus Syndrome

Sick sinus syndrome is the ischemia, degeneration and fibrosis of sinoatrial node and its adjacent tissue induced by

克。水煎服。

若胸闷、心痛者，加丹参15～30克，全瓜蒌15～30克。

3．阴阳两虚

主证：眩晕，耳鸣，健忘，心悸，倦怠乏力，腰膝酸软。偏于阳虚者，四肢不温，舌质淡，脉沉细；偏于阴虚者，五心烦热，舌质红，脉细数。

治则：育阴助阳。

处方：二仙汤加减。

仙茅9～15克，仙灵脾9～15克，巴戟天9克，当归9克，黄柏9克，知母9克，杜仲12克，怀牛膝12克。水煎服。

本方对妇女更年期出现的高血压亦有效。

第十一节　病态窦房结综合征

病态窦房结综合征是由各种原因所引起的窦房结及其周围组

various causes, resulting in marked sinus bradycardia as a major manifestation. In severe cases or in patients whose atrioventricular conductive junction system is also affected, it is called double nodal dysfunction, or dysfunction of the whole cardiac conduction system. The syndrome is included in the categories of *"mai chi"* (slow pulse), *"xin ji"* (plapitation), *"xuan yun"* (vertigo), *"xiong bi"* (obstruction of *qi* in the chest), *"jue zheng"* (cold limbs), etc.

MAIN POINTS OF DIAGNOSIS

1. Coronary heart disease, myocarditis and myocardiopathy are the common causes of sick sinus syndrome. Other organic heart diseases such as rheumatic heart disease, hypertensive heart disease, pericardial disease, degenerative disease and metabolic disease of the heart may be the causes. Some patients have no definite cause.

2. The commonest clinical manifestation is persistent sinus bradycardia, usually less than 50 beats / min. Based on bradycardia the patient may have sinus nodal arrest, sinoauricular block, and atrioventricular block. Some patients may have tachyarrhythmia such as atrial fibrillation or paroxysmal supraventricular tachhycardia. Sometimes there is bradycardia. Therefore, the disease is also called bradycardia-tachycardia syndrome. The change of heart rate or heart rhythm may cause decreased perfusion of the brain, heart and kidney, resulting in such symptoms as dizziness, syncope, chest distress, angina pectoris and even shock or sudden death.

3. Provocative tests

(1) Exercise test: In the submaximal exercise test, when the heart rate can not reach 100 beats / min or the sinoauricular block and escape rhythm appear, it is considered to be positive. But in this test there are more false-positive results.

(2) Atropine test: After intravenous injection of atropine 1–2 mg, the electrocardiograms at 1, 2, 3, 5, 10 and 15 minutes

织缺血、变性、纤维化等病变，从而导致以显著窦性心动过缓为主要表现的一种心律紊乱。病变严重或侵犯房室交界传导系统，称为双节病变或全传导系统病变。本病属中医"脉迟"、"心悸"、"眩晕"、"胸痹"、"厥证"等范畴。

【诊断要点】

1．病因中以冠心病、心肌炎、心肌病多见，其他器质性心脏病，如风心病、高心病、心包疾病和心脏退行性或代谢性疾病亦可引起。部分患者病因不明。

2．最常见的临床表现为持续性窦性心动过缓，常少于50次/分。在此基础上，可出现窦性停搏、窦房阻滞、房室传导阻滞等。部分患者有时出现快速性心律失常，如心房纤颤或阵发性室上性心动过速，有时出现缓慢心律失常，称为心动过缓—过速综合征。心率或心律变化可引起脑、心、肾供血不足的症状，患者可发生眩晕、晕厥、胸闷、心绞痛，甚至休克或猝死。

3．激发试验

（1）运动试验：次极量级运动试验患者心率达不到100次/分，或运动中出现窦房阻滞、逸搏心律等为阳性。运动试验假阳性较多。

（2）阿托品试验：静注阿托品1～2毫克后，观察并记录1、

are recorded. If the heart rates are less than 90 beats / min or junctional rhythm or ectopic tachycardia appears, it is considered to be positive. Atropine test is superior to the exercise test.

(3) Determinations of sinus node recovery time (SNRT), sinoatrial conduction time (SACT), and intrinsic sinus rate can be performed by atrial pacing through esophagus or electrophysiological study through catheterization. Among them, SNRT is most valuable and exceeds 2000 milliseconds in sick sinus syndrome.

The evaluation of the results from aforesaid tests should be carried out in combination with clinical data. In performing these tests, unless the effect of vagus nerve and sympthetic nerve on heart rate is eliminated, the results are less clinically significant.

DIFFERENTIATION AND TREATMENT OF COMMON SYNDROMES

1. Deficiency of the Heart-*yang* and Kidney-*yang*

Main Symptoms and Signs: Chest stuffiness, twinge in the precordial region, palpitation, shortness of breath, dizziness, occasional faint, fatigue and weakness, tinnitus, distress in the loins, aversion to cold, cold limbs, restlessness and insomnia, pale thick or dark red tongue, thready, slow and uneven or intermittent pulse.

Therapeutic Principle: Warming *yang* and replenishing *qi*.

Recipe: Modified prescriptions of Decoction for Protecting Primordial *Qi* and Decoction of Ephedra, Aconite and Asarum.

prepared aconite root, *Radix Aconiti Praeparata*   6–20g
red ginseng, *Radix Ginseng Rubra*   10–30g
or dangshen, *Radix Codonopsis Pilosulae*   20–40g
astragalus root, *Radix Astragali seu Hedysari*   30g
siberian solomonseal rhizome, *Rhizoma Polygonati*   30g
cinnamon twig, *Ramulus Cinnamomi*   10g
ephedra, *Herba Ephedrae*   6–12g

2、3、5、10、15分钟的心电图，如心率低于90次/分，或出现交界区心律或异位心动过速者为阳性。阿托品试验较运动试验优越。

（3）测定窦房结功能恢复时间、窦房传导时间和窦房结固有频率，通过食道心房调搏或导管法电生理检查均可测出。其中以窦房结功能恢复时间价值最大，本征常超过2000毫秒。

上述检查结果要结合临床资料综合评价，测试中要消除迷走神经和交感神经对心率的影响，其诊断意义才较大。

【辨证论治】

1．心肾阳虚

主证：胸闷，心前区刺痛，心悸，气短，头昏，偶有昏厥，神疲乏力，耳鸣腰酸，畏寒肢冷，心烦失眠，舌质淡胖或暗红，脉细迟涩或结代。

治则：温阳益气。

处方：保元汤合麻黄附子细辛汤加减。

附子6～20克，红参10～30克或党参20～40克，黄芪30克，

asarum herb, *Herba Asari*   3g

prepared liquorice, *Radix Glycyrrhizae Praeparata*   6–30g

All the above drugs are to be decocted in water for oral administration.

2. Deficiency of Both *Qi* and *Yin*

Main Symptoms and Signs: Chest stuffiness, shortness of breath, vague pain in the precordial region, dizziness, blurred vision, palpitation, insomnia, amnesia, spontaneous perspiration, dry mouth, pale or dark red tongue with thin and white fur, slow and thready or intermittent pulse.

Therapeutic Principle: Supplementing *qi* and nourishing *yin*.

Recipe: Modified Decoction of Prepared Licorice.

prepared licorice root, *Radix Glycyrrhizae Praeparata*
12–30g

dangshen, *Radix Codonopsis Pilosulae*   15–30g

astragalus root, *Radix Astragali seu Hedysari*   30g

siberian solomonseal rhizome, *Rhizoma Polygonati*   30g

dried rehmannia root, *Radix Rehmanniae*   20–30g

ophiopogon root, *Radix Ophiopogonis*   15g

sesame kernel, *Semen Sesami*   12g

cinnamon twig, *Ramulus Cinnamomi*   10g

Chinese-date, *Fructus Ziziphi Jujubae*   10 pieces

schisandra fruit, *Fructus Schisandrae*   10g

All the above drugs are to be decocted in water for oral administration.

The drugs for promoting blood circulation to remove blood stasis may be added to both the recipes mentioned above, such as red sage root (*Radix Salviae Miltiorrhizae*) 20g, Chinese angelica (*Radix Angelicae Sinensis*) 12g, safflower (*Flos Carthami*) 10g and red peony root (*Radix Paeoniae Rubra*) 12g. According to the patient's condition to select 1 or 2 ingredients each time to strengthen therapeutic effects.

黄精30克，桂枝10克，麻黄6～12克，细辛3克，炙甘草6～30克。水煎服。

2. 气阴两虚

主证：胸闷气短，心前区隐痛，头晕眼花，心悸怔忡，失眠健忘，自汗口干，舌质淡红或暗红，舌苔薄白，脉迟细或结代。

治则：益气养阴。

处方：炙甘草汤加减。

炙甘草12～30克，党参15～30克，黄芪30克，黄精30克，生地20～30克，麦冬15克，胡麻仁12克，桂枝10克，大枣10枚，五味子10克。水煎服。

以上两型均可加入活血化瘀药，如丹参20克，当归12克，红花10克，赤芍12克。以上可酌情选1～2味，以增强疗效。

Section 12
Hyperlipoproteinemia

Blood lipids are composed of cholesterol, triglyceride, phospholipid and free fatty acid. Hyperlipemia mainly implies the elevations of cholesterol and triglyceride in the plasma and is closely related to atherosclerosis. As blood lipids are transported in the form of lipoprotein, hyperlipemia also manifests as hyperlipoproteinemia. It is included in the categoreis of "*xuan yun*" (vertigo), "*tan zhuo*" (phlegm syndrome) and others in TCM.

MAIN POINTS OF DIAGNOSIS

1. Inquire closely about positive family history, diabetes, gout, hepatic diseases, nephroses and juvenile coronary heart disease.

2. During physical examination, pay attention to yellowish papules, xanthomas, premature corneal arcus and peripheral vascular disorders.

3. Hyperlipoproteinemia can be divided into 5 types.

Type I is chylomicronemia, a rare disorder due to congenital deficiency of lipoprotein lipase.

Type II is hyperbetalipoproteinemia, which is commonly seen with marked elevation of plasma cholesterol and the disorder closely related to atherosclerosis and coronary heart disease. Some patients are inherited and others are due to high-cholesterol diet or secondary to myeloma, nephrotic syndrome, hepatic disease, etc. Type II is subdivided into Type IIa and Type IIb.

Type III is an autosomal dominant disorder in which the plasma concentrations of cholesterol and triglyceride are both elevated. The disease occurs mostly after middle age. Patients usually have obesity, disturbance of carbohydrate meta-

第十二节　高脂蛋白血症

血中脂质包括胆固醇、甘油三脂、磷脂和非脂化脂肪酸四种。血中脂质增高主要指胆固醇和甘油三脂增高，并与动脉粥样硬化关系密切。由于血中脂质是以脂蛋白形式转运，所以高脂血症亦常反映高脂蛋白血症。本症属中医"眩晕"、"痰浊"等范畴。

【诊断要点】

1. 病史中注意有无家族倾向，有无糖尿病、痛风、肝肾疾患及青年期冠心病等。

2. 体检中注意有无黄脂斑、黄色瘤、早发角膜环及周围血管病变。

3. 高脂蛋白血症共分五型：

Ⅰ型：高乳糜微粒血症，系先天性脂蛋白酶缺乏，较罕见。

Ⅱ型：高脂蛋白血症，较常见。胆固醇增高明显，与动脉硬化及冠心病关系密切。部分病例系遗传所致，亦可因饮食胆固醇过多或继发于骨髓瘤、肾病综合征和肝病等。Ⅱ型又分Ⅱa和Ⅱb型。

Ⅲ型：血中胆固醇和甘油三脂均增高，呈家族性显性遗传，

bolism, etc.

Type IV is the most common disorder, in which endogenous plasma triglyceride is elevated due to the disturbance of carbohydrate metabolism which plasma cholesterol is not necessarily elevated.

Type V is very rare, a combination of Type I and Type IV and of little clinical significance.

DIFFERENTIATION AND TREATMENT OF COMMON SYNDROMES

1. Deficiency of the Liver-*yin* and Kidney-*yin*

Main Symptoms and Signs: Dizziness, tinnitus, blurred vision, irritability, amnesia, soreness and weakness of the loins and knees, red tongue with little fur, taut and thready pulse.

Therapeutic Principle: Nourishing the liver-*yin* and kidney-*yin*.

Recipe: Modified Pill of Fleece-flower for Longevity.

fleece-flower root, *Radix Polygoni Multiflori*   20–30g
sesame seed, *Semen Sesami*   30g
mulberry, *Fructus Mori*   30g
glossy privet fruit, *Fructus Ligustri Lucidi*   12g
eclipta, *Herba Ecliptae*   12g
honeysuckle flower, *Flos Lonicerae*   18g
chrysanthemum, *Flos Chrysanthemi*   10g
loranthus mulberry mistletoe, *Ramulus Loranthi*   15g
cherokee rose-hip, *Fructus Rosae Laevigatae*   18g
siberian solomonseal rhizome, *Rhizoma Polygonati*   20g
curcuma root, *Radix Curcumae*   12g

All the above drugs are to be decocted in water for oral administration.

In addition to the above drugs, supplementary ingredients are to be employed with respect to certain symptoms: cassia seed (*Semen Cassiae*) 30g, uncaria stem with hooks (*Ramulus Uncariae cum Uncis*) 20g and pueraria root (*Radix Puerariae*) 20g for the case complicated with hyperactivety of liver-*yang* mark-

多见于中年以后，常伴肥胖、糖代谢异常等。

Ⅳ型：最多见，为心源性甘油三脂增高，与碳水化合物代谢紊乱有关，而胆固醇不一定增高。

Ⅴ型：较罕见，为Ⅰ、Ⅳ型混合，临床意义较小。

【辨证论治】

1．肝肾阴虚

主证：头晕，头昏，耳鸣，视物昏花，心烦健忘,腰膝酸软，舌红少苔，脉弦细。

治则：滋补肝肾。

处方：首乌延寿丹加减。

何首乌20～30克，黑芝麻30克，桑椹子30克，女贞子12克，旱莲草12克，金银花18克，菊花10克，桑寄生15克,金樱子18克，黄精20克，郁金12克。水煎服。

若肝阳上亢，症见头痛、头胀明显者，加决明子30克，钩藤20克，葛根20克；气血不足症见心悸失眠、体倦纳减者，加黄芪

ed by obvious headache and feeling of distension in the head; astragalus root (*Radix Astragali seu Hedysari*) 15g and Chinese agnelica (*Radix Angelicae Sinensis*) 12g for the case with deficiency of both *qi* and blood marked by palpitation, insomnia, lassitude and anorexia; gastrodia tuber (*Radix Gastradiae*) 12g, mulberry twigs (*Ramulus Mori*) 30g and spatholobus stem (*Caulis Spatholobi*) 30g for the case with numbness and soreness of the limbs.

2. Retention of Damp-heat in the Interior

Main Symptoms and Signs: Dizziness, heavy sensation of the head, headache, distension and irritable feverish sensation in the chest, fatigue and listlessness, bitter taste, dry throat, fat stature, or dry stools, slightly red tongue with yellow and greasy fur, and smooth pulse.

Therapeutic Principle: Eliminating pathogenic dampness and heat.

Recipe: Modified Decoction of Gentian for Purging Liver-fire.

gentian root, *Radix Gentianae*   6g

plantain herb, *Herba Plantaginis*   12g

water-plantain tuber, *Rhizoma Alismatis*   15–30g

Bupleurum root, *Radix Bupleuri*   10g

oriental wormwood, *Herba Artemisiae Capillaris*   15–30g

cassia seed, *Semen Cassiae*   30g

poria, *Poria*   15g

rhubarb root, *Radix et Rhizoma Rhei*   3g (parched in wine)

hawthorn fruit, *Fructus Crataegi*   18g

All the above drugs are to be decocted in water for oral administration.

15克，当归12克；肢体麻木、疼痛者，加天麻12克，桑枝30克，

鸡血藤30克。

2. 湿热内蕴

主证：头晕，头重，头痛，烦热胸闷，体倦身困，口苦咽干，

体胖，或大便干，舌质偏红，舌苔黄腻，脉滑。

治则：清利湿热。

处方：龙胆泻肝汤加减。

龙胆草6克，车前草12克，泽泻15～30克，柴胡10克，茵陈

15～30克，决明子30克，茯苓15克，酒大黄3克，生山楂18克。

水煎服。

Section 13
Chronic Gastritis

Chronic gastritis is a chronic gastric lesion, pathologically characterized by nonspecific chronic inflammation of the gastric mucosa. Its etiology is not well understood, possibly related to administration of irritating drugs and food, bile regurgitation, buccal inflammation or autoimmunity. Chronic gastritis can be divided into two categories, primary and secondary. The former is further categorized into superficial, atrophic and hypertrophic types; the latter often complicates gastroduodenal ulcer and gastric cancer. Chronic gastritis occurs most frequently in the middle-aged people. This disease in TCM pertains to the categories of *"pi"* (feeling of fullness in the upper abdomen), *"wei wan tong"* (stomachache), etc.

MAIN POINTS OF DIAGNOSIS

1. The chief symptoms are chronic upper abdominal pain, fullness and discomfort, belching and acid regurgitation which often occur after meals. Mild hemorrhage of upper digestive tract may be induced by some precipitating factors in a few cases. Severe atrophic gastritis may be accompanied with anemia and pathologic leanness.

2. Physical examination reveals mild but diffuse tenderness in the upper abdominal region.

3. Laboratory examination

   (1) Gastric juice analysis: Gastric acid is normal in superficial gastritis, but mostly reduced or gone in atrophic gastritis.

   (2) X-ray barium examination: Positive rate is not high. Atrophic gastritis presents gastric hypotension, triviality or disappearance of gastric mucosal folds. The main purpose

第十三节　慢性胃炎

本病是以胃粘膜非特异性慢性炎症为主要病理变化的慢性胃部疾病。其病因不十分清楚，可能与服用刺激性药物和食物、胆汁返流、口腔炎症有关；亦有人认为和自身免疫有关。慢性胃炎可分为原发性和继发性两大类。前者又分为浅表性、萎缩性和肥厚性三种类型；后者多和溃疡病、胃癌等并存。慢性胃炎好发于中年以上。本病属中医"痞"、"胃脘痛"等范畴。

【诊断要点】

1．主要症状为慢性上腹痛、饱胀不适、嗳气、泛酸等，以餐后较普遍，部分患者可在某些因素诱发下发生少量上消化道出血，较严重的萎缩性胃炎可伴贫血和消瘦。

2．体检上腹有轻而弥漫压痛。

3．辅助检查

（1）胃液分析：浅表性胃炎胃酸正常，萎缩性胃炎胃酸多减少或缺乏。

（2）X线钡剂检查：阳性率不高，其中萎缩性胃炎胃张力较低，粘膜皱襞细小或消失。X线检查的主要目的在于排除消化性

of radiological examination is to exclude peptic ulcer and cancer.

(3) Gastrofiberscope: This method is most contributive in confirming diagnosis. Through it superficial mucosal erosion with hyperemia, swelling or red spots and increased ropy liquid could be discovered in chronic superficial gastritis; in chronic atrophic gastritis, such findings can be caught as thinned and greyish-pale mucosa, slenderized mucosal folds with exposure of submucosal vessels, and granular or nodular proliferation. The combined application of gastrofiberscope and biopsy proves to be an accurate method for the diagnosis of chronic gastritis.

DIFFERENTIATION AND TREATMENT OF COMMON SYNDROMES

1. Stagnation of the Stomach-*qi*

Main Symptoms and Signs: Epigastric distension and fullness or pain, loss of appetite, indigestion, or diarrhea, white coating of the tongue, and slippery pulse.

Therapeutic Principle: Regulating the stomach-*qi* to relieve distension and fullness.

Recipe: Pinellia Decoction for Purging Stomach-fire.

pinellia tuber, *Rhizoma Pinelliae*	9g	
dried ginger, *Rhizoma Zingiberis*	9g	
scutellaria root, *Radix Scutellariae*	9g	
coptis rhizome, *Rhizoma Coptididis*	6g	
dangshen, *Radix Codonopsis Pilosulae*	12g	
licorice root, *Rhizoma Glycyrrhizae*	9g	
Chinese-date, *Fructus Ziziphi Jujubae*	12 pieces	

All the above drugs are to be decocted in water for oral administration.

For the case of a more severe stomachache, 15 grams of white peony root (*Rhizoma Paeoniae Alba*) and 9 grams of corydalis tuber (*Rhizoma Corydalis*) may be employed.

2. Hyperactive Liver-*qi* Attacking the Stomach

溃疡和癌变。

（3）纤维胃镜检查：是有效的确诊方法。慢性浅表性胃炎可见粘膜浅表糜烂，伴充血、水肿或红斑，胃内有较多粘稠液体；慢性萎缩性胃炎可见粘膜变薄，色泽灰淡，粘膜皱襞变细，粘膜下血管显露，并可有颗粒状或结节状增生。纤维胃镜检查结合活检，是诊断本病的准确方法。

【辨证论治】

1. 胃呆气滞

主证：胃脘痞塞满闷，或有疼痛，食欲不振，消化不良，大便或稀，苔白脉滑。

治则：和胃消痞

处方：半夏泻心汤

半夏9克，干姜9克，黄芩9克，黄连6克，党参12克，甘草9克，大枣12枚。水煎服。

胃痛较重者，可加白芍15克，延胡索9克。

2. 肝气犯胃

Main Symptoms and Signs: Epigastric distension, pain, fullness, oppression and discomfort which is aggravated after meals, frequent belching which may be aggravated by emotional upset, thin and white coating of the tongue, and deep taut pulse.

Therapeutic Principle: Relieving hyperactive liver-*qi* and regulating the stomach.

Recipe: Modified Bupleurum Powder for Relieving Liver-*qi*.

bupleurum root, *Radix Bupleuri*   10g
cyperus tuber, *Rhizoma Cyperi*   10g
white peony root, *Radix Paeoniae Alba*   10g
bitter orange, *Fructus Aurantii*   10g
Sichuan chinaberry, *Fructus Meliae Toosendan*   10g
corydalis tuber, *Rhizoma Corydalis*   10g
tangerine peel, *Pericarpium Citri Reticulatae*   10g
perilla stem, *Caulis Perillae*   10g
licorice root, *Radix Glycyrrhizae*   6g

All the above drugs are to be decocted in water for oral administration.

If there are acid regurgitation, burning sensation and distress in the stomach, 15 grams of dandelion herb (*Herba Taraxaci*), 9 grams of coptis rhizome (*Rhizoma Coptidis*) and 6 grams of evodia fruit (*Fructus Evodiae*) are to be added to the recipe.

3. Insufficiency-cold of the Spleen and Stomach

Main Symptoms and Signs: Vague pain in the stomach, vomiting of watery fluid, preference for warmth and press, aggravation from cold, mental fatigue and weakness, loose stools, pale tongue, deep thready and weak pulse.

Therapeutic Principle: Warming middle-*jiao* and dispelling pathogenic cold.

Recipe: Modified Decoction of Astragalus for Tonifying Middle-*jiao*.

主证：胃脘胀痛，饱闷不适，食后尤甚，嗳气频作，每因情志刺激而加重，舌苔薄白，脉沉弦。

治则：疏肝和胃。

处方：柴胡疏肝散加减。

柴胡10克，香附10克，白芍10克，枳壳10克，川楝子10克，延胡索10克，陈皮10克，苏梗10克，甘草 6 克。水煎服。

胃脘部有烧灼感，泛酸嘈杂，可加蒲公英15克，黄连 9 克，吴茱萸 6 克。

3．脾胃虚寒

主证：胃痛隐隐，泛吐清水，喜暖喜按，遇冷加重，神疲乏力，大便溏薄，舌淡白，脉沉细无力。

治则：温中散寒

处方：黄芪建中汤加减

astragalus root, *Radix Astragali seu Hedysari*   30g

cinnamon twig, *Ramulus Cinnamomi*   9g

white peony root, *Radix Paeoniae Alba*   18g

aucklandia root, *Radix Aucklandiae*   9g

dried ginger, *Rhizoma Zingiberis*   6g

amomum fruit, *Fructus Amomi*   10g

Chinese-date, *Fructus Ziziphi Jujubae*   5 pieces

prepared licorice root, *Radix Glycyrrhizae Praeparata*   6g

All the above drugs are to be decocted in water for oral administration.

If the case is complicated with anorexia and belching with fetid odour, 10 grams of medicated leaven (*Massa Fermentata Medicinalis*) and 10 grams of germinated barley (*Fructus Hordei Germinatus*) may be administered; if the case with acid regurgitation, 30 grams of calcined ark shell (*Concha Arcae*) added; if the case with dominant cold of insufficiency type, 10 grams of dangshen (*Radix Codonopsis Pilosulae*), 10 grams of white atractylodes rhizome (*Rhizoma Atractylodis Macrocephalae*) and 10 grams of poria (*Poria*) included.

4. Deficiency of the Stomach-*yin* due to Stomach-heat

Main Symptoms and Signs: Irregular stomachache with burning sensation which is aggravated in the afternoon or on empty stomach and is relieved after meals, dry mouth and throat, or thirst, loss of appetite, dry stool, red tongue with yellowish and dry fur, and taut and thready or rapid pulse.

Therapeutic Principle: Clearing away heat from the stomach and nourishing the stomach-*yin*.

Recipe: Modified Decoction for Nourishing the Stomach.

glehnia root, *Radix Glehniae*   10g

ophiopogon root, *Radix Ophiopogonis*   10g

fragrant solomonseal rhizome, *Rhizoma Polygonati Odorati*
    10g

white peony root, *Radix Paeoniae Alba*   10g

scutellaria root, *Radix Scutellariae*   10g

黄芪30克，桂枝 9 克，白芍18克，木香 9 克，干姜 6 克，砂仁10克，大枣 5 枚，炙甘草 6 克。水煎服。

若兼纳呆、嗳腐者，加神曲10克，麦芽10克；泛酸者，加煅瓦楞30克；虚寒甚者，加党参10克，白术10克，茯苓10克。

4．胃热阴虚

主证：胃痛并有烧灼感，痛无定时，但下午或空腹时较重，得食较缓，口燥咽干，或口渴，纳少，大便干，舌质红，苔黄少津，脉弦细而数。

治则：清胃养阴。

处方：养胃汤加减。

沙参10克，麦冬10克，玉竹10克，白芍10克，黄芩10克，黄

coptis rhizome, *Rhizoma Coptidis*   10g
anemarrhena rhizome, *Rhizoma Anemarrhenae*   10g
tangerine peel, *Pericarpium Citri Reticulatae*   10g
dandelion herb, *Herba Taraxaci*   20g
licorice root, *Radix Glycyrrhizae*   6g

All the above drugs are to be decocted in water for oral administration.

Section 14
Peptic Ulcer

Peptic ulcer occurs most frequently in the stomach and duodenum. Its etiology, in spite of a variety of theories about it, has not been well understood. Gastric ulcer occurs predominantly in the lesser curvatuse and pyloric part. Duodenal ulcer mostly occurs in the duodenal bulb. The coexistance of gastric and duodenal ulcers is called complex ulcer. Peptic ulcers are more frequently found in males than females, and inclined to attack the young and middled-aged groups, but gastric ulcer usually occurs later than duodenal ulcer. The disease, in TCM, is categorized as *"weiwan tong"* (stomachache), *"outu"* (vomiting), etc.

MAIN POINTS OF DIAGNOSIS

1. Symptoms: Cardinal symptom of the disease is chronic epigastralgia which is marked by dull pain or pinching pain. Sometimes it is manifested as distending pain or burning pain which often radiates to the lumbar region or the back. The pains are closely related to meals. The rule of attack in gastric ulcer is food intake → pain → remission, while in duodenal ulcer the rule is pain → food intake → remission. The pain occurs periodically and is often induced by coldness, fatigue and improper food intake. The attack is frequently in winter and spring.

连10克，知母10克，陈皮10克，蒲公英20克，甘草6克。水煎服。

第十四节　消化性溃疡

消化性溃疡多发于胃和十二指肠，其原因和发病机理虽有多种学说，但仍不十分清楚。胃溃疡多发生于胃小弯及幽门部，十二指肠溃疡以球部为多。胃和十二指肠溃疡同时存在者，称复合性溃疡。本病男多于女，发病年龄多在中青年以上，胃溃疡较十二指肠溃疡稍晚。消化性溃疡属中医"胃脘痛"、"呕吐"等范畴。

【诊断要点】

1．症状：主要症状为慢性上腹疼痛。疼痛为隐性钝痛或刺痛。有时为胀痛或烧灼痛，常放射到腰背部。疼痛与进食有较密切的关系。通常胃溃疡的规律是进食→疼痛→缓解；而十二指肠溃疡则为疼痛→进食→缓解。疼痛常呈周期性，常因寒冷、疲劳、饮食不当所诱发。冬夏季节发病较多。

Other symptoms include acid regurgitation, belching, nausea and vomiting. In a few cases, perforation or bleeding may be the first clinical findings.

2. Signs: In active ulcer, there is often tenderness in the middle and upper abdominal regions. Tenderness on the left side of upper gastric region is found in gastric ulcer, while in duodenal ulcer it is found on the right side, often localized in 3—4 cm. Ulcer in the posterior wall may have pain hypersensitive area on the back at T11—12 level.

3. Laboratory examinations

(1) Fecal occult blood test (OB): OB positive reaction after 3-day vegetarian meals reveals that the active ulcer exists. OB positive result may turn into negative if the patient is treated properly. Persistent positive reaction indicates cancerous change of ulcer or gastric carcinoma.

(2) X-ray barium examination: It is of great value. Niche is often seen in gastric ulcer. Indirect signs such as irritation and disformity of duodenal bulbar region may occur in duodenal ulcer.

(3) Fiberscope examination: It is a main diagnostic method. Small and superficial ulcer can be seen directly. If fiberscopy is combined with biopsy, benign and cancerous changes can be differentiated. Gastric juice analysis is not used as a routine examination.

DIFFERENTIATION AND TREATMENT OF COMMON SYNDROMES

1. Insufficiency-cold Type

Main Symptoms and Signs: Latent pain in the upper abdomen with predilection for heat, and intolerance of cold which aggravates the pain, sallow complexion, lassitude and weakness, or loose stool, pale tongue with thin whitish fur, deep, slow and weak pulse.

Therapeutic Principle: Warming and invigorating middle-jiao.

其他症状有泛酸、嗳气、恶心、呕吐等。部分患者平素无症状，以穿孔或出血为首次表现。

2．体征：在溃疡活动期，中上腹常有压痛区。胃溃疡压痛区在上腹中线偏左，十二指肠溃疡在中线偏右。多局限于3～4厘米的范围。后壁溃疡在背部10～12胸椎旁可有皮肤过敏区。

3．辅助检查

（1）大便潜血试验：素食三天后潜血仍阳性者提示溃疡活动，治疗后可转阴，持续阳性提示溃疡恶变或胃癌。

（2）X线钡透：价值较大，胃溃疡可见龛影，十二指肠溃疡可见球部激惹变形等间接征象。

（3）纤维内窥镜检查：是诊断本病主要方法，可直接窥见浅小溃疡，且通过组织活检，可以鉴别是否有溃疡恶变。胃液测定通常不做常规检查。

【辨证论治】

1．虚寒型

主证：上腹隐痛，喜热怕冷，遇冷痛甚，面色萎黄，倦怠无力，大便或溏，舌质淡，苔薄白，脉沉细。

治则：温中补虚。

Recipe: Modified Decoction of Astragalus for Tonifying middle-*jiao*.

astragalus root, *Radix Astragali seu Hedysari*   30g
cinnamon twig, *Ramulus Cinnamomi*   9g
white peony root, *Radix Paeoniae Alba*   18g
cuttle-bone, *Os Sepiella seu Sepiae*   30g
dahurian angelica root, *Radix Angelicae Dahuricae*   30g
prepared licorice root, *Radix Glycyrrhizae Praeparata*   15g

All the above drugs are to be decocted in water for oral administration.

2. *Qi*-Stagnation Type

Main Symptoms and Signs: Epigastric distension and pain, distension and fullness in the hypochondria, belching, acid regurgitation, poor appetite, thin and whitish coating of the tongue, and taut pulse.

Therapeutic Principle: Soothing the liver, regulating the circulation of *qi* and regulating the function of stomach to relieve pain.

Recipe: Modified Powder for Treating Cold Limbs in combination with Sichuan Chinaberry Powder.

bupleurum root, *Radix Bupleuri*   9g
cyperus tuber, *Rhizoma Cyperi*   12g
white poeny root, *Radix Paeoniae Alba*   9g
bitter orange, *Frucuts Aurantii*   9g
tangerine peel, *Pericarpium Citri Reticulatae*   9g
Sichuan chinaberry, *Fructus Meliae Toosendan*   12g
corydalis tuber, *Rhizoma Corydalis*   12g
aucklandia root, *Radix Aucklandiae*   9g
perilla stem, *Caulis Perillae*   12g
ark shell, *Concha Arcae*   30g
finger citron, *Fructus Citri Sarcodactylis*   9g
prepared licorice root, *Radix Glycyrrhizae Praeparata*   6g

All the above drugs are to be decocted in water for oral administration.

处方：黄芪建中汤加减。

黄芪30克，桂枝9克，白芍18克，乌贼骨30克，白芷30克，

炙甘草15克。水煎服。

2．气滞型

主证：胃脘胀痛，两胁胀闷，嗳气吐酸，纳食减少，苔薄白，

脉弦。

治则：疏肝理气，和胃止痛。

处方：四逆散合金铃子散加减。

柴胡9克，香附12克，白芍9克，枳壳9克，陈皮9克，川

楝子12克，延胡索12克，木香9克，苏梗12克，煅瓦楞子30克，

佛手9克，炙甘草6克。水煎服。

3. Stagnated-heat Type

Main Symptoms and Signs: Epigastric pain which is aggravated after food intake, burning sensation in the stomach, dry mouth with bitter taste, fondness of cold drink, constipation, deep-coloured urine, red tongue with yellow fur, taut and rapid pulse.

Therapeutic Principle: Clearing away pathogenic heat and regulating the function of stomach.

Recipe: Modified Two Old Drugs Decoction in combination with Decoction for Eliminating Pathogenic Heat from the Liver.

coptis rhizome, *Rhizoma Coptidis*   9g
capejasmine fruit, *Fructus Gardeniae*   9g
scutellaria root, *Radix Scutellariae*   9g
anemarrhena rhizome, *Rhizoma Anemarrhenae*   10g
white peony root, *Radix Paeoniae Alba*   10g
tangerine peel, *Pericarpium Citri Reticulatae*   9g
pinellia tuber, *Rhizoma Pinelliae*   10g
poria, *Poria*   10g
finger citron, *Fructus Citri Sarcodactylis*   10g
dendrobium, *Herba Dendrobii*   10g
prepared licorice root, *Radix Glycyrrhizae Praeparata*   6g

All the above drug are to be decocted in water for oral administration.

If the case is complicated with insufficiency of the stomach-*yin* marked by latent pain in the epigastric region, dry mouth with reduced saliva, hot sensation in the palms and soles, red tongue with little fur or absence of fur and taut weak pulse, it is preferable to administer the Modified Decoction of Glehnia and Ophiopogon instead. Its compositions are: glehnia root (*Radix Glehniae*) 10g, ophiopogon root (*Radix Ophiopogonis*) 10g, fragrant solomonseal rhizome (*Rhizoma Polygonati Odorati*) 10g, white hyaciath bean (*Semen Dolichoris Album*) 10g, finger citron (*Fructus Citri Sarcodactylis*) 10g, dendrobium (*Herba Dendrobii*) 10g,

3．郁热型

主证：胃脘疼痛，食后加剧，胃中灼热，口干而苦，喜冷饮，便秘溲赤，舌质红，苔黄，脉弦数。

治则：清热和胃。

处方：二陈汤合化肝煎加减。

黄连9克，栀子9克，黄芩9克，知母10克，白芍10克，陈皮9克，半夏10克，茯苓10克，佛手10克，石斛10克，炙甘草6克。水煎服。

若胃阴不足，症见胃脘隐痛，口干少津，手足心热，舌红少苔或无苔，脉弦细者，可用沙参麦冬汤加减：沙参10克，麦冬10

prepared licorice root (*Radix Glycyrrhizae Praeparata*) 6g. All the drugs in the above recipe are to be decocted in water for oral administration.

If the case is manifested as severe symptom of blood stasis such as epigastric stabbing pain, or fixed pain just like knife-cutting, dark purple tongue or with ecchymoses, taut or unsmooth pulse, the modified Red Sage Drink in combination with Wonderful Powder for Relieving Blood Stagnation is preferable: red sage root (*Radix Salviae Miltiorrhizae*) 20g, amomum fruit (*Fructus Amomi*) 10g, cat-tail pollen (*Pollen Typhae*) 10g, trogopterus dung (*Faeces trogopterorum*) 10g, Sichuan chinaberry (*Fructus Meliae Toosendan*) 12g, corydalis tuber (*Rhizoma Corydalis*) 12g, Chinese angelica root (*Radix Angelicae Sinensis*) 12g, red peony root (*Radix Paeoniae Rubra*) 10g, prepared licorice root (*Radix Glycyrrhizae Praeparata*) 6g. All the above drugs are to be decocted in water for oral administration. For the case with hematemesis and tarry stools, 6 grams of powder of hyacinth bletilla (*Radix Bletillae*) and 3 grams of powder of notoginseng (*Radix Notoginseng*) should be added (administered orally after being mixed with the finished decoction). The above drugs except powder of notoginseng are to be decocted in water for oral administration.

Section 15
Chronic Nonspecific Ulcerative Colitis

The disease is also termed ulcerative colitis. Its etiology is still unknown, but in recent years, is associated with autoimmunity. The pathologic change attacks the rectum, sigmoid colon and descending colon. It is a kind of nonspecific inflammation which primarily involves mucosal layer. Precipitating factors include emotional tonus, psychic trauma and allergy to certain foods. It occurs more frequently in males than in females. In TCM, the disease is categorized as "*xie*

克，玉竹10克，白扁豆10克，佛手10克，石斛10克，炙甘草6克。

水煎服。

若属瘀血较重，症见胃脘刺痛，或痛如刀割，痛处不移，舌质紫暗或有瘀斑，脉弦或涩者，可用丹参饮合失笑散加减：丹参20克，砂仁10克，生蒲黄10克，五灵脂10克，川楝子12克，延胡索12克，当归12克，赤芍10克，炙甘草6克。水煎服。若吐血、便黑者，加白芨粉6克（冲），三七粉3克（冲）。

第十五节　慢性非特异性溃疡性结肠炎

本病亦称溃疡性结肠炎。其病因不明，近来认为与自身免疫有关。病变侵犯直肠、乙状结肠和降结肠，是一种非特异性炎症，主要累及粘膜层。情绪紧张、精神创伤和对某些食物过敏可诱发

xie" (diarrhea), *"chi bai li"* (dysentery), etc.

MAIN POINTS OF DIAGNOSIS

1. The chief clinical symptoms include diarrhea and abdominal pain. Diarrhea varies in severity. In severe cases it may occur dozens of times a day, accompanied with loose stool, mucous stool or bloody purulent stool and tenesmus. Diarrhea is often persistent or recurrent and resistant to treatment. In most cases, abdominal pain is localized in the left, middle or lower abdomen, pronounced before defecation and relieved after it. The patients may have fever, anorexia, nausea, loss of weight, anemia, edema, etc. Some patients may have erythema nodosum, arthritis, joint pain and other abenteric manifestations.

2. Ulcerative colitis can be divided into chronic recurrent type, chronic persistent type and fulminant type. The first one is more frequent, while the last one, though less frequent, is in critical condition and its prognosis is poor.

3. Laboratory examination: Routine stool test usually reveals nonspecific changes. Bacterial culture finds no pathogen. Barium enema shows colon spasm and deformity, disordered mucosal folds. In severe case, rigid or dented colon wall, colon stenosis or ulcers can be found. X-ray examination is most helpful in detecting the extent and scope of the disease, but runs a risk in acute phase.

Endoscopy is convenient and the most valuable in the diagnosis, since 95 percent of the patients have rectal involvement. Based on specific morphological changes and biopsy, the diagnosis can be confirmed, and differentiated from colonic or rectal carcinoma, colonic polys or chronic bacillary dysentery.

DIFFERENTIATION AND TREATMENT OF COMMON SYNDROMES

1. Downward Flow of Damp-heat (frequently found at the onset or in the duration of the attack)

Main Symptoms and Signs: Fever, abdominal pain, diar-

本病。患者女多于男。本病中医属"泄泻"、"赤白痢"等范畴。

【诊断要点】

1. 症状：主要临床症状为慢性腹泻和腹痛。腹泻轻重不一，重者每天可达数十次，可伴有稀便、粘液便和脓血便，常有里急后重，腹泻常持续或反复发作，顽固难愈。腹痛多局限于左中腹或下腹，便前为著，便后缓解。患者可有发热、厌食、恶心、体重减轻、贫血、水肿等症状，部分患者可有结节性红斑、关节炎、关节痛等肠外表现。

2. 根据病程和临床表现，可分为慢性复发性、慢性持续性和暴发型，以前者多见，暴发型虽较少见，但病情凶险，预后较差。

3. 辅助检查：粪便常规检查多呈非特异性改变，细菌培养无病原体可见；钡剂灌肠可见肠壁痉挛、袋影加深或消失，粘膜皱襞紊乱，重者可见结肠壁僵硬或呈锯齿形、肠管狭窄或呈溃疡。X线检查对了解病变程度和范围有较大帮助，但在急性期有一定危险性。

内窥镜检查价值最高。由于95%以上患者有直肠受累，因此本检查法方便可靠。根据病变特殊形态结合活组织检查，常可确诊并可与结肠、直肠癌及肠息肉、慢性菌痢等鉴别。

【辨证论治】

1. 湿热下注（多见于本病初起或发作时）

主证：发热，腹痛，腹泻，肛门灼热，或里急后重，大便夹

rhea, burning sensation in the anus, or tenesmus, bloody, purulent and mucous stool, red tongue with yellow, thick and
greasy fur, and slippery rapid pulse.

Therapeutic Principle: Clearing away pathogenic heat and
dampness.

Recipe: Decoction cf Pueraria, Scutellaria and Coptis with
additional ingredients.

pueraria root, *Radix Puerariae*   15g
scutellaria root, *Radix Scutellariae*   10g
coptis rhizome, *Rhizoma Coptidis*   10g
honeysuckle flower, *Flos Lonicerae*   30g
pulsatilla root, *Radix Pulsatillae*   15g
plantain seed, *Semen Plantaginis*   10g (wrapped in a
   piece of cloth before it is decocted)
aucklandia root, *Radix Aucklandiae*   10g
bitter orange, *Fructus Aurantii*   10g

All the above drugs are to be decocted in water for oral
administration.

2. Hyperactivity of the Liver and Insufficiency of the
Spleen (often induced by psychic factors)

Main Symptoms and Signs: Attacks often occurring after
emotional tonus and psychic trauma, manifested as abdominal
pain before diarrhea, after which the pain is relieved,
accompanied with distension and pain in the hypohcondrium,
epigastric fullness and anorexia, thin and whitish coating of the
tongue, and taut thready pulse.

Therapeutic Principle: Checking hyperfunction of the liver
and strengthening the spleen.

Recipe: Prescription of Importance for Diarrhea with
Pain with additional ingredients.

white peony root, *Radix Paeoniae Alba*   15g
white atractylodes rhizome, *Rhizoma Atractylodis* Macroce--
   phalae   15g
ledebouriella root, *Radix Ledebouriellae*   10g

有脓、血、粘冻，舌质红，苔厚腻，脉滑数。

治则：清热利湿。

处方：葛根芩连汤加味。

葛根15克，黄芩10克，黄连10克，金银花30克，白头翁15克，

车前子10克(布包煎)，木香10克，枳壳10克。水煎服。

2. 肝旺脾虚(多见于精神因素诱发者)

主证：多于情绪紧张或激动后发病，腹痛即泻，泻后痛减，

伴胸胁胀痛，脘闷纳呆，苔薄白，脉弦细。

治则：抑肝扶脾。

处方：痛泻要方加味。

白芍15克，白术15克，防风10克，陈皮10克，柴胡10克，苡

tangerine peel, *Pericarpium Citri Reticulatae*   10g
bupleurum root, *Radix Bupleuri*   10g
coix seed, *Semen Coicis*   15g
hyacinth bean, *Semen Dolichoris*   12g
parched hawthorn fruit, *Fructus Crataegi*   12g

All the above drugs are to be decocted in water for oral administration.

3. Insufficiency of the Spleen and Stomach (mostly occurring in patients with recurrent attacks)

Main Symptoms and Signs: Borborygmi, diarrhea with undigested food in the stool, anorexia, stuffiness in the abdomen, lassitude and fatigue, pale tongue with whitish fur, and deep weak pulse.

Therapeutic Principle: Reinforcing the spleen and stomach.

Recipe: Modified Powder of Ginseng, Poria and Bighead Astractylodes.

dangshen, *Radix Codonopsis Pilosulae*   15g
lotus seed, *Semen Nelumbinis*   12g
white astractylodes rhizome, *Rhizoma Astractylodis Macrocephalae*   12g
Chinese yam, *Rhizoma Dioscoreae*   12g
hyacinth bean, *Semen Dolichoris*   9g
poria, *Poria*   15g
coix seed, *Semen Coicis*   15g
tangerine peel, *Pericarpium Citri Reticulatae*   10g
prepared licorice root, *Radix Glycyrrhizae Praeparata*   6g

All the above drugs are to be decocted in water for oral administration.

Moreover, 6 grams of aucklandia root (*Radix Aucklandiae*) and 10 grams of coptis rhizome (*Rhizoma Coptidis*) ought to be employed for cases with residual heat; 30 grams of halloysite (*Halloysitum Rubrum*) and 10 grams of nutmeg (*Semen Myristicae*) for cases with severe diarrhea; 10 grams of chicken's gizzard-skin (*Endothelium Corneum Gigeriae Galli*) for cases with poor ap-

仁15克，扁豆12克，焦山楂12克。水煎服。

3．脾胃虚弱（多见于病情反复发作者）

主证：肠鸣腹泻，水谷不化，纳呆脘闷，倦怠乏力，舌质淡，

苔白，脉沉弱。

治则：健补脾胃。

处方：参苓白术散加减。

党参15克，莲子肉12克，白术12克，山药12克，扁豆 9 克，

茯苓15克，苡仁15克，陈皮10克，炙甘草 6 克。水煎服。

余热未清者，加木香 6 克，黄连10克；泻甚者，加赤石脂30

petite.

4. Insufficiency of the Spleen-*yang* and Kidney-*yang* (mostly occurring in the chronic case)

Main Symptoms and Signs: Diarrhea in the early morning, intolerance of cold, cold limbs, soreness and weakness of the loins, pale and tender tongue with whitish fur, deep, thready and weak pulse.

Therapeutic Principle: Warming and tonifying the spleen and kidney.

Recipe: Pill of Four Miraculous Drugs with additional ingredients.

psoralea fruit, *Fructus Psoraleae* 10g

nutmeg, *Semen Myristicae* 10g

schisandra fruit, *Fructus Schisandrae* 10g

evodia fruit, *Fructus Evodiae* 10g

prepared aconite root, *Radix Aconiti Praeparata* 10g

dangshen, *Radix Codonopsis Pilosulae* 12g

white atractylodes rhizome, *Rhizoma Atractylodis Macrocephalae* 12g

red halloysite, *Halloysitum Rubrum*. 30g

prepared licorice root, *Radix Glycyrrhizae Praeparata* 6g

All the above drugs are to be decocted in water for oral administration.

Section 16
Hepatocirrhosis

Hepatocirrhosis is the final outcome of diffuse inflammation of the liver, degeneration and necrosis of the hepatic cells and proliferation of fibrous tissue induced by various causes. Of the causes of the disease, posthepatitic cirrhosis is the most common one, second ones are the cardiac, biliary and alcoholic cirrhosis. Nodular cirrhosis is closely related to liver carcinoma.

克，肉豆蔻10克；食欲不振者，加鸡内金10克。

4. 脾肾阳虚（多见于病情迁延日久者）

主证：黎明腹泻，畏寒肢冷，腰酸乏力，舌淡嫩，苔白，脉沉细无力。

治则：温补脾肾。

处方：四神丸加味。

补骨脂10克，肉豆蔻10克，五味子10克，吴茱萸10克，附子10克，党参12克，白术 12 克，赤石脂 30 克，炙甘草 6 克。水煎服。

第十六节　肝硬化

肝硬化是由多种不同原因引起肝脏弥漫性炎症和肝细胞变性、坏死及纤维组织增生所导致的最终结果。病因中以肝炎后肝硬化最多见，心源性、胆汁性和酒精性肝硬化亦不少见。结节性

In TCM, this disease is included in the categories of "*gan yu*" (stagnation of liver-*qi*), "*zheng ji*" (mass in the abdomen), "*pi kuai*" (hepatosplenomegaly), "*gu zhang*" (tympanites), etc.

MAIN POINTS OF DIAGNOSIS

1. Compensatory Phase: Clinical manifestations include fatigue, loss of appetite, nausea, abdominal fullness and other symptoms of digestive tract. Slight edema and bleeding tendency may be present due to reduced liver function. The findings of physical examination are mild hepatomegaly with slight hardness, splenomegal, spider nevi and liver palms.

2. Decompensatory Phase

(1) Portal hypertension syndrome: Splenomegaly with hypersplenism, esophageal and gastric fundal venous varices which may result in hemorrhage of the upper digestive tract.

(2) Impaired liver function syndrome: Fatigue and symptoms of the digestive tract are aggravated, low fever, jaundice, edema and ascites are often present. Patients may have eminent bleeding tendency, darkish complexion and endocrine disorder. In severe cases complications such as hemorrhage of the upper digestive tract and hepatic coma may take their place.

3. Laboratory Examination

(1) Liver function test: It is found that icteric index has increased, A/G Ratio decreased or reversed, γ-globulin increased. Flocculation-turbidity test presents a positive; SGPT, transpeptidase and MAO, too elevated. The prothrombin time is often elongated.

(2) Ultrasonography (A and B Mode), liver scan, CT scanning and liver puncture are helpful in confirming the diagnosis and type of the disease. They are also valuable in differentiation from other liver disease such as hepatic carcinoma and liver abscess.

DIFFERENTIATION AND TREATMENT OF COMMON SYNDROMES

1. Stagnation of the Liver-*qi* and Deficiency of the Spleen

Main Symptoms and Signs: Anorexia, abdominal distress

肝硬变与肝癌关系密切。本病属中医"肝郁"、"癥积"、"痞块"、"臌胀"等范畴。

【诊断要点】

1. 代偿期：主要表现为乏力、食欲减退、恶心、腹胀等消化道症状，患者可因肝功能减退而出现较轻度浮肿和出血倾向。体检肝脏轻度肿大，质地偏硬，脾肿大亦常见，可见蜘蛛痣和肝掌。

2. 失代偿期

（1）门脉高压症候群：脾大伴脾功能亢进，食道和胃底静脉曲张并可导致上消化道出血。

（2）肝功能损害症候群：乏力和消化道症状加重，低热、黄疸、浮肿和腹水常见，患者常有较明显出血倾向，皮肤变黑，内分泌紊乱，严重者常出现上消化道出血和肝昏迷等并发症。

3. 辅助检查

（1）肝功能检查：可见黄疸指数增高，白蛋白球蛋白比例下降或倒置，γ—球蛋白增高，絮浊实验阳性，谷丙转氨酶、转肽酶和单胺氧化酶亦常增高，凝血酶原时间延长。

（2）A型和B型超声波、肝扫描、CT扫描、肝穿刺等对确诊有一定帮助，并可协助确定病变类型以及同其他肝脏病如肝癌、肝脓疡等的鉴别。

【辨证论治】

1. 肝郁脾虚

主证：食欲减退，胸腹闷胀，两胁隐痛，倦怠乏力，或有恶

and distension, vague hypochondriac pain, lassitude [and fatigue, or nausesa and loose stool, whitish coating of the tongue, and taut pulse.

Therapeutic Principle: Relieving the depressed liver-*qi* and invigorating the spleen, promoting blood circulation to remove blood stasis.

Recipe: Modified Ease Powder.

bupleurum root, *Radix Bupleuri*   12g

Chinese angelica root, *Radix Angelicae Sinensis*   15g

white peony root, *Radix Paeoniae Alba*   15g

white atractylodes rhizome, *Rhizoma Atractylodis Macrocephalae*   15g

poria, *Poria*   9g

cyperum tuber, *Rhizoma Cyperi*   9g

finger citron, *Fructus Citri Sarcodactylis*   12g

red sage root, *Radix Salviae Miltiorrhizae*   15g

chicken's gizzard-skin, *Endothelium Corneum Gigeriae Galli*   9g

prepared licorice root, *Radix Glycyrrhizae Praeparata*   6g

All the above drugs are to be decocted in water for oral administration.

Besides, 10 grams of atractylodes rhizome (*Rhizoma Atractylodis*) and 10 grams of magnoslia bark (*Cortex Magnoliae Officinalis*) ought to be administered for the case with thick coating of the tongue and distension of the abdomen due to abundance of pathogenic dampness; 12 grams of dangshen (*Radix Codonopsis Pilosulae*) and 12 grams of wolfberry fruit (*Fructus Lycii*) administered for the case with obvious fatigue.

2. Obstruction of the Liver-blood

Main Symptoms and Signs: Hepatomegaly and splemomegaly, twinge or distress in the hypochondrium, distension of the abdomen, anorexia, dim complexion, or accompanied with spider nevi and liver palms, deep-red tongue or with ecchymoses, taut and thready pulse.

Therapeutic Principle: Promoting blood circulation to re-

心便溏，苔白脉弦。

治则：疏肝健脾，活血化瘀。

处方：逍遥散加减。

柴胡12克，当归15克，白芍15克，白术15克，茯苓9克，香附9克，佛手12克，丹参15克，鸡内金9克，炙甘草6克。水煎服。

若湿邪较重苔厚腹胀者，加苍术10克，厚朴10克；困乏明显者，加党参12克，枸杞子12克。

2．肝血瘀阻

主证：肝脾肿大，胁下刺痛或闷痛，腹胀纳呆，面色晦暗，并有蜘蛛痣、肝掌，舌质暗红，或有瘀斑，脉弦细。

治则：活血化瘀，软坚通络。

move blood stasis, softening hard hepatosplenomegaly to remove obstruction in the liver-channel.

Recipe: Modified Decoction for Removing Blood Stasis.

Chinese angelica root, *Radix Angelicae Sinensis*   12g

red sage root, *Radix Salviae Miltiorrhizae*   15g

peach kernel, *Semen Persicae*   10g

safflower, *Flos Carthami*   10g

curcuma root, *Radix Curcumae*   10g

bupleurum root, *Radix Bupleuri*   10g

green tangerine peel, *Pericarpium Citri Reticulatae Viride*   10g

fresh-water turtle shell, *Carapex Trionycis*   15g

pangolin scales, *Squama Manitis*   10g

oyster shell, *Concha ostreae*   30g

white atractylodes rhizome, *Rhizoma Atractylodis Macrocephalae*   12g

prepared licorice root, *Radix Glycyrrhizae Praeparata*   6g

All the above drugs are to be decocted in water for oral administration.

In addition, the administration of dangshen (*Radix Codonopsis Pilosulae*) 12g and astragalus root (*Radix Astragali seu Hedysari*) 15g is for patients with symptoms of deficiency of *qi*; dried rehmannia root (*Radix Rehmanniae*) 12g and dendrobium (*Herba Dendrobii*) 10g for patients with manifestations of impairment of *yin*.

3. Retention of Water within the Body

Main Symptoms and Signs: Tympanites which is firm and full when pressed, epigastric distress, anorexia, scanty urine, red tongue, taut and thready pulse.

Therapeutic Principle: Regulating the flow of *qi* to induce diuresis, removing blood stasis to soften hard hepatosplenomigaly.

Recipe: Modified Stomach Decoction with Poria.

atractylodes rhizome, *Rhizoma Atractylodis*   10g

处方：化瘀汤加减。

当归12克，丹参15克，桃仁10克，红花10克，郁金10克，柴
胡10克，青皮10克，鳖甲15克，穿山甲10克，牡蛎30克，白术12
克，炙甘草6克。水煎服。

若症见气虚者，加党参12克，黄芪15克；阴伤者，加生地12
克，石斛10克。

3. 水湿内阻

主证：腹胀如鼓，按之坚满，脘闷纳呆，小便短少,舌质红，
脉弦细。

治则：理气行水，化瘀软坚。

处方：胃苓汤加减。

white atractylodes rhizome, *Rhizoma Atactylodis Macrocephalae* 10g

magnolia bark, *Cortex Magnoliae Officinalis* 10g

poria, *Poria* 15g

umbellate pore lungus, *Polyporus Umbellatus* 12g

water-plantain tuber, *Rhizoma Alismatis* 15g

shell of areca nut, *Pericarpium Arecae* 15g

plantain seed, *Semen Plantaginis* 20g (wrapped in a piece of cloth for decoction)

aucklandia root, *Radix Aucklandiae* 10g

red sage root, *Radix Salviae Miltiorrhizae* 15g

fresh-water turtle shell, *Carapax Trionycis* 15g

peach kernel, *Semen Persicae* 10g

prepared licorice root, *Radix Glycyrrhizae Praeparata* 6g

All the above drugs are to be decocted in water for oral administration.

If the case is complicated with deficiency of the liver-*yin* and kidney-*yin* marked by abdominal distension with dry mouth and lips, hot sensation in the palms and soles, deep-red tongue with very little fur or none, and taut, thready and rapid pulse, the treatment should be concentrated on nourishing the liver and kidney, and nourishing *yin* and inducing diuresis. The modified Decoction for Nourishing the Liver and Kidney is preferable for the very treatment. The compositions are: glehnia root (*Radix Glehniae*) 10g, ophiopogon root (*Radix Ophiopogonis*) 10g, dried rehmannia root (*Radix Rehmanniae*) 15g, wolfberry fruit (*Fructus Lycii*) 12g, umbellate pore-fungus (*Polyporus Umblelatus*) 15g, water-plantain tuber (*Rhizoma Alismatis*) 15g, poria (*Poria*) 15g, tale (*Talcum*) 12g, oyster shell (*Concha Ostreae*) 30g, red sage root (*Radix Salviae Miltiorrhizae*) 15g, fresh-water turtle shell (*Carapax Trionycis*) 15g. All the drugs are to be decocted in water for oral administration.

苍术10克，白术10克，厚朴10克，茯苓15克，猪苓12克，泽

泻15克，大腹皮15克，车前子20克（包煎），木香10克，丹参15克，

鳖甲15克，桃仁10克，炙甘草6克。水煎服。

若兼肝肾阴虚，症见腹胀而兼有口干唇燥，手足心热，舌质

红绛，少苔或无苔，脉弦细数，治宜滋养肝肾，育阴利水，可用

一贯煎加减：沙参10克，麦冬10克，生地15克，枸杞子12克，猪

苓15克，泽泻15克，茯苓15克，滑石12克，牡蛎30克，丹参15克，

鳖甲15克。水煎服。

Section 17
Cholecystitis

Acute cholecystitis is caused mainly by bacterial infection and biliary tract obstruction; chronic cholecystitis usually coexists with gallstone besides a history of acute cholecystitis. In TCM, this disease is categorized as *"xie tong"* (hypochondriac pain), *"huang dan"* (jaundice), etc.

MAIN POINTS OF DIAGNOSIS

1. Acute cholecystitis has an acute onset and persistent pain in the right upper quadrant radiating to the right shoulder accompanied with nausea vomiting and fever. Jaundice may be present in some patients. Physical examination reveals prominent tenderness, rebounding tenderness and muscular tension in the right upper adbomen, sometimes the enlarged gallbladder is palpable.

2. Patients suffering from chronic cholecystitis usually have such chronic symptoms as discomfort in the right upper quadrant, vague pain, abdominal distension, aversion to greasy food, eruction and other dyspeptic manifestations. Physical examination may reveal slight tenderness or no specific signs.

3. Laboratory examination

(1) In the stage of acute attack, leucocytosis, elevated icterus index and hepatic lesion to some extent may be present.

(2) Abdominal X-ray plain film may show positive radioopaque stone, enlarged gallbladder and calcified opacity. Cholecystography reveals the form of gallbladder and its concentrating function or radio-opaque stone. It is helpful for the diagnosis of chronic cholecystitis.

(3) Duodenal drainage is valuable in detecting the pathogen as well as confirming the diagnosis, giving some hints for treatment. Ultrasonic examination is practical to evaluate the

第十七节　胆囊炎

急性胆囊炎主要由细菌感染和胆道阻塞引起；慢性胆囊炎除可有急性胆囊炎病史外，多与结石并存。本病属中医"胁痛"、"黄疸"等范畴。

【诊断要点】

1．急性胆囊炎起病急骤，持续性右上腹痛向右肩部放射，伴发热，恶心和呕吐。部分患者可有黄疸，体检右上腹明显压痛、反跳痛和肌卫，有时可触及肿大的胆囊。

2．慢性胆囊炎患者常有右上腹不适、隐痛以及腹胀、厌油、嗳气等消化不良症状，经久不愈。体检上腹可有轻压痛或无特殊体征。

3．辅助检查

（1）急性发作期可见白细胞增高、黄疸指数增高和一定程度的肝脏损害表现。

（2）腹部X线平片可显示阳性结石阴影，部分患者可见胆囊肿大和钙化影；胆囊造影可显示胆囊形态、浓缩功能和结石阴影，对慢性患者较适用。

（3）十二指肠引流价值较大，除可确诊病变，尚可发现病原体，有助于指导治疗。超声检查方便可行，对估价胆囊功能和提

function of gallbladder and suggest the existence of gallstones.

DIFFERENTIATION AND TREATMENT OF COMMON SYNDROMES

1. Damp-heat in the Liver and Gallbladder (frequently occurring in acute cholecystitis or in acute attack of chronic form)

Main Symptoms and Signs: Alternate spells of fever and chill or fever without chill, pain in the right upper abdomen or right ribs, poor appetite, bitterness in the mouth, even accompanied with nausea and vomiting, constipation, deep-coloured urine, sometimes with jaundice, red tongue with yellow and greasy fur, and taut rapid pulse.

Therapeutic Principle: Clearing away pathogenic heat and dampness, soothing the liver and normalizing the function of gallbladder.

Recipe: The combination of Oriental Wormwood Decoction and Decoction of Gentian for Purging Liver-fire with additional ingredients.

oriental wormwood, *Herba Artemisiae Capillaris*   30g
capejasmine fruit, *Fructus Gardeniae*   12g
rhubarb, *Radix et Rhizoma Rhei*   9g
scutellaria root, *Radix Scutellariae*   15g
bupleurum root, *Radix Bupleuri*   15g
curcuma root, *Radix Curcumae*   15g
honeysuckle flower, *Flos Lonicerae*   30g
forsythia fruit, *Fructus Forsythiae*   15g
gentian root, *Radix Gentianae*   12g
immature bitter orange, *Fructus Aurantii Immaturus*   9g
aucklandia root, *Radix Aucklandiae*   9g
licorice root, *Radix Glycyrrhizae*   9g

All the above drugs are to be decocted in water for oral administration.

In addition to the above ingredients, 30 grams of gypsum (*Gypsum Fibrosum*) and 30 grams of isatis root (*Radix Isatidis*) ought to be employed for the case with high fever; 9 grams of

示有无结石很有帮助。

【辨证论治】

1. 肝胆湿热（多见于急性胆囊炎或慢性胆囊炎急性发作）

主证：寒热往来或但热不寒，右上腹或右胁痛，纳呆口苦，甚则恶心呕吐，大便秘结，小便色赤，或有黄疸，舌质红，苔黄腻，脉弦数。

治则：清热利湿，疏肝利胆。

处方：茵陈蒿汤合龙胆泻肝汤加味。

茵陈30克，栀子12克，大黄9克，黄芩15克，柴胡15克，郁金15克，金银花30克，连翘15克，龙胆草12克，枳实9克，木香9克，甘草9克。

高热者，加生石膏30克，板蓝根30克；恶心、呕吐者，加半

pinellia tuber (*Rhizoma Pinelliae*) and 9 grams of bamboo shavings *Caulis Bambusae in Taeniam*) for the case with nausea and vomiting; 9 grams of chicken's gizzard-skin (*Endothelium Corneum GigeriaeGalli*) 9 grams of parched hawthorn fruit (*Fructus Crataegik*) 9 grams of parched medicated leaven (*Massa Fermentata Medicinalis*) and 9 grams of parched germinated barley (*Fructus Hordei Germinatus*) for the case with poor appetite.

2. Stagnation in the Liver and Gallbladder (frequently occurring in chonic cholecystitis)

Main Symptoms and Signs: Right-sided hypochondriac pain which sometimes radiates to the right shoulder and back, epigastric distension and fullness, which are aggravated by anger or intake of greasy foods, poor appetite, eruction, nausea, red tongue with thin yellowish fur, and taut pulse.

Therapeutic Principle: Soothing the liver and normalizing the function of gallbladder.

Recipe: Modified Major Bupleurum Decoction.

bupleurum root, *Radix Bupleuri*   9g
scutellaria root, *Radix Scutellariae*   9g
curcuma root, *Radix Curcumae*   15g
chicken's gizzard-skin, *Endothelium Corneum Gigeriae Galli*   9g
blimbing fern spore, *Spora Lygodii*   15g
bitter orange, *Fructus Aurantii*   9g
aucklandia root, *Radix Aucklandiae*   9g
honeysuckle flower, *Flos Lonicerae*   30g
forsythia fruit, *Fructus Forsythiae*   15g
white peony root, *Radix Paeoniae Alba*   15g
rhubarb, *Radix et Rhizoma Rhei*   6g
licorice root, *Radix Glycyrrhizae*   6g

All the above drugs are to be decocted in water for oral administration.

Moreover, for the case with poor appetite, 9 grams of parched hawthorn fruit (*Fructus Crataegi*), 9 grams of parched

夏9克，竹茹9克；食欲不振者，加鸡内金（研冲）9克，焦三仙

9克。

2. 肝胆郁滞（多见于慢性胆囊炎）

主证：右胁胀痛，或牵引右肩背不适，胃脘胀闷，发怒或进

食油腻后加重，食欲不振，嗳气恶心，舌质红，苔薄黄，脉弦。

治则：疏肝利胆。

处方：大柴胡汤加减。

柴胡9克，黄芩9克，郁金15克，鸡内金9克，海金砂15克，

枳壳9克，木香9克，金银花30克，连翘15克，白芍15克，大黄

6克，生甘草6克。水煎服。

食欲不振，加焦三仙各9克；脾虚明显者，加白术9克，党

medicated leaven (*Massa Fermentata Medicinalis*) and 9 grams of parched germinated barley (*Fructus Hordei Germinatus*) should be administered; for the case with distinct symptoms of spleen deficiency, 9 grams of white atractylodes rhizome (*Rhizoma Atractylodis Macrocephalae*), 9 grams of dangshen (*Radix Codonopsis Pilosulae*) and 9 grams of poria (*Poria*) be administered.

Section 18
Aplastic Anemia

Aplastic anemia is a clinical syndrome caused by a variety of etiological factors (some of them are unknown) which lead to hematopoietic disorder of bone marrow. Clinically, it is characterized by panhematopenia resulting in anemia, hemorrhage and infections. The disease often occurs in young adults. It is more common in males than in females. In TCM, it is categorized as "*xu lao*" (consumptive disease), "*xue zheng*" (blood trouble), etc.

MAIN POINTS OF DIAGNOSIS

According to the clinical features and pictures of bone marrow, the disease can be divided into two types — acute and chronic.

1. Acute aplastic anemia: The onset is abrupt with rapid progress of the disease. There are marked symptoms of anemia, hemorrhage and infection, particularly symptoms of severe and extensive bleeding. Intracranial hemorrhage is the leading cause of death.

2. Chronic aplastic anemia: The onset of the disease is slow, and the course is persistent. Anemia is the major symptom, while the symptoms of hemorrhage and infection are relatively mild and easy to be controlled.

3. Physical examination generally finds no enlargement of liver and spleen except the manifestations of anemia and he-

参9克，茯苓9克。

第十八节　再生障碍性贫血

再生障碍性贫血是由于不同病因（部分原因不明）所引起的一组骨髓造血障碍综合症。临床上以全血细胞减少为特征，表现为贫血、出血和感染。好发于青壮年，男较女多见。本病属中医"虚劳"、"血证"等范畴。

【诊断要点】

根据临床表现和骨髓象特点可分为急、慢两型。

1．急性型：起病急，病情进展迅速，贫血、出血和感染症状明显，尤以出血广泛而严重。颅内出血常为致死原因。

2．慢性型：起病缓慢，病程迁延，以贫血为主要症状，出血较轻微，感染亦较轻，易控制。

morrhage.

4. The blood picture shows the decrease in whole blood cells, normochromic anemia, reticulocytopenia, thrombocytopenia and increased serum iron. The picture of bone marrow in acute type presents obvious hypoplasia, characterized by the decrease of three blood cell systems and elevation of non-producing blood cells. In chronic type, relatively mild retardation of proliferation may be the feature in bone marrow, associated with right shift of classification.

DIFFERENTIATION AND TREATMENT OF COMMON SYNDROMES

1. Deficiency of Both *Qi* and Blood

Main Symptoms and Signs: Slow onset, dizziness, palpitation, shortness of breath, fatigue and weakness, pale complexion and pale tongue with white fur, deep and thready pulse.

Therapeutic Principle: Supplementing *qi* and nourishing blood.

Recipe: Modified Eight Precious Ingredients Decoction.

dangshen, *Radix Codonopsis Pilosulae*   15g

white atractylodes rhizome, *Rhizoma Atractylodis Macrocephalae*   10g

poria, *Poria*   10g

prepared liquorice, *Raidx Glycyrrhizae Praeparata*   6g

Chinese angelica, *Radix Angelicae Sinensis*   12g

prepared rehmannia root, *Radix Rehmanniae Praeparata*   12g

white peony root, *Radix Paeoniae Alba*   10g

astragalus root, *Radix Astragali seu Hedysari*   18g

donkey-hide gelatin, *Colla Corii Asini*   10g

All the above drugs, except donkey-hide gelatin which is to be melted in the finished decoction, are to be decocted in water for oral administration.

In addition to the above ingredients, 30 grams of hairy vein agrimony (*Herba Agrimoniae*) and 10 grams of stir-baked argyi leaf (*Folium Arthmisiae Argyi*) ought to be employed if there

3．体检除贫血、出血表现外，一般无肝脾肿大。

4．血象全血细胞减少、正色素性贫血，网织红细胞减少，血小板亦减少，血清铁增加。骨髓象急性呈增生明显低下，三象细胞减少，非造血细胞增多；慢性呈增生不良，但程度较轻，分类右移。

【辨证论治】

1．气血两虚

主证：起病缓慢，头晕眼花，心悸气短，疲乏无力，面色苍白，舌质淡，苔白，脉沉细。

治则：益气养血。

处方：八珍汤加减。

党参15克，白术10克，茯苓10克，炙甘草6克，当归12克，熟地12克，白芍10克，黄芪18克，阿胶10克（烊化）。水煎服。

若有出血者，可加仙鹤草30克，艾叶炭10克；发热者，可加

is bleeding; 10 grams of bupleurum root (*Radix Bupleuri*), 10 grams of scutellaria root (*Radix Scutellariae*) and 20 grams of honeysuckle flower (*Flos Lonicerae*) be administered if the case is accompanied with fever.

2. Deficiency of the Liver-*yin* and Kidney-*yin*

Main Symptoms and Signs: Dizziness, tinnitus, aching pain of the waist and knees, hot sensation in the palms and soles, or low fever in the afternoon, dry mouth, night sweat, insomnia, excessive dreaming, menorrhagia, red tongue with little fur, thready and rapid pulse.

Therapeutic Principle: Nourishing the liver and kidney.

Recipe: Modified prescriptions of Decoction for Invigorating Primodial *Qi* and of Glossy Privet Fruit and Eclipta Pill.

dangshen, *Radix Codonopsis Pilosulae*   15g
dried rehmannia root, *Radix Rehmanniae*   15g
prepared rehmannia root, *Radix Rehmanniae Praeparata*   15g
Chinese angelica, *Radix Angelicae Sinensis*   10g
siberian solomonseal rhizome, *Rhizoma Polygonati*   15g
wolfberry fruit, *Fructus Lycii*   15g
glossy privet fruit, *Fructus Ligustri Lucidi*   10g
eclipta, *Herba Ecliptae*   15g
dogwood fruit, *Fructus Corni*   12g
fleece-flower root, *Radix Polygoni Multiflori*   15g
mulberry, *Fructus Mori*   18g
prepared liquorice, *Radix Glycyrrhizae Praeparata*   6g

All the above drugs are to be decocted in water for oral administration.

For the case with fever, 12 grams of sweet wormwood (*Herba Artemisiae*), 12 grams of wolfberry bark (*Cortex Lycii Radicis*) and 10 grams of anemarrhena rhizome (*Rhizoma Anemarrhenae*) should be added; For the case with marked bleeding, additional drugs are stir-baked sanguisorba root (*Radix Sanguisorbae*) 12g, donkey-hide glue (*Colla Corii Asini*) 10g and biota tops (*Cacumen Biotae*)

柴胡10克，黄芩10克，银花20克。

2. 肝肾阴虚

主证：头昏耳鸣，腰膝酸痛，手足心热，或午后低热，口干

盗汗，失眠多梦，妇女则月经过多，舌质红，苔少，脉细数。

治则：滋补肝肾。

处方：大补元煎合二至丸加减。

党参15克，生地15克，熟地15克，当归10克，黄精15克，枸

杞15克，女贞子10克，旱莲草15克，山萸肉12克，何首乌15克，

桑椹18克，炙甘草6克。水煎服。

若发热者，加青蒿12克，地骨皮12克，知母10克，出血明显

10g.

3. Deficiency of the Spleen-*yang* and Kidney-*yang*

Main Symptoms and Signs: Mental debility, disinclination to talk, aching pain of the waist and weakness of the legs, aversion to cold, cold limbs, spontaneous perspiration, edema, loose stool, pale complexion, corpulent and pale tongue with thin and white fur, deep and thready pulse.

Therapeutic Principle: Invigorating the spleen and warming the kidney.

Recipe: Modified prescriptions of Decoction of Four Noble Drugs and Kidney-*yang*-reinforcing Bolus.

dangshen, *Radix Codonopsis Pilosulae*   18g

astragalus root, *Radix Astragali seu Hedysari*   18g

white atractylodes rhizome, *Rhizoma Atractylodis Macrocephalae*   12g

Chinese yam, *Rhizoma Dioscoreae*   12g

tangerine peel, *Pericarpium Citri Reticulatae*   9g

prepared rehmannia root, *Radix Rehmanniae Praeparata*   15g

Chinese angelica, *Radix Angelicae Sinensis*   10g

psoralae fruit, *Fructus Psoraleae*   10g

antler glue, *Colla Cornus Cervi*   10g

cinnamon bark, *Cortex Cinnamomi*   3g

morinda root, *Radix Morindae Officinalis*   10g

epimedium, *Herba Epimedii*   10g

All the above drugs are to be decocted in water for oral administration.

Section 19
Thrombocytopenic Purpura

Thrombocytopenic purpura is an autoimmune disease. This disease also involves the spleen and often occurs in children and young adults. The incidence in females is

者，加地榆炭12克，阿胶珠10克，侧柏叶10克。

3．脾肾阳虚

主证：神疲懒言，腰酸腿软，畏寒肢冷，自汗浮肿，大便溏稀，面色㿠白，舌胖质淡，苔薄白，脉沉细。

治则：健脾温肾。

处方：四君子汤合右归丸加减。

党参18克，黄芪18克，白术12克，山药12克，陈皮9克，熟地15克，当归10克，补骨脂10克，鹿角胶10克，肉桂3克，巴戟天10克，仙灵脾10克。水煎服。

第十九节　血小板减少性紫癜

血小板减少性紫癜是一种自身免疫性疾病，发病中脾脏因素

higher than in males. In TCM, the disease is categorized as *"ji niu"* (subcutaneous hemorrhage) *"fa ban"* (purpura), etc.

MAIN POINTS OF DIAGNOSIS

The disease can be divided into acute type and chronic type according to the clinical manifestations and courses.

1. Acute type of thrombocytopenic purpura is commonly found in adolescents. In most cases, the patients have a previous history of viral infection. The onset of the disease is sudden, manifested as chill, fever and obvious hemorrhage in skin and mucosa. Chronic type of the disease is often seen in females. The onset is slow with mild ymptoms. There may appear alternation of attack and remission in a certain period.

2. Physical examination of acute type reveals no particular signs but infection and hemorrhage, while in chronic type which is recurrent in attack, spelenomegaly may be the only finding.

3. Laboratory test: Blood test shows a sharp reduction of platelet count in acute type, usually less than 20×10^9/L, with the life of platelets being markedly shorter than normal. The range of platelet count in chronic type is frequently from 30 to 80×10^9/L. The bleeding time is prolonged associated with poor contraction of blood clot.

The picture of bone marrow in acute type shows an increased promegakaryocytes, with smaller bodies and few granules inside the cells, most of which are immature, and there is no formation of platelets, while in chronic type, there is an increase of megalocaryocytes, in which mature cells dominate in number, but granulae inside are smaller in number, indicating their poor function of producing blood.

DIFFERENTIATION AND TREATMENT OF COMMON SYNDROMES

1. Bleeding due to Blood-heat

Main Symptoms and Signs: Sudden onset with fever, pur-

亦起到一定作用。本病多见于青少年，女性多于男性，属中医"肌衄"、"发斑"等范畴。

【诊断要点】

根据临床表现和病程，可分为急性型和慢性型。

1. 急性型常见于青少年，起病前多有病毒感染史，病情急，发热、畏寒常见，皮肤粘膜出血明显；慢性型多见于成年女性，起病缓慢，症状较轻微，缓解和发作常交替出现。

2. 体检急性型除出血感染表现外，余无特殊体征；慢性型反复发作，可见脾肿大。

3. 实验室检查：急性型血小板明显下降，常低于$20 \times 10^9/L$血小板寿命明显缩短，慢性型血小板多在$30 \sim 80 \times 10^9/L$，出血时间延长，血块收缩不良。

骨髓检查：急性型幼巨核细胞增多，但体积小，无颗粒，未成熟者多，无血小板形成；慢性型除巨核细胞增加外，成熟者亦多，但颗粒较少，显示功能低下。

【辨证论治】

1. 血热妄行

主证：起较急，初有发热，斑色紫赤，量多成片，或衄血、

ple and deep-coloured purpuras which are great in quantities and in stretches or epistaxis and hematuria with bright colour, flushed face, irritability, deep-red tongue with dry and yellowish fur, slippery and rapid pulse.

Therapeutic Principle: Clearing away pathogenic heat and toxic materials, cooling blood to stop bleeding.

Recipe: Decoction of Rhinoceros Horn and Rehmannia with additional ingredients.

rhinoceros horn, *Cornu Rhinocerotis*   1g (ground)
or buffalo horn, *Cornu Bubali*   30g (decocted prior to others)
dried rehmannia root, *Radix Rehmanniae*   20g
red peony root, *Radix Paeoniae Rubra*   10g
moutan bark, *Cortex Moutan Radicis*   10g
scrophularia root, *Radix Scrophulariae*   10g
arnebia root, *Radix Arnebiae seu Lithospermi*   12g
forsythia fruit, *Fructus Forsythiae*   15g
field thistle, *Herba Cephalanoploris*   30g

All the above drugs, except rhinoceros horn which is to be mixed with the finished decoction, are to be decocted in water for oral administration.

In addition to the above ingredients, 15 grams of rubia root (*Radix Rubiae*) and 30 grams of hairy vein agrimony (*Herba Agrimoniae*) should be prescribed for treating cases with profuse bleeding; 30 grams of gypsum (*Gypsum Fibrosum*) and 10 grams of anemarrhena rhizome (*Rhizoma Anemarrhenae*) for cases with thirst and fondness for cold drink; 6 grams of rhubarb (*Radix et Rhizoma Rhei*) (decocted later) for cases with restlessness and constipation.

2. Hyperactivity of Fire due to *Yin* Deficiency

Main Symptoms and Signs: More purpuras in purple and red colour, especially in the low extremities and appearing and fading at frequent internals, dizziness, tinnitus, hot sensation in the palms and soles, irritability, night sweat, bleeding from the gum, epistaxis, profuse menstruation, red tongue with re-

尿血，血色鲜红，面赤心烦，舌色红绛，苔黄燥，脉滑数。

治则：清热解毒，凉血止血。

处方：犀角地黄汤加味。

犀角 1 克(磨汁冲服)或水牛角30克(先煎)，生地20克，赤芍

10克，丹皮10克，元参10克，紫草12克，连翘15克，小蓟30克。

水煎服。

出血量多者，加茜草15克，仙鹤草30克；口渴喜冷饮者，加

生石膏30克，知母10克，烦躁便秘者，加大黄 6 克(后入)。

2．阴虚火旺

主证：紫斑较多，颜色紫红，下肢尤甚，时发时止，头晕耳

duced saliva, thready and rapid pulse.

Therapeutic Principle: Nourishing *yin* and removing pathogenic heat from blood to arrest bleeding.

Recipe: Modified Bolus for Replenishing **Vital** Essence.

dried rehmannia root, *Radix Rehmanniae*   20g

prepared rehmannia root, *Radix Rehmanniae Praeparata*   20g

tortoise plastron, *Plastrum Testudinis*   15g

anemarrhena rhizome, *Rhizoma Anemarrhenae*   12g

phellodendron bark, *Cortex Phellodendri*   10g

eclipta, *Herba Ecliptae*   15g

glossy privet fruit, *Fructus Ligustri Lucidii*   12g

donkey-hide gelatin, *Colla Corii Asini*   10g

moutan bark, *Cortex Moutan Radicis*   10g

wolfberry bark, *Cortex Lycii Radicis*   10g

biota tops, *Cacumen Biotae*   10g

All the above drugs are to be decocted in water for oral administration.

3. Deficiency of the Spleen-*qi*

Main Symptoms and Signs: Pink purpuras which appear and fade from time to time, sallow complexion, lassitude and listlessness, dizziness, palpitation, poor appetite, pale tongue with little fur, weak pulse.

Therapeutic Principle: Reinforcing the spleen and tonifying *qi* and guiding blood to go back to the vessels.

Recipe: Modified Decoction for Invigorating the Spleen and Nourishing the Heart.

astragalus root, *Radix Astragali seu Hedysari*   20g

dangshen, *Radix Codonopsis Pilosulae*   15g

white atractylodes rhizome, *Rhizoma Atractylodis Macrocephalae*   10g

poria, *Poria*   10g

Chinese angelica, *Radix Angelicae Sinensis*   10g

white peony root, *Radix Paeoniae Alba*   10g

鸣，手足心热，心烦盗汗，齿衄，鼻衄，月经量多，舌红少津，脉细数。

治则：滋阴清热，凉血止血。

处方：大补阴丸加减。

生地20克，熟地20克，龟板15克，知母12克，黄柏10克，旱莲草15克，女贞子12克，阿胶珠10克，丹皮10克，地骨皮10克，侧柏叶10克。水煎服。

3. 脾气亏虚

主证：斑色淡红，时发时愈，面色萎黄，神疲乏力，头晕心悸，食欲不振，舌质淡，少苔，脉虚弱。

治则：健脾益气，引血归经。

处方：归脾汤加减。

黄芪20克，党参15克，白术10克，茯苓10克，当归10克，白

longan aril, *Arillus Longan*   10g

eclipta, *Herba Ecliptae*   12g

donkey-hide gelatin, *Colla Corii Asini*   10g

Chinese-date, *Fructus Ziziphi Jujubae*   5 pieces

prepared licorice root, *Radix Glycyrrhizae Praeparata*   6g

All the above drugs are to be decocted in water for oral administration.

As for cases with persistent purpuras and splenomegaly, add 3 grams of notoginseng powder (*Radix Notoginseng*) (taken after being mixed with the finished decoction), 6 grams of prepared aconite root (*Radix Aconiti Praeparata*) are added for chronic cases marked with aversion to cold, cold limbs, aching pain of the loins and loose stool.

Section 20
Leukopenia

Leukopenia exists whenever the number of the white blood cells in the peripheral circulation is continually lower than $4 \times 10^9/L$, and the percentage of neutrophilic granulocytes is normal or slightly decreased. In most cases, the disease is related to the decrease of neutrophilic granulocytes, and granulocytopenia is defined as the absolute number of granulocytes is reduced below $1.8 - 2 \times 10^9/L$. In TCM, this disease is grouped into the categories of "*xuan yun*" (vertigo), "*xu lao*" (consumptive diseases), etc.

MAIN POINTS OF DIAGNOSIS

1. There must be a history of facilitating the result of leukopenia, e.g. contact with X-ray or radioactive materials, administration of drugs that affect leucocytes, such as Amidopyrine, Butazolidin, Thiouracil, Sulfonamides and antitumor agents, etc. Virus infection, desmosis and hepersplenism may also cause leukopenia.

芍10克，龙眼肉10克，旱莲草12克，阿胶珠10克，大枣5枚，炙甘草6克。水煎服。

瘀斑难以消退，脾脏肿大者，加三七粉3克（冲服）；病程日久，畏寒肢冷，腰酸便溏者，加附子6克。

第二十节　白细胞减少症

周围血液中白细胞数持续低于$4\times10^9/L$，中性粒细胞百分比正常或稍减少，称为白细胞减少症。多数情况下，白细胞减少症是由中性粒细胞减少所致，若粒细胞绝对值低于$1.8\sim2\times10^9/L$称为粒细胞减少症。本病属中医"眩晕"、"虚劳"等范畴。

【诊断要点】

1. 有引起白细胞减少的病史，如接触X线、放射性物质，服用影响白细胞药物如氨基比林、保泰松、硫氧嘧啶、磺胺类及抗肿瘤药物等。病毒性感染、结缔组织疾病、脾功能亢进等疾病，亦可引起白细胞减少。

2. The patient may be sick with such symptoms as dizziness, fatigue, mild fever, amprexoa and insomnia. The disease is chronic and is frequently accompanied with infections.

3. Leukocyte countranges 2—4×10⁹/L, with normal or slightly reduced percentage of granulocytes. The picture of bone marrow shows no specific change.

4. The provocative test of adrenalin is helpful for identifying the false leukopenia. Hydrocortisone test can be used to test the reserving energy of bone marrow, indicating treatment and prognosis.

DIFFERENTIATION AND TREATMENT OF COMMON SYNDROMES

1. Deficiency of Both *Qi* and *Yin*

Main Symptoms and Signs: Dim complexion, dizziness, blurred vision, lassitude and weakness, dysphoria with feverish sensation in the chest, palms and soles, pink tongue with little fur, thready and weak or thready and rapid pulse.

Therapeutic Principle: Supplementing *qi* and nourishing *yin*.

Recipe: Pulse-activating Powder with additional ingredients.

pseudostellaria root, *Radix Pseudostellariae*   15g
ophiopogon root, *Radix Ophiopogonis*   10g
schisandra fruit, *Fructus Schisandrae*   10g
astragalus root, *Radix Astragali seu Hedysari*   15g
siberian solomonseal rhizome, *Rhizoma Polygonati*   15g
spatholobus stem, *Caulis Spotholobi*   20g
tortoise plastron, *Plastrum Testudinis*   12g
prepared liquorice, *Radix Glycyrrhizae Praeparata*   6g

All the above drugs are to be decocted in water for oral administration.

In addition to the above ingredients, drugs of prepared rehmannia root (*Radix Rehmanniae Praeparata*) 15g, dogwood fruit (*Fructus Corni*) 12g and wolfberry fruit (*Fructus Lycii*) 15g are needed for cases with severe deficiency of the liver-*yin* and

2. 患者可有头晕、乏力、低热、纳差和失眠等症状,病程缓慢,易并发感染。

3. 白细胞计数在 $2\sim4\times10^9/L$ 之间,粒细胞百分比正常程度减低。骨髓象无特异性改变。

4. 肾上腺素激发试验有助于鉴别假性白细胞减少症;氢化考的松试验等可以测定骨髓储备能力,指示治疗和预后。

【辨证论治】

1. 气阴两亏

主证:面色少华,头昏目眩,倦怠乏力,五心烦热,舌淡红,少苔,脉细弱或细数。

治则:益气养阴。

处方:生脉散加味。

太子参15克,麦冬10克,五味子10克,黄芪15克,黄精15克,鸡血藤20克,龟板12克,炙甘草6克。水煎服。

若肝肾阴虚较重,症见健忘耳鸣,腰膝酸软,潮热盗汗者,

kidney-*yin* marked by amnesia, tinnitus, soreness and weakness in the loins and knees, tidal fever, night sweat, etc.

2. Insufficiency of Both the Spleen and Stomach

Main Symptoms and Signs: Vertigo, emaciation, lassitude, anorexia, indigestion, abdominal distension and fullness, sallow complexion, loose stool, pale tongue with whitish fur, thready and weak pulse.

Therapeutic Principle: Strengthening the spleen and replenishing *qi*.

Recipe: Modified prescriptions of Decoction of Four Noble Drugs and Astragalus Decoction for Tonifying the Middle-*jiao*.

dangshen, *Radix Codonopsis Pilosulae*   12g

white atractylodes rhizome, *Rhizoma Atractglodis Mascrocephalae*   10g

poria, *Poria*   10g

prepared liquorice, *Radix Glycyrrhizae Praeparata*   6g

astragalus root, *Radix Astragali seu Hedysari*   15g

cinnamon twig, *Ramulus Cinnamomi*   6g

white peony root, *Radix Paeoniae Alba*   10g

Chinese-date, *Fructus Ziziphi Jujubae*   5 pieces

hyacinth bean, *Semen Dolicoris*   10g

Chinese yam, *Rhizoma Dioscoreae*   10g

amomum fruit, *Fructus Amomi*   10g

chicken's gizzard-skin, *Endothelium Corneum Gigeriae Galli* 10g

All the above drugs are to be decocted in water for oral administration.

3. Deficiency of the Spleen-*yang* and Kidney-*yang*

Main Symptoms and Signs: Dizziness, tinnitus, fatigue and weakness, deficiency of *qi*, disinclination to talk, intolerance of cold, cold limbs, aching pain and weakness in the loins and knees, poor appetite, loose stool, or puffy face and edema of limbs, pale and tender tongue with thin and whitish or whitish and greasy fur, deep, thready and weak pulse.

Therapeutic Principle: Warming and replenishing the

加熟地15克，山萸肉12克，枸杞子15克。

2. 脾胃虚弱

主证：头晕眼花，消瘦无力，食少纳呆，脘腹胀满，面色萎黄，或见大便溏薄，舌质淡，苔白，脉细弱。

治则：健脾益气。

处方：四君子汤合黄芪建中汤加味。

党参12克，白术10克，茯苓10克，炙甘草6克，黄芪15克，桂枝6克，白芍10克，大枣5枚，扁豆10克，山药10克，砂仁10克，鸡内金10克。水煎服。

3. 脾肾阳虚

主证：头昏耳鸣，神疲乏力，少气懒言，畏寒肢冷，腰膝酸软，纳差便溏，或面浮肢肿，舌质淡嫩，苔薄白或白腻，脉沉细弱。

spleen and kidney.

Recipe: Modified prescriptions of Aconite Decoction for Regulating the Function of Middle-*jiao* and Kidney-*yang* Reinforcing Bolus.

    prepared aconite root, *Radix Aconiti Praeparata*   10g

    dried ginger, *Rhizoma Zingiberis*   6g

    dangshen, *Radix Codonopsis Pilosulae*   12g

    white atractylodes rhizome, *Rhizoma Atractylodis Macrocephalae*   10g

    poria, *Poria*   10g

    eucommia bark, *Cortex Eucommiae*   10g

    antler glue, *Colla Cornus Cervi*   10g (melted in boiling water)

    dodder seed, *Semen Cuscutae*   12g

    astragalus root, *Radix Astragali seu Hedysari*   12g

    prepared liquorice, *Radix Glycyrrhizae Praeparata*   6g

All the above drugs are to be decocted in water for oral administration.

Section 21
Acute Nephritis

Acute nephritis is an immunoreactive disease caused by the deposition of immune complex in the glomeruli mainly after hemolytic streptococcal infection. The disease can also be caused by other organisms, or is involved as a part of the manifestations of other disease. It occurs mostly in children with males predominating. Most patients can recover completely. A few cases may progress to chronic nephritis. This disease pertains to the category of "*feng shui*" (wind edema) in TCM.

MAIN POINTS OF DIAGNOSIS

1. A vast majority of patients have hemolytic streptococcal infection 1—3 weeks prior to the onset of acute nephritis.

治则：温补脾肾。

处方：附子理中汤合右归丸加减。

附子10克，干姜6克，党参12克，白术10克，茯苓10克，杜仲10克，鹿角胶10克(开水化服)，菟丝子12克，黄芪12克，炙甘草6克。水煎服。

第二十一节　急性肾炎

急性肾炎是一种免疫反应性疾病，多由溶血性链球菌感染后体内产生免疫复合物沉积于肾小球所致，亦可为其他病原体感染引起，或为其他疾病表现的一部分。本病多见于儿童，男多于女。大多数患者病后可以恢复，少数迁延不愈转为慢性肾炎。急性肾小球肾炎多属于中医"风水"范畴。

【诊断要点】

1. 病前1～3周多有溶血性链球菌感染，如扁桃体炎、咽

such as tonsillitis, angina, scarlet fever or purulent infection of the skin.

2. The onset is sudden. Edema, hypertension, albuminuria are the major manifestations accompanied with hematuria and cylindruria. In mild cases, only slight edema of eyelids and urinary changes may be present. In severe cases there may be heart failure, hypertensive encephalogpathy or even renal failure.

3. Laboratory examination shows moderate albuminuria with erythrocytes and casts in the urine. Serum creatinine may rise slightly. ESR (erythrocyte sedimentation rate) may grow at speed and ASO (antistreptolysin O) may be positive. In some cases, throat swab culture may give a positive result of group A hemolytic streptococci.

DIFFERENTIATION AND TREATMENT OF COMMON SYNDROMES

1. Wind Edema

Main Symptoms and Signs: Sudden onset, fever and chill characterized by higher fever and slight chill, dry mouth, sore throat, scanty and deep-coloured urine, facial edema at the beginning followed by edema all over the body especially of the face and head, red tongue with thin whitish fur, floating and rapid pulse.

Therapeutic Principle: Dispelling pathogenic wind, removing pathogenic heat and ventilating the lung to induce diuresis.

Recipe: Modified Decoction for Relieving Edema.

ephedra, *Herba Ephedrae*   6g
gypsum, *Gypsum Fibrosum*   30g
honeysuckle flower, *Flos Lonicerae*   20g
motherwort, *Herba Leonuri*   20g
cogongrass rhizome, *Rhizoma Imperatae*   30g
lophatherum, *Herba Lophatheri*   10g
licorice root, *Radix Glycyrrhizae*   3g

All the above drugs are to be decocted in water for oral

峡炎、猩红热或化脓性皮肤感染等。

2. 起病急，有浮肿、高血压、蛋白尿，或伴血尿、管型尿等。轻型者仅轻微眼睑浮肿和尿改变；重者可出现心力衰竭、高血压脑病，甚至肾功衰竭。

3. 化验检查常见中等蛋白尿，可伴红细胞和管型，血肌酐常轻度升高，血沉可增快，抗O测定阳性，咽拭子培养可见A组溶血性链球菌 。

【辨证论治】

1. 风水

主证：发病急，发热恶寒，热重寒轻，口干咽痛，尿少而赤，初起颜面浮肿，继则全身浮肿，以头面为甚，舌质红，苔薄黄，脉浮数。

治则：疏风清热，宣肺利水。

处方：越婢汤加减。

麻黄6克，生石膏30克，金银花20克，益母草20克，白茅根

administration.

In addition to the above ingredients, the employment of the following drugs is necessary for accessory treatment: scrophularia root (*Radix Scrophulariae*) 12g and isatis root (*Radix Isatidis*) 20g for the case with marked sore throat; mulberry bark (*Cortex Mori Radicis*) 10g and lepidium seed (*Semen Lepidii seu Descurainiae*) 10g for the case suffering from cough with dispnea; chrysanthemum (*Flos Chrysanthemi*) 10g and mulberry leaf (*Folium Mori*) 10g to treat headache; field thistle (*Herba Cephalanoploris*) 30g to treat hematuria; and plantain herb (*Herba Plantaginis*) 12g to treat severe edema.

If the disorder is considered exterior syndrome of wind-cold manifested as fever, chill, stuffy nose and headache, aching pain of the body and limbs, facial edema, puffiness of eyelids, scanty urine, thin and white coating of the tongue, floating and tight pulse, The treatment should be aimed at relieving the exterior syndrome with drugs pungent in flavor and warm in property and ventilating the lung to induce diuresis. The preferable recipe for it is modified prescriptions of Ephedra Decoction with Bighead Atractylodes and Decoction of Peel of Five Drugs. The compositions are: ephedra (*Herba Ephedrae*) 10g, cinnamon twig (*Ramulus Cinnamomi*) 6g, bitter apricot kernel (*Semen Armeniacae Amarum*) 6g, bighead atractylodes rhizome (*Rhizoma Atractylodis Macrocephalae*) 10g, trangerine peel (*Pericarpium Citri Reticulatae*) 10g, shell of areca nut (*Pericarpium Arecae*) 12g, poria peel (*Pericar Poriae*) 15g, water plantain rhizome (*Rhizoma Alismatis*) 12g. All the above drugs are to be decocted in water for oral administration.

2. Heat-toxin Edema

Main Symptoms and Signs: Boils and carbuncles on the skin, edema of the body and limbs, dry mouth, dysphoria, scanty and deep-coloured urine, dry stool, red tongue with yellowish fur, slippery and rapid pusle.

Therapeutic Principle: Clearing away pathogenic heat

30克，竹叶10克，甘草 3 克。水煎服。

若咽痛明显者，加元参12克，板兰根20克；咳喘者，加桑白皮10克，葶苈子10克；头痛者，加菊花10克，桑叶10克；血尿者，加小蓟30克；浮肿甚者，加车前草12克。

若症见发热恶寒、鼻塞头痛、肢体酸痛、颜面及眼睑浮肿、小便短少、舌苔薄白、脉浮紧等风寒表证时，治宜辛温解表，宣肺利水。可用麻黄加术汤合五皮饮加减：麻黄10克，桂枝 6 克，杏仁 6 克，白术10克，陈皮10克，大腹皮12克，茯苓皮15克，泽泻12克。水煎服。

2．热毒

主证：皮肤疖疮，肢体水肿，口干心烦，小便短赤，大便干结，舌质红，苔黄，脉滑数。

and toxic materials and inducing diuresis to reduce edema.

Recipe: Modified Antiphlogistic Decoction of Five Drugs.

honeysuckle flower, *Flos Lonicerae*   30g

forsythia fruit, *Fructus Forsythiae*   15g

dandelion herb, *Herba Taraxaci*   30g

Chinese violet, *Herba Violae*   15g

rhubarb root, *Radix et Rhizoma Rhei*   6g (decocted later)

scutellaria root, *Radix Scutellariae*   10g

cogongrass rhizome, *Rhizoma Imperatae*   30g

plantain herb, *Herba Plantaginis*   12g

All the above drugs are to be decocted in water for oral administration.

3. Water-dampness Edema

Main Symptoms and Signs: Indistinct symptoms of exterior syndrome, facial edema, edema of the body and limbs, fatigue and bodily heaviness, distension in the stomach, anorexia, oliguria, white and greasy coating of the tongue, deep and slow pulse.

Therapeutic Principle: Invigorating the spleen for excreting dampness and activating *yang* to induce diuresis.

Recipe: Modified prescriptions of Powder of Five Drugs with Poria and Decoction of Peel of Five Drugs.

cinnamon twig, *Ramulus Cinnamomi*   10g

umbellate pore-fungus, *Polyporus Umbellatus*   10g

water-plantain tuber, *Rhizoma Alismatis*   10g

white atractylodes rhizome, *Rhizoma Atractylodis Macrocephalae*   10g

poria, *Poria*   12g

shell of areca nut, *Pericarpium Arecae*   12g

fuling peel, *Pericar Poriae*   15g

waxgourd peel, *Exocarpium Benincasae*   15g

plantain herb, *Herba Plantaginis*   12g

All the above drugs are to be decocted in water for oral administration.

治则：清热解毒，利湿消肿。

处方：五味消毒饮加减。

金银花30克，连翘15克，蒲公英30克，地丁15克，大黄6克（后入），黄芩10克，白茅根30克，车前草12克。水煎服。

3．水湿

主证：表证不明显，颜面及肢体浮肿，身体困重，脘胀纳少，小便短少，舌苔白腻，脉沉缓。

治则：健脾渗湿，通阳利水。

处方：五苓散合五皮饮加减。

桂枝10克，猪苓10克，泽泻10克，白术10克，茯苓12克，大腹皮12克，茯苓皮15克，冬瓜皮15克，车前草12克。水煎服。

In case of stagnation of dampness-heat manifested as edema of the whole body, bitter taste in the mouth, dry throat, fullness in the chest, distension in the abdomen, scanty dark urine, yellow and greasy coating of the tongue, smooth and rapid pulse, the treatment is aimed at clearing up pathogenic heat and dampness. The preferable recipe is modified prescriptions of Two Wonderful Drugs Powder and Decoction for Diuresis. The compositions are: atractylodes rhizome (*Rhizoma Atractylodis*) 10g, phellodendron bark (*Cortex Phellodendri*) 10g, tetrandra root (*Radix Stephaniae Tetrandrae*) 10g, umbellate pore-fungus (*Polyporus Umbellatus*) 10g, oriental water-plantain rhizome (*Rhizoma Alismatis*) 10g, shell of areca nut (*Pericarpium Arecae*) 12g, poria (*Poria*) 15g, Sichuan clemalis stem (*Caulis Clematidis Armandii*) 10g, red bean (*Semen Phaseoli*) 30g, cogongrass rhizome (*Rhizoma Imperatae*) 30g. All the ingredients are to be decocted in water for oral administration.

Section 22
Chronic Nephritis

Chronic nephritis is an allergic disease caused by a wide variety of etiological factors. Only a small percentage of cases are obviously due to the progression of acute nephritis. The majority of patients with chronic nephritis have no history of acute nephritis. The disease is common in young adults and middle aged people. Its course is long and the prognosis is poor. In TCM, this disease is categorized as *"shui zhong"* (edema), *"xu lao"* (consumptive diseases), *"yao tong"* (lumbago), etc.

MAIN POINTS OF DIAGNOSIS

There are three types of chronic nephritis according to the clinical features.

1. Common type: The course of this type is persistent.

若湿热蕴结，症见全身浮肿，口苦咽干，胸腹胀满，小便短赤，舌苔黄腻，脉滑数，治宜清热利湿，方用二妙散合疏凿饮子加减：苍术10克，黄柏10克，防己10克，猪苓10克，泽泻10克，大腹皮12克，茯苓15克，木通10克，赤小豆30克，白茅根30克。水煎服。

第二十二节　慢性肾炎

慢性肾炎是由多种病因所引起的一种变态反应性疾病。患者可由急性肾炎演变而来，但多无急性肾炎病史。好发于中青年，病程长，预后较差。本病属中医"水肿"、"虚劳"、"腰痛"等范畴。

【诊断要点】

根据临床表现，本病可分为三型：

1. 普通型：病程较迁延，24小时尿蛋白定量在1.5～3.5克

The quantitative examiniation of urinary protein is at a range between 1.5g and 3.5g per day. Patients may have hypertension, hematuria, cylinduria and decrease of renal function.

2. Nephrotic type: In addition to the features of the common type, quantitative examination of urinary protein is greater than 3.5g per day, the serum albumin is less than 3.5g percent. Marked edema is the characteristic feature of this type.

3. Hypertensive type: A persistent hypertension is the predominant manifestation of this type of chronic nephritis besides the features of the common type.

DIFFERENTIATION AND TREATMENT OF COMMON SYNDROMES

1. Deficiency of the Spleen-*yang* and Kidney-*yang*

Main Symptoms and Signs: Pale complexion, lassitudde, listlessness, aversion to cold, cold limbs, high-grade edema, abdominal distension, anorexia, soreness of the waist, oliguria, thin and whitish coating of the tongue, deep and fine pulse.

Therapeutic Principle: Warming *yang* of the spleen and kidney to promote diuresis

Recipe: Modified Decoction for Reinforcing the Spleen.

astragalus root, *Radix Astragali seu Hedysari*   15g

dangshen, *Radix Codonopsis Pilosulae*   15g

white atractylodes rhizome, *Rhizoma Atractylodis Macrocephalae*   15g

poria, *Poria*   15g

prepared aconite root, *Radix Aconiti Praeparata*   10g

cinnamon bark, *Cortex Cinnamomi*   6g

shell of areca nut, *Pericarpium Arecae*   12g

water-plantain tuber, *Rhizoma Alismatis*   15g

plantain seed, *Semen Plantaginis*   30g (wrapped in a piece of cloth before decoction)

All the above drugs are to be decocted in water for oral administration.

之间，可有血压增高、血尿、管型尿和肾功能减退。

2．肾病型：除上述普通型特点外，24小时尿蛋白定量＞3.5克，血浆白蛋白＜3.5克％，总蛋白降低，浮肿多较明显。

3．高血压型：除上述普通型特点外，常以持续中度以上高血压为突出表现。

【辨证论治】

1．脾肾阳虚

主证：面色㿠白，倦怠乏力，形寒肢冷，高度浮肿，腹胀纳呆，腰酸尿少，苔薄白，脉沉细。

治则：温阳利水。

处方：实脾饮加减。

黄芪15克，党参15克，白术15克，茯苓15克，附子15克，肉桂6克，大腹皮12克，泽泻15克，车前子30克（布包煎）。水煎服。

If the edema is mild but persistent, it suggests the deficiency of spleen-*qi*, the treatment should be aimed at replenishing *qi* and invigorating the spleen to induce diuresis. Modified Tetrandra and Astragalus Decoction is preferred for the treatment. The compositions are: tetrandra root (*Radix Stephaniae Tetrandrae*) 10g, astragalus root (*Radix Astragali seu Hedysari*) 15g, white atractylodes rhizome (*Rhizoma Atractylodis Macrocephalae*) 15g, dangshen (*Radix Codonopsis Pilosulae*) 15g, poria (*Poria*) 15g, umbellate pore-fungus (*Polyporus Umbellatus*) 12g, water-plantain tuber (*Rhizoma Alismatis*) 12g, tangerine peel (*Pericarpium Citri Reticulatae*) 10g, prepared licorice root (*Radix Glycyrrhizae Praeparata*) 3g. All the above drugs are to be decocted in water for oral administration.

2. Hyperactivity of *Yang* due to Deficiency of *Yin*

Main Symptoms and Signs: Indistinct edema, headache, dizziness, tinnitus, dry mouth, irritability, feverish sensation in the palms and soles, palpitation, insomnia, red tongue, taut and thready pulse.

Therapeutic Principle: Nourishing *yin* and suppressing hyperactive *yang*.

Recipe: Bolus of Six Drugs Including Rehmannia and Adding Wolfberry and Chrysanthemum with additional ingredients.

wolfberry fruit, *Fructus Lycii*   15g

chrysanthemum, *Flos Chrysanthemi*   10g

dried rehmannia root, *Radix Rehmanniae*   15g

prepared rehmannia root, *Radix Rehmanniae Praeparata* 15g

dogwood fruit, *Fructus Corni*   12g.

moutan bark, *Cortex Moutan Radicis*   10g

Chinese yam, *Rhizoma Dioscoreae*   15g

poria, *Poria*   12g

water-plantain tuber, *Rhizoma Alismatis*   10g

tortoise plastron, *Plastrum Testudinis*   15g

若浮肿较轻，但持续较久者，属脾气虚弱。治宜益气健脾利

水。可用防己黄芪汤加减：防己10克，黄芪15克，白术15克，党

参15克，茯苓15克，猪苓12克，泽泻12克，陈皮10克，炙甘草3

克。水煎服。

2. 阴虚阳亢

主证：浮肿不明显，头痛，头晕，耳鸣，口干心烦，手足心

热，心悸失眠，舌质红，脉弦细。

治则：滋阴潜阳。

处方：杞菊地黄丸加味。

枸杞子15克，菊花10克，生地15克，熟地15克，山萸肉12克，

uncaria stem with hooks, *Ramulus Uncariae cum Uncis*   20g
eucommia bark, *Cortex Eucommiae*   10g
abalone shell, *Concha Haliotidis*   30g

All the above drugs are to be decocted in water for oral administration.

3. Retention of Damp-heat in the Body

Main Symptoms and Signs: Flushed face, obesity, edema, distension of head, headache, dry mouth, irritability, constipation, prolonged hormonotherapy, thin and yellowish or yellowish and greasy coating of the tongue, taut and rapid or slippery and rapid pulse.

Therapeutic Principle: Clearing away pathogenic heat and dampness.

Recipe: Modified Decoction of Gentian for Purging Liver-fire.

gentian root, *Radix Gentianae*   10g
scutellaria root, *Radix Scutellariae*   10g
capejasmine fruit, *Fructus Gardeniae*   10g
Sichuan clematis stem, *Caulis Clematidis Armandii*   10g
water-plantain tuber, Rhizoma *Alismatis*   10g
plantain seed, *Semen Plantaginis*   12g (wrapped in a piece of cloth during decocting)
dried rehmannia root, *Radix Rehmanniae*   12g
phellodendron bark, *Cortex Phellodendri*   10g
dandelion herb, *Herba Taraxaci*   20g
cogongrass rhizome, *Rhizoma Imperatae*   30g

All the above drugs are to be decocted in water for oral administration.

Sectioh 23
Nephrotic Syndrome

Nephrotic syndrome can be caused by a wide variety of

丹皮10克，山药15克，茯苓12克，泽泻10克，龟板15克，钩藤20

克，杜仲10克，石决明30克。水煎服。

3. 湿热内蕴

主证：面红体胖，肢体浮肿，头胀头痛，口干心烦，大便秘

结，久用皮质激素，苔薄黄或黄腻，脉弦数或滑数。

治则：清热利湿。

处方：龙胆泻肝汤加减。

龙胆草10克，黄芩10克，栀子10克，木通10克，泽泻10克，

车前子12克（布包煎），生地12克，黄柏10克，蒲公英20克，白茅

根30克。水煎服。

第二十三节　肾病综合征

肾病综合征可由多种肾小球病变所引起，亦可继发于细菌、

glomerular diseases. It may follow bacterial or viral infections, malignant tumors and administration of some drugs. Some immune diseases, such as systemic lupus erythematosus, allergic purpura and diabetes mellitus can be complicated by nephrotic syndrome. This disease is included in the categories of "*shui zhong*" (edema), and "*xu lao*" (consumptive diseases) in TCM.

MAIN POINTS OF DIAGNOSIS

1. Heavy proteinuria, accompanied with edema and hypoproteinemia, are three major manifestations of this syndrome. Urinary protein excretion exceeds 3.5g per day. The serum albumin is lower than 30g per liter. Severe edema may appear if serum albumin is lower than 15g per liter.

2. The alteration of blood pressure varies with different types of the disease. Hyperlipemia is common, particularly increased cholesterol.

3. About 75 per cent of cases with nephrotic syndrome are caused by primary glomerular diseases. In children nearly 80 per cent of cases are nephrotic syndrome of minute lesion type. The rest are secondary to other diseases. Renopuncture biopsy is of much help in confirming the cases of the disease and indicating treatment.

DIFFERENTIATION AND TREATMENT OF COMMON SYNDROMES

1. Insufficiency of the Spleen-*yang* and Kidney-*yang*

Main Symptoms and Signs: Sallow complexion, mental fatigue, cold extremities, bodily edema which is more severe in the region below the waist, anorexia, loose stool, weakness of the loins, oliguria, pale or plump moist tongue with whitish smooth fur, deep, thready and weak pulse.

Therapeutic Principle: Warming the kidney, strengthening the spleen and inducing diuresis to alleviate edema.

Recipe: Modified Drink for Reinforcing the Spleen in combination with Diuretic Decoction for Strengthening *Yang*

病毒等感染，恶性肿瘤，或使用某些药物以后。部分免疫性疾病，如系统性红斑狼疮、过敏性紫癜、糖尿病等，亦可并发本征。肾病综合征属中医"水肿"、"虚劳"范畴。

【诊断要点】

1. 大量蛋白尿伴浮肿及低蛋白血症是本病三大特点。24小时尿蛋白多超过 3.5 克。血浆白蛋白多在 30 克/L 以下，低于 51 克/L 可出现严重浮肿。

2. 血压改变随病种而异，高脂血症常见，以胆固醇增高为主。

3. 约75%的患者由原发性肾小球疾病所致。儿童中80%为微小病变型肾病,余多为继发性病变。肾穿刺活检对于明确病因,指导治疗很有帮助。

【辨证论治】

1. 脾肾阳虚

主证：面色萎黄，神倦肢冷，肢体浮肿，腰下尤甚，纳少便溏，腰酸尿少，舌质淡或胖润，苔白滑，脉沉细而弱。

治则：温肾健脾，利水消肿。

of the Spleen and Kidney.

    astragalus root, *Radix Astragali seu Hedysari*   30g

    dangshen, *Radix Codonopsis Pilosulae*   15g

    white atractylodes rhizome, *Rhizoma Atractylodis Macroce-phalae*   15g

    poria, *Poria*   15g

    coix seed, *Semen Coicis*   15g

    prepared aconite root, *Radix Aconiti Praeparata*   10g

    cinnamon bark, *Cortex Cinnamomi*   5g

    umbellate pore-fungus, *Polyporus Umbellatus*   12g

    aucklandia root, *Radix Aucklamdiae*   5g

    epimedium, *Herba Epimedii*   10g

All the above drugs are to be decocted in water for oral administration.

2. Weakness of the Kidney-*qi*

Main Symptoms and Signs: Pale complexion, general debility with desire for sleep, aversion to cold, pitting edema, hydrops in the scrotum or hydrothorax and ascites, frequent urination at night (with profuse proteinuria), pale, swollen and teeth-printed tongue with whitish fur, deep and slow pulse.

Therapeutic Principle: Strengthening the function of the kidney to stop proteinuria.

Recipe: Kidney-*yang*-reinforcing Bolus with additional ingredients.

    prepared rehmannia root, *Radix Rehmanniae Praeparata* 15g

    Chinese yam, *Rhizoma Dioscoreae*   15g

    dogwood fruit, *Fructus Corni*   12g

    wolfberry fruit, *Fructus Lycii*   12g

    dodder seed, *Semen Cuscutae*   15g

    prepared aconite root, *Radix Aconiti Praeparata*   10g

    cinnamon bark, *Cortex Cinnamomi*   5g

    astragalus root, *Radix Astragali seu Hedysari*   30g

    dangshen, *Radix Codonopsis Pilosulae*   15g

处方：实脾饮合真武汤加减。

黄芪30克，党参15克，白术15克，茯苓15克，苡仁15克，附子10克，肉桂5克，猪苓12克，木香5克，仙灵脾10克。水煎服。

2. 肾气亏虚

主证：面色㿠白，神疲欲寐，身踡畏寒，全身浮肿，按之凹陷不起，阴囊或胸、腹积液，夜尿多(大量蛋白尿)，舌质淡，胖嫩，有齿痕，苔白，脉沉迟。

治则：强肾固精。

处方：右归丸加味。

熟地15克，山药15克，山茱萸12克，枸杞子12克，菟丝子15

lotus seed, *Semen Nelumbinis*   15g
cherokee rose-hip, *Fructus Rosae Laevigatae*   15g
gordon euryale seed, *Semen Euryales*   15g
poria, *Poria*   15g
unbellate pore-fungus, *Polyporus Umbellatus*   12g

All the above drugs are to be decocted in water for oral administration.

If the case is complicated with symptoms of dampness and heat, 10 grams of phellodendron bark (*Cortex Phellodendri*), 15 grams of tale (*Talcum*) and 20 grams of coix seed (*Semen Coicis*) ought to be added to the recipe.

Section 24
Diabetes Mellitus

Diabetes mellitus is a common metabolic endocrinopathy resulting from absolute or relative deficiency of insuline and leading to metabolic disturbance of carbohydrate, fat and protein. The disease is frequently followed by water-electrolyte imbalance and acid-base disturbance. According to the age of the patients, clinical manifestations and requirements for insulin, diabetes mellitus can be divided into many types. In TCM, the disease is categorized as *"xiao ke"* which means diabetes.

MAIN POINTS OF DIAGNOSIS

1. The characteristics of a typical case of diabetes mellitus are often polyphagia, polydipsia, polyuria and loss of body weight. Early or asymptomatic patients only show abnormal release of cortical hormone and insuline inside the body. The level of fasting blood sugar is elevated with abnormal glucose tolerance test. Symptomatic patients are frequently complicated by other symptoms of dermal, neural and endocrinous disorders, besides polyphogia, polydipsia, polyuria and loss of body weight.

克，附子10克，肉桂5克，黄芪30克，党参15克，莲子15克，金樱子15克，芡实15克，茯苓15克，猪苓12克。水煎服。

若兼湿热者，加黄柏10克，滑石15克，薏仁20克。

第二十四节 糖尿病

糖尿病是一种常见的代谢内分泌疾病，其主要病理改变为胰岛素绝对或相对不足，引起糖、脂肪、蛋白质等代谢紊乱，并可继发水、电解质和酸碱平衡方面失调。本病按发病年龄和临床表现以及对胰岛素的需求，可分为许多类型。中医称之为"消渴"。

【诊断要点】

1. 典型病例有"三多一少"，即多食、多饮、多尿和体重减轻。早期或无症状期，患者仅有体内皮质激素和胰岛素释放异常，表现为空腹血糖增高和糖耐量异常；症状期患者除三多一少表现外，还常伴有皮肤、神经和其他内分泌功能紊乱症状。

2. The main complications and concomitant diseases of diabetes mellitus are diabetic ketoacidosis, cardiovascular diseases, diabetic renopathy and peripheral neuropathy. Cardiovascualr complications are the chief causes of death.

3. Diabetes mellitus is classified into juvenile and adult types according to the clinical features. The age of onset of the juvenile type is young and has a tendency to inheritance. Blood sugar fluctuates widely and is quite sensitive to insulin. Treatment is difficult and is easily complicated by ketoacidosis and hypoglycemia, and so it is often named insulin-depending diabetes or unstable diabetes. The age of onset of adult type is above 40. This type is relatively mild and can be controlled by dietary restriction or oral antidiabetics. Therefore it is also named non-insulin depending diabetes or stable diabetes.

4. Accessory examination

(1) Fasting blood-glucose is higher than 130 mg. Blood glucose after meal is more than 160–180 mg. Urine is positive for glucose. If complicated by ketosis, urine is positive for ketone bodies.

(2) Glucose tolerance test can be used to diagnose early or suspected cases and is the principal test in diagnosis.

(3) New diagnostic techniques such as testing blood insuline levels are quite helpful in understanding the pathological changes of pancreas and in obtaining information concerning treatment.

DIFFERENTIATION AND TREATMENT OF COMMON SYNDROMES

1. Dryness-heat in the Lung and Stomach

Main Symptoms and Signs: Restlessness, polydipsia, polyphagia with tendency to hunger, dryness of the mouth and tongue, polyuria, red tongue with yellowish fur, slippery and rapid pulse.

Therapeutic Principle: Nourishing *yin* and clearing away pathogenic heat.

2．主要并发症和伴发病有糖尿病性酮症酸中毒、心血管病变、糖尿病肾病和周围神经病变，心血管并发症是死亡的重要病因之一。

3．根据临床上发病特点，可将本病分为幼年型糖尿病和成年型糖尿病。前者发病年龄轻，多有遗传倾向，血糖波动大，对胰岛素较敏感，治疗困难，容易发生酮症酸中毒或低血糖，故又称胰岛素依赖型糖尿病或不稳定型糖尿病；后者病情较轻，发病年龄多在40岁以上，可用饮食或口服降糖药物控制，故亦称非胰岛素依赖型或稳定型糖尿病。

4．辅助检查

（1）空腹血糖超过 130 毫克％或餐后血糖 超过 160～180 毫克％，尿糖阳性，合并酮症者尿中酮体亦阳性。

（2）葡萄糖耐量试验用以诊断早期或可疑患者，为诊断本病主要方法。

（3）新的诊断技术如测定血中胰岛素，对明确胰脏病变情况，指导治疗有帮助。

【辨证论治】

1．肺胃燥热

主证：烦渴多饮，多食易饥，口干舌燥，小便频多，舌质红，苔黄，脉滑数。

治则：养阴清热。

Recipe: Modified Gypsum Decoction in combination with Nourishing the Stomach Decoction.

gypsum, *Gypsum Fibrosum*   25g

anemarrhena rhizome, *Rhizoma Anemarrhenae*   12ge

glehnia root, *Radix Glehniae*   20g

ophiopogon root, *Radix Ophiopogonis*   15g

dried rehmannia root, *Radix Rehmanniae*   20g

fragrant solomonseal rhizome, *Rhizoma Polygonati Odorati*   15g

trichesanthes root, *Radix Trichosanthis*   30g

wolfberry bark, *Cortex Lycii Radicis*   12g

scrophularia root, *Radix Scrophulariae*   12g

licorice root, *Radix Glycyrrhizae*   6g

All the above drugs are to be decocted in water for oral administration.

Besides, the following additional ingredients ought to be employed for accessory treatment: rhubarb (*Radix et Rhizoma Rhei*) 10g (decocted later) for the case complicated with constipation; coptis rhizome (*Rhizoma Coptidis*) 10g and honeysuckle flower (*Flos Lonicerae*) 20g for the case with ulcerations of the mouth and tongue; dangshen (*Radix Codonopsis Pilosulae*) 10g, astragalus root (*Radix Astragali seu Hedysari*) 15g and schisandra fruit (*Fructus Schisandrae*) 10g for the case with shortness of breath, fatigue, spontaneous perspiration and thready weak pulse.

2. Deficiency of the Kidney-*yin*

Main Symptoms and Signs: Polyuria with turbid discharge, soreness and debility of the lumbus, dryness of the mouth and tongue, dysphoria with feverish sensation in the chest, palms and soles, red tongue, deep, thready and rapid pulse.

Therapeutic Principle: Nourishing *yin* and supplementing the kidney.

Recipe: Modified Bolus of Six Drugs Including Rehmannia.

dried rehmannia root, *Radix Rehmanniae*   15g

prepared rehmannia root, *Radix Rehmanniae Praeparata*

处方：玉女煎合益胃汤加减。

石膏25克，知母12克，沙参20克，麦冬15克，生地20克，玉竹15克，天花粉30克，地骨皮12克，玄参12克，甘草6克。水煎服。

大便秘结者，加大黄10克（后入）；口舌生疮者，加黄连10克，银花20克；气短疲倦，易汗出，脉细弱者，加党参10克，黄芪15克，五味子10克。

2．肾阴亏损

主证：尿频量多，浊如脂膏，腰酸无力，口干舌燥，五心烦热，舌质红，脉沉细数。

治则：滋阴补肾。

处方：六味地黄汤加减。

生地15克，熟地15克，山药20克，茯苓10克，山萸肉10克，

15g

Chinese yam, *Rhizoma Dioscoreae*   20g

poria, *Poria*   10g

dogwood fruit, *Fructus Corni*   10g

moutan bark, *Cortex Moutan Radicis*   10g

schisandra fruit, *Fructus Schisandrae*   10g

arisaema tuber, *Rhizoma Arisaematis*   12g

All the above drugs are to be decocted in water for oral administration.

Special attention should be paid to accessory treatment in which supplementary ingredients should be employed: anemarrhena rhizome (*Rhizoma Anemarrhenae*) 12g and phellodendron bark (*Cortex Phellodendri*) 10g for the treatment of dysphoria with feverish sensation in the chest, palms and soles and night sweat; dangshen (*Radix Codonopsis Pilosulae*) 15g and astragalus root (*Radix Astragali seu Hedysari*) 15g for the case indicating impairment of both *qi* and *yin* manifested as fatigue, thready and weak pulse; wolfberry fruit (*Fructus Lycii*) 12g and glossy privet fruit (*Fructus Ligustri Lucidi*) 12g for the case ascribable to the deficiency of *yin* in the liver and kidney marked by dizziness, blurred vision, and tinnitus; If the course is so prolonged that deficiency of *yin* affects *yang*, resulting in deficiency of both *yin* and *yang*, manifested as aversion to cold, cold limbs, edema, diarrhea, pale tongue whith whitish fur, deep thready and weak pulse, the treatment should be aimed at nourishing the kidney-*yin* and warming its *yang*, modified Bolus for Tonifying the Kidney-*qi* is recommended for it. The ingredients are: prepared rehmannia root (*Radix Rehmanniae Praeparata*) 25g, Chinese yam (*Rhizoma Dioscoreae*) 15g, dogwood fruit (*Fructus Corni*) 12g, poria (*Poria*) 12g, moutan bark (*Cortex Moutan Radicis*) 10g, water-plantain tuber (*Rhizoma Alismatis*) 10g, cinnamon bark (*Cortex Cinnamomi*) 6g, prepared aconite root (*Radix Aconiti Praeparata*) 6g, wolfberry fruit (*Fructus Lycii*) 12g, dodder seed (*Semen Cuscutae*) 12g, astragalus root (*Radix Astragali seu Hedysari*) 12g. All the

丹皮10克，五味子10克，天冬12克。水煎服。

若五心烦热，盗汗者，加知母12克，黄柏10克；若疲乏无力，

脉细弱，气阴两伤者，可加党参15克，黄芪15克；若头晕眼花，

耳鸣证属肝肾阴虚者，加枸杞子12克，女贞子12克；若久病阴损

及阳，致阴阳两虚，症见畏寒肢冷，浮肿腹泻，舌淡苔白，脉沉

细无力者，治宜滋肾温阳，可用金匮肾气丸加减：熟地25克，山

药15克，山萸肉12克，茯苓12克，丹皮10克，泽泻10克，肉桂6

drugs are to be decocted in water for oral administration.

Section 25
Diabetes Insipidus

The syndrome is caused by heposecretion of antidiuretic hormone resulting from hypothalamus-pituitary lesion. It can also be secondary to other diseases. The state of illness may be mild or severe, transient or permanent. The disease belongs to the category of *"xiao ke"* in TCM.

MAIN POINTS OF DIAGNOSIS

1. Polyuria, polydipsia and increased water intake are the principal features. If water intake is restricted, severe dehydration may occur.

2. The etiology of primary diabetes insipidus remains indeterminate. Secondary cases may be initiated by tumor, infection or trauma of the hypothalamus-pituitary system or the adjacent tissues. There they have the corresponding histories and clinical symptoms and signs.

3. Accessory examinations

(1) The specific gravity of urine is reduced and usually less than 1.006. The osmotic pressure of urine is also reduced.

(2) The osmotic pressure of plasma is elevated. There may appear dizziness, dysphoria, tachycardia or disorder of consciousness, the so-called hyperosmotic syndrome.

(3) Water-deprivation test and hypertonic saline test are used to distinguish diabetes insipidus from psychogenic polydipsia and polyuria. Water-deprivation test is dangerous, and now is rarely performed.

DIFFERENTIATION AND TREATMENT OF COMMON SYNDROMES

Deficiency of the Kidney-*qi*

Main Symptoms and Signs: Polydipsia, frequent and profuse urination, emaciation, aching pain in the lumbus, las-

克，附子 6 克，枸杞子12克，菟丝子12克，黄芪12克。水煎服。

第二十五节　尿崩症

尿崩症是由于下丘脑—垂体损害引起的抗利尿激素分泌减少所致，亦可继发于其他疾病。病情可轻可重，可为暂时性，或为永久性。本病亦属中医"消渴"范畴。

【诊断要点】

1. 多尿、烦渴　多饮为突出特点，如限制饮水可引起严重失水症。

2. 原发性尿崩症病因难以确定。继发性者多由下丘脑—垂体或其附近肿瘤、感染或创伤所致，并有相应病史和临床表现。

3. 辅助检查

（1）尿比重减低，常低于 1.006，尿渗透压减低。

（2）血浆渗透压增高，并可出现头晕、烦躁、心动过速或意识障碍等高渗综合征表现。

（3）禁水试验和高渗盐水试验用以和精神性多饮、多尿鉴别。但前者有一定危险，目前已很少用。

【辨证论治】

肾气亏虚

主证：大渴引饮，尿频而多，形体消瘦，腰酸乏力。肾阴偏

situde. The case exhibiting more symptoms and signs of deficiency of the kidney-*yin* is marked as feverish sensation in the palms and soles, restlessness, red tongue with little fur, deep, thready and rapid pulse; while the case presenting more symptoms and signs of deficiency of the kidney-*yang* is manifested as light colour urine, aversion to cold, impotence, pale tongue with whitish fur, and deep, thready and weak pulse.

Therapeutic Principle: Tonifying the kidney and arresting polyuria.

Recipe: Modified Decoction of Six Drugs Including Rehmannia.

prepared rehmannia root, *Radix Rehmanniae Praeparata* 15g

dogwood fruit, *Fructus Corni*　15g

Chinese yam, *Rhizoma Dioscoreae*　15g

wolfberry fruit, *Fructus Lycii*　15g

dodder seed, *Semen Cuscutae*　12g

opiopogon root, *Radix Ophiopogonis*　15g

schisandra fruit, *Fructus Schisandrae*　10g

mantis egg-case, *Oothca Mantidis*　20g

licorice root, *Radix Glycyrrhizae*　15g

All the above drugs are to be decocted in water for oral administration.

In addition to the above recipe, for treating those presenting more symptoms and signs of deficiency of the kidney-*yin*, 15 grams of dried rehmannia root (*Radix Rehmanniae*), 12 grams of scrophularia root (*Radix Scrophulariae*), 18 grams of trichosanthes root (*Radix Trichosanthis*) and 10 grams of Chinese gall (*Galla Sinensis*) should be added. For treating those exhibiting more symptoms and signs of deficiency of the kidney-*yang*, the following ingredients are added; prepared aconite root (*Radix Aconiti Praeparata*) 10g, cinnamon bark (*Cortex Cinnamomi*) 6g, psoralea fruit (*Fructus Psoraleae*) 12g, bitter cardamon (*Fructus Alpiniae Oxyphyllae*) 10g, raspberry (*Fructus Rubi*) 12g, astragalus

虚者，伴有手足心热，烦躁，舌红少苔，脉沉细数；肾阳偏虚者，

尿色清白，畏寒，阳萎，舌淡苔白，脉沉细无力。

治则：补肾固摄。

处方：六味地黄汤加减。

熟地15克，山萸肉15克，山药15克，枸杞子15克，菟丝子12克，

麦冬15克，五味子10克，桑螵蛸20克，生甘草15克。水煎服。

若肾阴偏虚者，加生地15克，玄参12克，天花粉18克，五倍

子10克，肾阳偏虚者，加附子10克，肉桂6克，补骨脂12克，益

root (*Radix Astragali seu Hedysari*) 15g.

Section 26
Systemic Lupus Erythematosus (SLE)

The cause of SLE is unknown, but most of scholars hold the view that it may be related to autoimmunity and genetic factors. Many organs and connective tissues of the body may be involved. The disease is often accompanied with many serological and immunological changes. It is seen more often in young females. In TCM the disease is categorized as *"xu lao"* (comsumptive diseases), *"shui zhong"* (edema), *"bi zheng"* (arthralgia-syndrome) *"wen du fa ban"* (epidemic disease with eruptions), etc.

MAIN POINTS OF DIAGNOSIS

1. The onset of disease is slow, early symptoms include fatigue, anorexia, emaciation, arthralgia, low fever, skin rash, photosensitization, etc. The initial symptoms are usually atypical, and diagnosis is difficult.

2. Functional damages of multiple organs: As the disease progresses, there appear functional damages of the liver, kidney, cardiovascular, digestive and nervous systems. Cardiovascular and renal damages are predominant features and renal failure is the major cause of death.

3. Accessory examinations

(1) Blood picture shows anemia, decreased numbers of white blood cells and platelets. ESR may be increased.

(2) Serum albumin is reduced, with elevated globulin. IgG (Immune globulin G) is elevated markedly, elevation of α_2 globulin in patients with prominent renal lesions. Some of the patients are positive for rheumatoid factor (RF).

(3) Lupus cells are positive in 70—80 percent of the patients, ANA (antinuclear antibody) is positive, up to 95 percent; sensitivity to anti-DNA-antibody is high in some cases;

智仁10克，覆盆子12克，黄芪15克。

第二十六节　系统性红斑狼疮

本病病因不明，多数学者认为与自身免疫和遗传因素有关。病变可累及多个机体器官及结缔组织，并伴有多种血清学和免疫学上的变化，以青年女性为多者。系统性红斑狼疮属中医"虚劳"、"水肿"、"痹证"、"温毒发斑"等范畴。

【诊断要点】

1. 起病多缓慢，早期可有乏力、纳差、消瘦、关节疼、低热、皮疹、光敏等表现，症状多不典型，诊断较困难。

2. 多器官功能损害：病程进展后，可出现肝、肾、心血管、消化、神经等系统损害的表现，但以心、肾损害为最常见，晚期肾功能衰竭常是死亡原因。

3. 辅助检查

（1）血象多数有贫血，白细胞、血小板亦有下降，血沉增快。

（2）血清白蛋白下降，球蛋白升高；免疫球蛋白G升高明显，α_2球蛋白在肾病型中亦升高，部分患者类风湿因子阳性。

（3）狼疮细胞多次检查有70～80%阳性率；抗核抗体95%

serum total complements and C_3 can be used to determine whether SLE is complicated by lupus nephritis. Skin biopsy is specific for diagnosis.

DIFFERENTIATION AND TREATMENT OF COMMON SYNDROMES

1. Domination of Heat-toxin

Main Symptoms and Signs: Sudden onset, high fever, flushed face, fresh red-coloured skin rash, purpura dotted over the skin, irritability, thirst, even coma and delirium in severe cases, arthralgia, constipation, scanty and dark urine, deep red tongue with yellow greasy fur, full and rapid or taut and rapid pluse.

Therapeutic Principle: Clearing away pathogenic heat and toxic materials, cooling blood and nourishing *yin*.

Recipe: Modified Antipyretic and Antitoxic Decoction.

rhinoceros horn powder, *Cornu Rhinocerotis*   3g (taken after being mixed with the finished decoction)

dried rehmannia root, *Radix Rehmanniae*   30g

red peony root, *Radix Paeoniae Rubra*   12g

moutan bark, *Cortex Moutan Radicis*   10g

gypsum, *Gypsum Fibrosum*   30g

anemarrhena rhizome, *Rhizoma Anemarrhenae*   10g

scrophularia root, *Radix Scrophulariae*   15g

honeysuckle flower, *Flos Lonicerae*   30g

forsythia fruit, *Fructus Forsythiae*   15g

arnebia or lithosperm root, *Radix Arnebiae seu Lithospermi*   12g

ophiopogon root, *Radix Ophiopogonis*   12g

cogongrass rhizome, *Rhizoma Imperatae*   15g

All the above drugs except rhinoceros horn powder are to be decocted in water for oral administration.

2. Internal Heat due to *Yin*-Deficiency

Main Symptoms and Signs: Low-graded fever or hectic fever in the afternoon, feverish sensation in the palms and soles,

以上阳性；抗 DNA 抗体敏感度较高，血清总补体和 C_3 用于检查是否合并有狼疮肾炎；皮肤活检是本病特异检查方法。

【辨证论治】

1. 热毒炽盛

主证：骤然发病，高热面赤，皮疹嫩红，皮肤紫斑，烦躁口渴，甚或神昏谵妄，关节疼痛，大便秘结，小便短赤，舌质红绛，苔黄腻，脉洪数或弦数。

治则：清热解毒，凉血养阴。

处方：清瘟败毒饮加减。

犀角粉 3 克（冲服），生地 30 克，赤芍 12 克，丹皮 10 克，生石膏 30 克，知母 10 克，玄参 15 克，银花 30 克，连翘 15 克，紫草 12 克，麦冬 12 克，白茅根 15 克。水煎服。

2. 阴虚内热

主证：低热或午后潮热，手足心热，斑疹黯红，盗汗乏力，

deep red-coloured eruption, night sweat, fatigue, irritability, insomnia, aching pain of joints, soreness of waist, baldness, red tongue with thin yellowish fur or mirror-like tongue, thready and rapid pulse.

Therapeutic Principle: Nourishing *yin* and clearing away pathogenic heat, cooling blood and removing toxic material.

Recipe: Modified Sweet Wormwood and Turtle Shell Decoction in combination with Bolus for Replenishing Vital Essence.

sweet wormwood, *Herba Artemisiae*   12g
stellaria root, *Radix Stellariae*   10g
wolfberry bark, *Cortex Lycii Radicis*   15g
picrorhiza rhizome, *Rhizoma Picrorhizae*   10g
dried rehmannia root, *Radix Rehmanniae*   30g
scrophularia root, *Radix Scrophulariae*   12g
anemarrhena rhizome, *Rhizoma Anemarrhenae*   12g
phellodendron bark, *Cortex Phellodendri*   10g
arisaema tuber, *Rhizoma Ariszematis*   12g
ophiopogon root, *Radix Ophiopogonis*   12g
fresh-water turtle shell, *Carapax Trionycis*   15g
prepared licorice root, *Radix Glycyrrhizae Praeparata*   6g

All the above drugs are to be decocted in water for oral administration.

In case of deficiency of the liver-*yin* and kidney-*yin* manifested as vertigo, blurred vision, tinnitus, dryness of mouth and throat, 12 grams of glossy privet fruit (*Fructus Ligustri Lucidi*) and 12 grams of eclipta (*Herba Ecliptae*) should be included in the above prescription.

If the case is marked by jaundice, hypochondriac distension and pain, abdominal distension and anorexia, hematemesis, nosebleed and hepatosplenomegaly, belonging to impairment of the liver due to heat, treatment should be aimed at soothing the liver, regulating the circulation of *qi* and promoting blood circulation to remove stasis. The recipe preferred for it is mo-

心烦不寐，关节酸痛，腰酸脱发，舌质红，苔薄黄或见镜面舌，

脉细数。

治则：滋阴清热，凉血解毒。

处方：青蒿鳖甲汤合大补阴丸加减。

青蒿 12 克，银柴胡 10 克，地骨皮 15 克，胡黄连 10 克，生

地 30 克，玄参 12 克，知母 12 克，黄柏 10 克，天冬 12 克，麦

冬 12 克，鳖甲 15 克，炙甘草 6 克。水煎服。

若肝肾阴虚，伴有头晕目眩、耳鸣、口燥咽干等症者，加女

贞子 12 克，旱莲草 12 克。

若症见黄疸，胸胁胀痛，腹胀纳呆，吐血衄血，肝脾肿大，

证属邪热伤肝者，治宜舒肝理气，活血化瘀为主，可用膈下逐瘀

dified Decoction for Dissipating Blood Stasis under the Diaphram. The compositions are bupleurum root (*Radix Bupleuri*) 10g, Chinese angelica (*Radix Angelicae Sinensis*) 10g, red peony root (*Radix Paeoniae Rubra*) 10g, white peony root (*Radix Paeoniae Alba*) 10g, giant knot-weed rhizome (*Rhizoma Polygoni Cuspidati*) 10g, Sichuan chinaberry (*Fructus Meliae Toosendan*) 10g, corydalis tuber (*Rhizoma Corydalis*) 10g, curcuma root (*Radix Curcumae*) 12g, globethistle (*Radix Thapontici seu Echinopsis*) 10g. All the above drugs are to be decocted in water for oral administration.

If the articular symptoms are dominant marked by migratory arthralgia, heat, pain and swelling in the affected region, difficulty in flexion and extension, etc., the suitable treatment should be aimed at clearing away heat, dispelling wind and removing dampness to drege the channels and collaterals. The chosen recipe is modified White Tiger Decoction and Pubescent Angelica and Loranthus Decoction. The compositions are pubescent angelica root (*Radix Angelicae Pubescentis*) 10g, loranthus mulberry mistletoe (*Ramulus Loranthi*) 18g, large-leaf gentian root (*Radix Gentianae Macrophyllae*) 15g, notopterygium root (*Rhizoma seu Radix Nothpterygii*) 10g, Ledebouriella (*Radix Ledebouriellae*) 10g, spatholobus stem (*Caulis Spatholobi*) 30g, achyranthes root (*Radix Achyranthis Bidentatae*) 10g, anemarrhena rhizome (*Rhizoma Anemarrhenae*) 10g, gypsum (*Gypsum Fibrosum*) 30g, Chinese angelica (*Radix Angelicae Sinensis*) 10g, hypoglauca yam (*Rhizoma Dioscoreae Hypoglaucae*) 12g, giant knotweed rhizome (*Rhizoma Polygnoi Cuspidati*) 12g, honeysuckle stem (*Caulis Lonicerae*) 30g. All the drugs are to be decocted in water for oral administration.

3. Deficiency of the Spleen-*yang* and Kidney-*yang*

Main Symptoms and Signs: Pale complexion, puffy face, edema of limbs, distension and fullness of abdomen, cold extremities, shortness of breath, disinclination to talk, disturbance of urination, loose stool, pale tongue with whitish moist fur, deep and thready or thready and weak pulse.

汤加减：柴胡 10 克，当归 10 克，赤芍 10 克，白芍 10 克，虎杖 10 克，川楝子 10 克，延胡索 10 克，郁金 12 克，漏芦 10 克。水煎服。

若以关节症状为主要表现，症见关节疼痛，游走不定，局部灼热红肿，屈伸不利等，治宜清热祛风，利湿通络，可用白虎汤合独活寄生汤加减：独活 10 克，桑寄生 18 克，秦艽 15 克，羌活 10 克，防风 10 克，鸡血藤 30 克，牛膝 10 克，知母 10 克，生石膏 30 克，当归 10 克，草薢 12 克，虎杖 12 克，忍冬藤 30 克。水煎服。

3. 脾肾阳虚

主证：面色㿠白，面目四肢浮肿，腹部胀满，手足不温，气短懒言，小便不利，大便溏薄，舌质淡，苔白润，脉沉细或细弱。

Therapeutic Principle: Warming and invigorating the spleen and kidney and activating *yang* to promote diuresis.

Recipe: Modified Decoction of Two Immortals Drugs combined with Powder of Five Drugs with Poria.

curculigo rhizome, *Rhizoma Curculiginis*   15g

epimedium, *Herba Epimedii*   15g

astragalus root, *Radix Astragali seu Hedysari*   15g

dodder seed, *Semen Cuscutae*   15g

dangshen, *Radix Codonopsis Pilosulae*   15g

cinnamon twig, *Ramulus Cinnamomi*   10g

umbellate pore-fungus, *Polyporus Umbellatus*   10g

poria, *Poria*   15g

water-plantain tuber, *Rhizoma Alismatis*   10g

white atractylodes rhizome, *Rhizoma Atractylodis Macrocephalae*   10g

waxgourd peel, *Exocarpium Benincasae*   20g

cogongrass rhizome, *Rhizoma Imperatae*   30g

All the above drugs are to be decocted in water for oral administration.

Section 27
Cerebral Thrombosis

Cerebral thrombosis is also recognized as atherosclerotic and thrombotic cerebral infarction and is caused by the pathological changes of cerebral arterial wall together with elevation of blood coagulability, leading to vascular narrowness, obstruction and ischemic changes of the corresponding cerebral tissue, which may be followed by necrosis. This disease, in TCM, is included in the category of "*zhong feng*" (apoplexy).

MAIN POINTS OF DIAGNOSIS

1. The disease is more common in middle-aged and old people. There may be transient numbness of limbs, fatigue

治则：温补脾肾，通阳利水。

处方：二仙汤合五苓散加减。

仙茅 15 克，仙灵脾 15 克，黄芪 15 克，菟丝子 15 克，党参 15 克，桂枝 10 克，猪苓 10 克，茯苓 15 克，泽泻 10 克，白术 10 克，冬瓜皮 20 克，茅根 30 克。水煎服。

第二十七节　脑血栓形成

本病又称为动脉粥样硬化性血栓形成性脑梗塞，系由于颅内动脉管壁病变和血液凝固性增高，使管腔狭窄或闭塞，从而相应部位组织缺血，并进一步发生坏死所致。属中医"中风"范畴。

【诊断要点】

1. 本病多见于中老年患者，发病前可有一过性肢体麻木、

and aphasia before the onset of the disease.

2. The attack often occurs in sleep, when the blood pressure is lower and blood flow is slower. A few cases may be seen after strenuous exercise.

3. Neural manifestations include central monoplegia and hemiplegia. They may be accompanied with aphasia, but are often with hemihypoesthesia and hemianopia. There may also be disphagia and disturbance of consciousness. Unilateral optic atrophy and Horner's syndrome may be present.

4. Cerebrospinal fluid examination shows no change in pressure and cell content. This can be used to distinguish cerebral thrombosis form cerebral hemorrhage. CT scanning is helpful in the determination of location and extent of cerebral necrosis.

DIFFERENTIATION AND TREATMENT OF COMMON SYNDROMES

Blood Staiss due to Deficiency of *Qi*

Main Symptoms and Signs: Slow onset, attacks occurring mostly in rest or sleep, full consciousness, deviation of the eye and mouth, aphasia, hemiplegia, dark purple tongue with thin and white fur, thready and weak pulse.

Therapeutic Principle: Supplementing *qi* and nourishing blood, promoting blood circulation to remove obstruction in the channels.

Recipe: Modified Decoction Invigorating *Yang* for Recuperation.

astragalus root, *Radix Astragali seu Hedysari*   30g
cinnamon twig, *Ramulus Cinnamomi*   10g
peach kernel, *Semen Persicae*   10g
safflower, *Flos Carthami*   10g
Chinese angelica, *Radix Angelicae Sinensis*   12g
Chuanxiong rhizome, *Rhizoma Ligustici Chuanxiong*   12g
red peony root, *Radix Paeoniae Rubra*   12g
earthworm, *Lumbricus*   12g

乏力或语言障碍。

2．发病多在睡眠中发生，此和睡眠中血压偏低和血流变慢有关，少数患者可在剧烈活动后发生。

3．神经系统表现为中枢性单瘫、偏瘫，伴或不伴失语，常伴偏身性感觉障碍及偏盲。亦可有吞咽困难和意识障碍、一侧视神经萎缩和贺纳氏综合征。

4．脑脊液检查多无压力和细胞学改变，并有助于和脑出血等并发症相鉴别，CT检查对确立脑组织坏死部位和程度很有帮助。

【辨证论治】

气虚血瘀

主证：起病缓慢，多在休息或睡眠时发病，神志清楚，口眼歪斜，言语不利，半身不遂，舌质紫暗，苔薄白，脉细弱。

治则：益气养血，活血通络。

处方：补阳还五汤加减。

黄芪30克，桂枝10克，桃仁10克，红花10克，当归尾12

red sage root, *Radix Salviae Miltiorrhizae*   30g

achyranthes root, *Radix Achyranthis Bidentatae*   15g

All the above drugs are to be decocted in water for oral administration.

Apart from the above recipe, supplementary ingredients should be employed: 6 grams of ground beetle (*Eupolyphaga seu Steleophaga*) should be administered for cases with severe blood stasis; 15 grams of dangshen (*Radix Codonopsis Pilosulae*) for those with extreme deficiency of *qi*; 6 grams of prepared aconite root (*Radix Aconiti Praeparata*) for those with dominative cold; 10 grams of pinellia tuber (*Rhizoma Pinelliae*) and 10 grams of tabasheer (*Concretio Silicea Bambusae*) for those with profuse sputum; 10 grams of grassleaved sweetflag rhizome (*Rhizoma Acori Graminei*) and 10 grams of polygala root (*Radix Polygalae*) for those with aphasia. If the patient's blood pressure is normal, astragalus root can be dosed as much as 60 grams or even more; and if the patient has hypertension, the dosage of astragalus root should be decreased in accordance with practical conditions. To treat the case with deviation of eye and mouth, 10 grams of batryticated silkworm (*Bombyx Batryticatus*), 6 grams of giant typhonium tuber (*Rhizoma Typhonii*) and 6 grams of scorpion (*Scorpio*) should be administered; to treat constipation, 10 grams of hemp seed (*Fructus Cannabis*) administered; to treat those whose major symptom is paralyses of lower extremities, the ingredients for nourishing the liver and kidney are to be included, such as 15 grams of loranthus mulberry mistletoe (*Ramulus Loranthi*), 15 grams of prepared rehmannia root (*Radix Rehmanniae Praeparata*) and 15 grams of fleece-flower root (*Radix Polygoni Multiflori*).

Section 28
Neurosis

Neurosis is caused by long-term mental stress which results

克，川芎 12 克，赤芍 12 克，地龙 12 克，丹参 30 克，牛膝 15 克。

水煎服。

瘀血甚者加地鳖虫 6 克；气虚甚者，加党参 15 克；偏寒者，

加附子 6 克；痰多者，加半夏 10 克，天竺黄 10 克；语言不利者，

加菖蒲 10 克，远志 10 克；血压不高者，可重用黄芪，其用量可

达 60 克或更多，血压高者则黄芪量酌减；口眼歪斜者，加僵蚕

10 克，白附子 6 克，全蝎 6 克；大便秘结者，加麻子仁 10 克；

以下肢瘫痪为主，加补肝肾之品，如桑寄生 15 克，熟地 15 克，

何首乌 15 克。

第二十八节　神经官能症

本病系由于长期精神紧张，致使大脑皮层的兴奋和抑制失调

in imbalance of excito-inhibitory process of cerebral cortex. The patients get excited or fatigue easily, and are frequently accompanied with various forms of somatic discomfort. It is more common in middle-aged females. In TCM, this disease is categorized as *"bu mei"* (sleeplessness), *"xin ji"* (palpitation), *"yu zheng"* (melancholia), *"yi jing"* (emission), *"yang wei"* (impotence), *"zang zao"* (hysteria), *"xu xun"* (consumption), etc.

MAIN POINTS OF DIAGNOSIS

1. There is a history of mental conflict, or a long period of mental stress.

2. Major clinical manifestations

(1) Dyssomnia and reduced cerebral functions: such as insomnia, dreaminess, waking up easily, distractibility and bad memory.

(2) The emotion is easy to be changed, accompanied with restlessness, hypersensitivity, poor tolerance to the sound and light.

(3) Functional disorders of the viscera: The patients frequently complain of palpitation, abdominal distension, belching, anorexia, constipation, frequency of micturition, impotence, etc.

3. The organic diseases should be excluded after examinations of nervous and visceral functions.

DIFFERENTIATION AND TREATMENT OF COMMON SYNDROMES

1. Stagnation of the Liver-*qi*

Main Symptoms and Signs: Emotional depression, doubting mania, anxiety, vertigo, blurred vision, fullness in the abdomen, eructation, anorexia, feeling of oppression in the chest, hypochondriac pain, irregular menstruation, reddish tongue with whitish fur, taut and thready pulse.

Therapeutic Principle: Dispersing depressed liver-*qi* to relieve emotional depression.

Recipe: Modified Bupleurum Powder for Relieving Liver-

所致。患者易于兴奋，亦易于疲劳，常伴各种躯体不适，以中年女性为多。神经官能症属中医"不寐"、"心悸"、"郁证"、"遗精"、"阳萎"、"脏躁"、"虚损"等范畴。

【诊断要点】

1. 患者多有精神受刺激史，或神经活动长期紧张史。

2. 主要临床表现

（1）睡眠障碍、脑力衰弱：如失眠、多梦、易醒、注意力不集中及记忆力减退等。

（2）情绪易波动，焦虑不安，敏感性增加，对声光刺激耐受性差。

（3）内脏功能失调：常有心悸、腹胀、嗳气、食欲不振、便秘、尿频、阳萎等。

3. 通过神经、内脏功能检查排除器质性疾病。

【辨证论治】

1. 肝气郁结

主证：精神抑郁，多疑善虑，头晕目眩，腹胀嗳气，食欲不振，胸闷胁痛，女子月经不调，舌质淡红，苔白，脉弦细。

治则：舒肝解郁。

处方：柴胡舒肝散加减。

bupleurum root, *Radix Bupleuri*   10g
nutgrass flatsedge, *Rhizoma Cyperi*   10g
curcuma root, *Radix Curcumae*   10g
fruit of citron, *Fructus Aurantii*   10g
white peony root, *Radix Paeoniae Alba*   10g
albizia flower, *Flos Albiziae*   12g
red sage root, *Radix Salviae Miltiorrhizae*   10g

All the above drugs are to be decocted in water for oral administration.

In addition, the recipe should include 10 grams of both medicated leaven (*Massa Fermentata Medicinalis*) and membrane of chicken's gizzard (*Endothelium Corneum Gigeriae Galli*) if the case is with indigestion; 12 grams of pinellia tuber (*Rhizoma Pinelliae*), 10 grams of tangerine peel (*Pericarpium Citri Reticulatae*) for the case with eructation and oppressed sensation in the chest; 10 grams of moutan bark (*Cortex Moutan Radicis*) and 10 grams of capejasmine (*Fructus Gardeniae*) when a disorder is ascribed to the fire-transmission due to stagnation of *qi* marked by bitter taste in the mouth, restlessness, headache, conjunctival congestion, red tongue with yellow fur, and taut rapid pulse; 10 grams of chrysanthemum (*Flos Chrysanthemi*) and 15 grams of uncaria stem with hooks (*Ramulus Uncariae cum Uncis*) to treat such symptoms as dizziness and feeling of fullness in the head.

2. Hyperactivity of Fire due to *Yin* Deficiency

Main Symptoms and Signs: Anxiety, insomnia, dizziness, tinnitus, feverish sensation in the palms and soles, dry mouth with a few saliva, nocturnal emission, spermatorrhoea, premature ejaculation, palpitation, amnesia, soreness of waist, red tongue with yellowish fur, thready and rapid pulse.

Therapeutic Principle: Nourishing *yin* to clear away pathogenic fire.

Recipe: Modified prescriptions of Decoction of Coptis and Donkey-hide Gelatin and Heart-tonifying Bolus.

柴胡 10 克，香附 10 克，郁金 10 克，枳壳 10 克，白芍10克，

合欢花 12 克，丹参 10 克。水煎服。

若有食滞者，加陈曲 10 克，鸡内金 10 克；嗳气胸闷者，加

半夏 12 克，陈皮 10 克。若气郁化火，症见口苦烦躁、头痛目赤、

舌质红、苔黄、脉弦数者，加丹皮 10 克，栀子 10 克。若头晕胀

者，加菊花 10 克，钩藤 15 克。

2. 阴虚火旺

主证：心烦失眠，头晕耳鸣，手足心热，口干津少，梦遗滑

泄，心悸健忘，腰酸，舌质红，苔黄，脉细数。

治则：滋阴清火。

处方：黄连阿胶汤合补心丹加减。

dried rehmannia root, *Radix Rehmanniae*   15g
Chinese angelica, *Radix Angelicae Sinensis*   10g
white peony root, *Radix Paeoniae Alba*   10g
ophiopogon root, *Radix Ophiopogonis*   10g
coptis root, *Rhizoma Coptidis*   6g
spiny jujube seed, *Semen Ziziphi Spinosae*   12g
fleece-flower stem, *Caulis Polygoni Multifori*   30g
schisandra fruit, *Fructus Schisandrae*   10g
poria with hostwood, *Poria cum Ligno Hospite*   10g
red sage root, *Radix Salviae Miltiorrhizae*   10g
prepared licorice root, *Radix Glycyrrhizae Praeparata*   6g
donkey-hide gelatin, *Colla Corii Asini*   10g

All the above drugs are to be decocted in water for oral administration. Besides, donkey-hide gelatin is melted with the decoction for oral use.

If the patient is extremely disturbed by insomnia, 30 grams of raw fossil fragments (*Os Draconis*) and 30 grams of oyster shell (*Concha Ostreae*) ought to be administered. If deficiency of the liver-*yin* and kidney-*yin* is remarkable with symptoms of soreness and weakness of the loins and knees, 20 grams of prepared rehmannia root (*Radix Rehmanniae Praeparata*) and 12 grams of wolfberry fruit (*Fructus Lycii*) be included. When a disorder is caused by insufficiency of the kidney-*yang* manifested as spermatorrhea, impotence, premature ejaculation, aversion to cold, cold limbs, listlessness, pale tongue, weak and deep pulse, the treatment should be aimed at tonifying the kidney-*yang*. The preferred recipe is modified Kidney-*yang*-reinforcing Bolus. The compositions are: prepared rehmannia root (*Radix Rehmanniae Praeparata*) 20g, Chinese yam (*Rhizoma Dioscoreae*) 12g, wolfberry fruit (*Fructus Lycii*) 12g, fruit of medicinal cornel (*Fructus Corni*) 12g, dodder seed (*Semen Cuscutae*) 12g, morinda root (*Radix Morindae*) 12g antler glue (*Colla Cornus Cervi*) 10g (melted in boiling water for oral administration with the decoction), red raspberry (*Fructus Rubi*) 10g, prepared aconite root (*Radix*

生地 15 克，当归 10 克，白芍 10 克，麦冬 10 克，黄连 6 克，

枣仁 12 克，夜交藤 30 克，五味子 10 克，茯神 10 克，丹参 10 克，

炙甘草 6 克，阿胶10克（烊化）。水煎服。

若失眠甚者，加生龙、牡各30克；若腰膝酸软，肝肾阴虚

明显者，加熟地 20 克，枸杞子 12 克；若症见滑精、阳萎、早泄、

畏寒肢冷、精神萎靡、舌质淡、脉沉弱者，属肾阳不足，治宜补

肾助阳，方选右归丸加减：熟地 20 克，山药 12 克，枸杞子 12 克，

萸肉 12 克，菟丝子 12 克，巴戟天 12 克，鹿角胶 10 克（开水化

Aconini Praeparata) 6g, epimedium (*Herba Epimedii*) 10g, curculigo rhizome (*Rhizoma Curvuliginis*) 10g. All the drugs are to be decocted in water for oral administration.

3. Deficiency of the Heart and Spleen

Main Symptoms and Signs: Dreaminess and being easy to wake, palpitation, amnesia, fatigue and weakness, anorexia, sallow complexion, pale tongue with thin whitish fur, thready and weak pulse.

Therapeutic Principle: Invigorating the heart and spleen.

Recipe: Modified Decoction for Invigorating the Spleen and Nourishing the Heart.

astragalus root, *Radix Astragali seu Hedysari*   15g

dangshen, *Radix Codonopsis Pilosulae*   12g

bighead atractylodes rhizome, *Rhizoma Atractylodis Macrocephalae*   10g

poria, *Poria*   10g

Chinese angelica, *Radix Angelicae Sinensis*   10g

spiny jujuba seed, *Semen Ziziphi Spinosae*   12g

dried longan pulp, *Arillus Longan*   12g

polygala root, *Radix Polygalae*   10g

aucklandia root, *Radix Aucklandiae*   6g

prepared licorice root, *Radix Glycyrrhizae Praeparata*   3g

All the above drugs are to be decocted in water for oral administration.

If the patient is troubled by frequent insomnia, the recipe should include schisandra fruit (*Fructus Schisandrae*) 10g, fleece-flower stem (*Caulis Polygoni Multiflori*) 30g, or arborvitae seed (*Semen Biotae*) 10g, raw fossil fragments (*Os Draconis*) 20g, oyster shell (*Concha Ostreae*) 20g, and if the patient complains of anorexia, 10 grams of membrane of chicken's gizzard (*Endothelium Corneum Gigeriae Galli*). When a disorder is persistant depression resulting in impairment of the mind characterized by trance, dysphoria, sadness and melancholy and tending to cry, pale tongue with thin whitish fur, string-like and thready pulse, the treatment

服），覆盆子 10 克，附子 6 克，仙灵脾 12 克，仙茅 10 克。水煎服。

3. 心脾亏虚

主证：多梦易醒，心悸健忘，神疲乏力，饮食无味，面色少华，舌质淡，苔薄白，脉细弱。

治则：补益心脾。

处方：归脾汤加减。

黄芪 15 克，党参 12 克，白术 10 克，茯苓 10 克，当归 10 克，酸枣仁 12 克，桂圆肉 12 克，远志 10 克，木香 6 克，炙甘草 3 克。水煎服。

若失眠较甚者，加五味子 10 克，夜交藤 30 克，或柏子仁 10 克，生龙、牡各 20 克；纳食不香者，加鸡内金 10 克。若久郁伤神，症见精神恍惚、心神不宁、悲忧欲哭、舌质淡、苔薄白、脉

should be aimed at nourishing the heart to tranquilize the mind. Decoction of Licoirce, Wheat and Chinese-Date with additional ingredients can be chosen for the case. It includes the following drugs:

prepared licorice root, *Radix Glycyrrhizae Praeparata*　　10g

light wheat, *Fructus Tritici Levis*　　30g

Chinese-date, *Fructus Ziziphi Jujubae*　　10 pieces

spiny jujuba seed, *Semen Ziziphi Spinosae*　　12g

arborvitae seed, *Semen Biotae*　　12g

albizia flower, *Flos Albiziae*　　15g

dragon's teeth, *Dens Draconis*　　20g

curcuma root, *Radix Curcumae*　　10g

All the above drugs are to be decocted in water for oral administration.

Section 29

Schizophrenia

Schizophrenia is the most common psychosis. Its etiology has not been well understood despite many years of studies. Generally, genetic and environmental factors are considered to be involved in causing the disease. Schizophrenia frequently occurs in young adults. The ratio of incidence between males and females is roughly equal. In TCM, this disease is included in the categories of *"yu zheng"* (melancholia), *"dian"* (depressive psychosis), *"kuang"* (mania), etc.

MAIN POINTS OF DIAGNOSIS

1. Most patients have distortion, introversion, sensitiveness, doubting mania, fantasy and other features before the attack, which are associated with weak neural type.

2. The major psychogenic symptoms include the obstacle of thinking (split of thought and incoherence of thinking), obstacles of affect and volition. Delusion is a common symptom and may become a noticing manifestation. Auditory and visual

弦细者，治宜养心安神为主，可用甘麦大枣汤加味：炙甘草10克，浮小麦30克，大枣10枚，酸枣仁12克，柏子仁12克，合欢花15克，龙齿20克，郁金10克。水煎服。

第二十九节　精神分裂症

精神分裂症是最常见的一种精神病。其病因迄今尚未明了，一般认为与遗传因素、环境因素等有关。多发于青年人，男女发病率无明显差异。本病属中医"郁证"、"癫"、"狂"等范畴。

【诊断要点】

1. 多数患者病前有性格孤僻、内向、敏感、多疑和幻想等特点，其神经类型多属弱型。

2. 精神症状主要包括思维障碍（思维破裂和思维散漫）、情感障碍和意志活动障碍。妄想很常见，可成为病人的突出症状。

hallucination and depersonalization may appear in some patients.

3. Clinically, the disease can be divided into different types according to their manifestations: simple type, hebephrenic type, catatonic type and paranoid type. The last is the most common of all.

4. The general physical examination, nervous examination and tests of blood, urine and stool show no anbormal changes. Diagnosis depends chiefly on the history of the illness and symptoms.

DIFFERENTIATION AND TREATMENT OF COMMON SYNDROMES

1. Syndrome of Depressive Psychosis (Stagnancy of Phlegm and *Qi*)

Main Symptoms and Signs: Emotional depression, apathy, dementia, divagation or mutter to oneself, frequent cry or laugh for no apparent reason, caprice, no desire for diet, white greasy coating of the tongue, taut and slippery pulse.

Therapeutic Principle: Resolving phlegm, alleviating mental depression and regulating the flow of *qi* to treat psychosis.

Recipe: Modified Decoction for Regulating the Flow of *Qi* and Expelling Phlegm.

tangerine peel, *Pericarpium Citri Reticulatae*   10g
pinellia tuber, *Rhizoma Pinelliae*   10g
poria, *Poria*   10g
licorice root, *Radix Glycyrrhizae*   6g
arisaema with bile, *Arisaema cum Bile*   10g
immature bitter orange, *Fructus Aurantii Immaturus*   10g
polygala root, *Radix Polygalae*   10g
grass-leaved sweetflag, *Rhizoma Acori Graminei*   10g
nutgrass flatsedge *Rhizoma Cyperi*   10g
curcuma root, *Radix Curcumae*   12g

All the above drugs are to be decocted in water for oral administration.

Besides, 10 grams of coptis root (*Radix Coptidis*) are to be

部分患者可有幻听、幻视或人格解体等。

3．根据其临床表现，可分为单纯型、青春型、紧张型和偏执型(或妄想型)等，其中以妄想型最为常见。

4．一般体格检查、神经系统检查及血、尿、大便常规检查均无异常发现。诊断主要依据病史和临床症状。

【辨证论治】

1．癫证(痰气郁结)

主证：精神抑郁，表情淡漠，神志痴呆，语无伦次或喃喃独语，时哭时笑，喜怒无常，不思饮食，舌苔白腻，脉弦滑。

治则：化痰解郁，理气醒神。

处方：顺气导痰汤加减。

陈皮10克，半夏10克，茯苓10克，甘草6克，胆星10克，枳实10克，远志10克，菖蒲10克，香附10克，郁金12克。水煎服。

烦躁不安，苔黄脉数者，加黄连10克；便秘者，加大黄10

added for the case with the symptoms of restlessness, yellowish coating of the tongue and rapid pulse; and 10 grams of rhubarb (*Radix et Rhizoma Rhei*) added (to be decocted later) for the case with constipation; If the patient suffers from insomnia and is easy to be scared, 12 grams of wild jujuba seed (*Semen Ziziphi Spinosae*), 30 grams of raw dragon's teeth (*Dens Draconis*) and 30 grams of magnetite (*Magnetitum*) included. Still if the patient's depressive psychosis lasts for a long time resulting in the loss of *qi* and blood of the heart and spleen, with the symptoms of palpitation, insomnia dreaminess and trance, 10 grams of dangshen (*Radix Codonopsis Pilosulae*), 10 grams of Chinese angelica (*Radix Angelicae Sinensis*), 10 grams of red sage root (*Radix Salviae Miltiorrhizae*) and 10 grams of wild jujuba seed (*Semen Ziziphi Spinosae*) supplemented.

2. **Syndorme of Manic Psychosis (Flaring Up of Phlegm-fire)**

Main Symptoms and Signs: Sudden onset, irritability, flushed face, blood-shot eyes, mania, restlessness, constant scolding and beating, climbing up to a high place and singing, unusual strength, anorexia and insomnia, red tongue with yellow and greasy fur, slippery and rapid pulse.

Therapeutic Principle: Purging liver-fire, tranquilizing the mind and removing phlegm.

Recipe: Modified prescriptions of Pill for Removing Phlegm and Pig Iron Cinder Drink.

chlorite-schist, *Lapis Chloriti*　　20g
rhubarb, *Radix et Rhizoma Rhei*　　10g (decocted later)
scutellaria root, *Radix Scutellariae*　　12g
coptis root, *Radix Coptidis*　　10g
gentian root, *Radix Gentianae*　　10g
immature bitter orange, *Fructus Aurantii Immaturus*　　10g
pinellia tuber, *Rhizoma Pinelliae*　　10g
arisaema with bile, *Arisaema cum Bile*　　10g
grass-leaved sweetflag rhizome, *Rhizoma Acori Graminei*　10g

克(后入)；失眠易惊者，加酸枣仁 12 克，生龙齿 30 克，磁石 30

克；癫病日久，心脾气血耗损，症见心悸、少寐、多梦、神思恍

惚者，加党参 10 克，当归 10 克，丹参 10 克，酸枣仁 10 克。

2. 狂证（痰火上扰）

主证：起病急骤，急躁易怒，面红目赤，狂躁不安，打骂不

休，登高而歌，气力逾常，少食少眠，舌质红，苔黄腻，脉滑

数。

治则：清肝泻火，镇心涤痰。

处方：滚痰丸合生铁落饮加减。

青礞石 20 克，大黄 10 克（后入），黄芩 12 克，黄连 10 克，

tabasheer, *Concretio Silicea Bambusae*   10g

All the above drugs are to be decocted in water for oral administration.

If the patient suffers from mamia for a long period of time, excessive fire will hurt *yin*, which is manifested as restlessness and easy scare, emaciation, flushed face, red tongue, fine and rapid pulse. In such a case the above recipe should include dried rehmannia root (*Radix Rehmanniae*) 15g, ophiopogon root (*Radix Ophiopogonis*) 10g and scrophularia root (*Radix Scrophulariae*) 12g.

龙胆草 10 克，枳实 10 克，半夏 10 克，胆星 10 克，菖蒲 10 克，天竺黄 10 克。水煎服。

若狂病日久，火盛伤阴，症见烦躁善惊、形瘦面红、脉细数者，加生地 15 克，麦冬 10 克，玄参 12 克。

Chapter Two

THE COMMON DISEASES OF OBSTETRICS AND GYNECOLOGY

Section 1
Menoxenia

Menoxenia in TCM (Traditional Chinese Medicine) re-fers to the disorders in menstrual cycle and period, and abnor-malities in the amount, colour and nature of menstrual blood. In this category of disorders, the commonest are preceded men-strual cycle, delayed menstrual cycle, irregular menstrual cycle, menorrhagia, scanty menstruation, etc.

MAIN POINTS OF DIAGNOSIS

1. The condition in which menstruation occurs 7 or more days or even 10 days or more earlier than usual is referred to as preceded menstrual cycle; while the condition in which men-struation occurs a week or more later, or comes in 40—50 days, is termed delayed menstrual cycle. And if menstruation oc-curs over 7 days either earlier or later irregularly, it is called irregular menstrual cycle.

2. The condition in which the amount of menstrual blood is obviously more than usual but the cycle is basically normal is termed menorrhagia. If the amount of menstrual blood is obviously less than usual and the cycle is basically normal, this condition is referred to as scanty menstruation.

DIFFERENTIATION AND TREATMENT OF COMMON SYNDROMES

1. Heat in the Blood

第二章

妇产科常见疾病

第一节　月经失调

中医所称的"月经失调"，是指月经的周期、经期、经量、经色、经质发生异常。常见的有月经先期、月经后期、月经先后无定期、月经过多、月经过少等。

【诊断要点】

1. 月经周期提前七天以上，甚至十余日者，称为"月经先期"；月经周期延后七天以上，甚或四、五十日一至者，称为"月经后期"；月经周期时而提前、时而延后在七天以上者，称为"月经先后无定期"。

2. 月经量较以往明显增多，周期基本正常者，称为"月经过多"；月经量明显减少，甚或点滴即净，月经周期基本正常者，称为"月经过少"。

【辨证论治】

1. 血热型

Main Symptoms and Signs: Preceded menstrual cycle or profuse menstruation which is bright or dark red, thick and sticky, accompanied with restlessness and dry mouth, yellowish urine, constipation, redness of the tongue proper with yellow fur, rapid pulse.

Therapeutic Principle: Clearing heat from the blood to regulate menstruation.

Recipe: Modified Powder for Clearing Menstruation-heat

moutan bark, *Cortex Moutan Radicis*   9g
wolfberry bark, *Cortex Lycii Radicis*   15g
white peony root, *Radix Paeoniae Alba*   9g
dried rehmannia root, *Radix Rehmanniae*   9g
sweet wormwood, *Herba Artemisiae*   6g
phellodendron bark, *Cortex Phellodendri*   3g
motherwort, *Herba Leonuri*   15g
raw sanguisorba root, *Radix Sanguisorbae*   15g

All the above drugs are to be decocted in water for oral administration.

If, before menstruation, there is a feeling of distension and fullness in the breasts, and distending pain in the lower abdomen, fidgets, bitter taste, exclude motherwort (*Herba Leonuri*) and phellodendron bark (*Cortex Phellodendri*) and add 9 grams of capejasmine fruit (*Fructus Gardeniae*), 9 grams of bupleurum root (*Radix Bupleuri*) and 9 grams of rose (*Flos Rosae Rugosae*). If the menstrual blood is scanty accompanied with tidal fever, flushing of zygomatic region, feverish sensation in the palms and soles, then subtract sweet wormwood (*Herba Artemisiae*) phellodendron (*Cortex Phellodendri*) and raw sanguisorba root (*Radix Sanguisorbae*) and add 12 grams of scrophularia root (*Radix Scrophulariae*), 9 grams of donkey-hide gelatin (*Colla Corii Asini*) (to be melted and mixed in the finished decoction), 9 grams of glossy privet fruit (*Fructus Ligustri Lucidi*) and 9 grams of eclipta (*Herba Ecliptae*).

2. Deficiency of *Qi*

Main Symptoms and Signs: Advanced menstruation or pro-

主证：月经先期而至，或经来量多，**色鲜红**或深红，质粘稠，伴烦躁口干、尿黄便结，舌质红，苔黄，脉数。

治则：清热凉血调经。

处方：清经散加减。

丹皮9克，地骨皮15克，白芍9克，生地9克，青蒿6克，黄柏3克，益母草15克，生地榆15克。水煎服。

若经前乳胀、少腹胀痛、心烦口苦者，去益母草、黄柏，加山栀9克，柴胡9克，玫瑰花9克；若经来量少、潮热颧红、手足心热者，去青蒿、黄柏、生地榆，加玄参12克，阿胶9克(烊化)，女贞子9克，旱莲草9克。

2. 气虚型

主证：经来先期，或经来量多，色淡，质稀，伴神疲肢倦、

fuse menstruation, thin blood with light colour, lack of vitality, tiredness in the extremeties, short of breath and want of speech, pale tongue with white fur, thready and weak pulse.

Therapeutic Principle: Regulating menstruation by invigorating *qi* and keeping the blood flowing within the vessels.

Recipe: Modified Decoction for Reinforcing the Middle-*jiao* and Replenishing *qi*.

dangshen, *Radix Codonopsis Pilosulae*   15g
astragalus root, *Radix Astragali seu Hedysari*   15g
bighead atractylodes rhizome, *Rhizoma Atractylodis Macro-*
    cephalae   9g
prepared licorice root, *Radix Glycyrrhizae Praeparata*   9g
Chinese angelica root, *Radix Angelicae Sinensis*   9g
motherwort, *Herba Leonuri*   15g
tangerine peel, *Pericarpium Citri Reticulatae*   6g
cimicifuga rhizome, *Rhizoma Cimicifugae*   9g
bupleurum root, *Radix Bupleuri*   3g

All the above drugs are to be decocted in water for oral administration.

If palpitation or severe palpitation is present, 9 grams of poria with hostwood (*Poria cum Ligno Hospite*) and 15 grams of wild jujuba seed (*Semen Ziziphi Spinosae*) should be added; if accompained with soreness of waist and loose stool, 9 grams of antler glue (*Colla Cornus Cervi*) which is to be melted and mixed in the finished decoction and 9 grams of eucommia bark (*Cortex Eucommiae*) should be added.

3. Blood Stasis

Main Symptoms and Signs: Delayed menstrual cycle, scanty menstruation, dark-coloured menstrual blood with clots, pain in the lower abdomen, dark-coloured tongue or with ecchymoses, taut and unsmooth pulse.

Therapeutic Principle: Promoting blood circulation and removing blood stasis to regulate menstruation.

Recipe: Modified Four-ingredient Decoction plus Peach

气短懒言，舌质淡、苔白，脉细弱。

治则：补气摄血调经。

处方：补中益气汤加减。

党参15克，黄芪15克，白术9克，炙甘草9克，当归9克，益母草15克，陈皮6克，升麻9克，柴胡3克。水煎服。

若兼征忡、心悸者，加茯神9克，酸枣仁15克；若伴腰酸便溏者，加鹿角胶9克(烊化)，杜仲9克。

3．血瘀型

主证：经期延后、量少，色暗有块，小腹疼痛，舌质紫暗或有瘀点，脉弦涩。

治则：活血祛瘀调经。

Kernel and Safflower.

  peach kernel, *Semen Persicae*   9g
  safflower, *Flos Carthami*   9g
  motherwort, *Herba Leonuri*   15g
  rubia root, *Radix Rubiae*   12g
  Chinese angelica root, *Radix Angelicae Sinensis*   9g
  white peony root, *Radix Paeoniae Alba*   9g
  chuanxiong rhizome, *Rhizoma Ligustici Chuanxiong*   9g
  dried rehmannia root, *Radix Rehmanniae*   9g
  parched cat-tail pollen, *Pollen Typhae*   6g
  parched trogopterus dung, *Faeces Trogopterorum*   9g

All the drugs mentioned above are to be decocted in water
for oral administration.

If there are symptoms of cold-pain in the lower abdomen
which can be relieved by warmth, and intolerance of cold with
cold limbs, the following drugs should be added:

  baked ginger, *Rhizoma Zingiberis Praeparata*   6g
  bark of Chinese cassia tree, *Cortex Cinnamomi*   6g
  evodia fruit, *Fructus Evodiae*   9g
  common fennel fruit, *Fructus Foeniculi*   6g

Section 2
Dysfunctional Uterine Bleeding

Dysfunctional uterine bleeding is an abnormal uterine
bleeding caused by ovarian dysfunction. Its clinical manifestations are disorder of menstrual cycle, prolonged and heavy bleeding. This disease belongs to the category of *"beng"* (metrorrhagia) or *"lou"* (metrostaxis) in TCM.

MAIN POINTS OF DIAGNOSIS

1. Menstruation comes irregularly with heavy bleeding
or metrostaxis lasts even for a month in every cycle.

2. The blood can be bright or dark in colour; sticky or wa-

处方：桃红四物汤加减。

桃仁9克，红花9克，益母草15克，茜草12克，当归9克，白芍9克，川芎9克，生地9克，炒蒲黄6克，炒灵脂9克。水煎服。

若小腹冷痛、得热减轻、畏寒肢冷者，加炮姜6克，肉桂心6克，吴茱萸9克，小茴香6克。

第二节　功能性子宫出血

功能失调性子宫出血系指由于卵巢功能失调而引起的子宫异常出血。临床表现为月经周期紊乱、出血时间长、经量增多，甚至大量出血或淋漓不止。本病属中医"崩漏"范畴。

【诊断要点】

1. 月经不按周期而妄行，出血量多如注，或淋漓不断，甚至屡月未有尽时。

2. 血色或鲜明，或暗淡，血质或稠粘，或清稀如水，或有

tery in quality, sometimes with clots, fish-stench.

3. Physical and gynecological examinations show no abnormal findings.

DIFFERENTIATION AND TREATMENT OF COMMON SYNDROMES

1. Heat in the Blood

Main Symptoms and Signs: Sudden, abnormal bursts of profuse menstrual bleeding or uterine bleeding prolonged and sustained for many days, with the blood being bright red, thick and sticky, accompanied with tidal fever, thin and yellow fur of the tongue, thready and rapid pulse.

Therapeutic Principle: Nourishing *yin*, clearing away heat and arresting bleeding to regulate menstruation.

Recipe: Modified Decoction for Protecting *Yin*.

dried rehmannia root, *Radix Rehmanniae*   9g

scutellaria root, *Radix Scutellariae*   9g

phellodendron bark, *Cortex Phellodendri*   9g

donkey-hide gelatin, *Colla Corii Asini*   9g (melted)

glossy privet fruit, *Fructus Ligustri Lucidi*   12g

eclipta, *Herba Ecliptae*   12g

motherwort, *Herba Leonuri*   15g

white peony root, *Radix Paeoniae Alba*   9g

Chinese yam, *Rhizoma Dioscoreae*   9g

All the above drugs are to be decocted in water except the donkey-hide gelatin which is to be melted and then mixed with the decoction for oral administration.

For patients with dark-red and thick menstrual blood, dry mouth, dysphoria with smothery sensation, modified Hemostatic Decoction by Clearing Away Heat is recommended.

scutellaria root, *Radix Scutellariae*   9g

stir-fried capejasmine fruit, *Fructus Gardeniae*   9g

dried rehmannia root, *Radix Rehmanniae*   9g

wolfberry bark, *Cortex Lycii Radicis*   9g

raw sanguisorba root, *Radix Sanguisorbae*   15g

血块，气腥或秽。

3. 全身及妇科检查，多无异常发现。

【辨证论治】

1. 血热型

主证：经血非时突然而下，量多势急或淋漓日久，色鲜红。

质稠，心烦潮热，苔薄黄，脉细数。

治则：滋阴清热，止血调经。

处方：保阴煎加减。

生地9克，黄芩9克，黄柏9克，阿胶9克(烊化)，女贞子

12克，旱莲草12克，益母草12克，白芍9克，山药9克。水煎服。

若血色深红、质稠、口渴烦热者，改用清热固经汤加减：黄

芩9克，炒山栀9克，生地9克，地骨皮9克，生地榆15克，益

motherwort, *Herba Leonuri*   15g

donkey-hide gelatin, *Colla Corii Asini*   9g (melted)

long-stored carbonized petiole of windmill palm, *Petiolus Trachycarpi Carbonisatus*   15g

calcined oyster shell, *Concha Ostreae Usta*   24g

The drugs are to be decocted in water except the donkey-hide gelatin which is to be melted and then mixed with the decoction for oral administration.

2. Blood Stasis

Main Symptoms and Signs: Abnormal and frequent bursts of menstrual bleeding, manifested as metrorrhagia or metrostaxis, marked by dark-coloured blood with clots, accompanied with distending pain in the lower abdomen, dull-purple tongue with white and thin fur, unsmooth pulse.

Therapeutic Principle: Promoting blood circulation, removing blood stasis and arresting bleeding to regulate menstruation.

Recipe: Modified recipe of Four-ingredient Decoction plus Peach Kernel and Safflower.

prepared rehmannia root, *Radix Rehmanniae Praeparata*   9g

Chinese angelica root, *Radix Angelicae Sinensis*   9g

stri-fried white peony root, *Radix Paeoniae Alba Praeparata*   9g

peach kernel, *Semen Persicae*   9g

safflower, *Flos Carthami*   9g

stir-fried trogopterus dung, *Faeces Trogopterorum Praeparata* 9g

stir-fried cat-tail pollen, *Pollen Typhae Praeparata*   9g

rubia root, *Radix Rubiae*   12g

carbonized field thistle, *Herba Cephalanoploris Praeparata*   9g

notoginseng powder, *Radix Notoginseng*   3g (infused)

Decoct the above drugs in water and mix notoginseng powder with the finished decoction for oral administration.

In case of severe abdominal distension, add 12 grams of Sichuan chinaberry (*Fructus Medliae Toosendan*) and 9 grams of nutgrass flatsedge rhizome (*Rhizoma Cyperi*). For those having

母草15克，阿胶 9 克(烊化)，陈棕炭 15 克，煅牡蛎 24 克。水煎

服。

2. 血瘀型

主证：经血非时而下，时下时止，或崩中漏下，色紫暗有

块，伴小腹胀痛，舌质紫暗，苔薄白，脉涩。

治则：活血化瘀，止血调经。

处方：桃红四物汤加减。

熟地 9 克，当归 9 克，炒白芍 9 克，桃仁 9 克，红花 9 克，

炒灵脂 9 克，炒蒲黄 9 克，茜草12克，小蓟炭 9 克，三七粉 3 克

(冲)。水煎服。

若腹胀甚者，加川楝子12克，香附 9 克；口干苦、血色红量

a dry mouth with bitter taste or profuse bleeding with the blood red in colour, add 30 grams of hairy vein agrimony (*Herba Agrimoniae*) 15 grams of sanguisorba root (*Radix Sanguisorbae*) and 15 grams of rubia root (*Radix Rubiae*).

3. Insufficiency of the Spleen

Main Symptoms and Signs: Irregular menstrual cycle, manifested as metrorrhagia or metrostaxis, prolonged menstruation, light-coloured and thin menstrual blood, accompanied with shortness of breath, spiritlessness, pale complexion, pale tongue with thin white fur, weak pulse.

Therapeutic Principle: Hemostasis by invigorating *qi* and enriching blood to regulate menstruation.

Recipe: Modified Decoction for Curing Metrorrhagia by Reinforcing Body Resistance.

ginseng, *Radix Ginseng*   6g

astragalus root, *Radix Astragali seu Hedysari*   15g

bighead atractylodes rhizome, *Rhizoma Atractylodis Macrocephalae*   12g

prepared rehmannia root, *Radix Rehmanniae Praeparata*   12g

cimicifuga rhizome, *Rhizoma Cimicifugae*   9g

Chinese yam, *Rhizoma Dioscoreae*   15g

cuttle-bone, *Os Sepiella seu Sepiae*   9g

baked ginger, *Rhizoma Zingiberis Praeparata*   9g

motherwort, *Herba Leonuri*   15g

All the above drugs are to be decocted in water for oral administration.

In addition to the above described symptoms, there might be intolerance of cold, cold limbs and lassitude in loins and legs. In this case, omit prepared rehmannia root (*Radix Rehmanniae Praeparata*), Chinese yam (*Rhizoma Dioscoreae*) and cuttlebone (*Os Sepiella seu Sepiae*), add 9 grams of melted antler glue (*Colla Cornus Cervi*), 9 grams of dodder seed (*Semen Cuscutae*) and 9 grams of eucommia bark (*Cortex Eucommiae*) instead. In case that the

多者，加仙鹤草30克，地榆15克，茜草根15克。

3. 脾虚型

主证：经来无期，崩中漏下，淋漓日久，色淡，质稀，伴气

短神疲、面色㿠白，舌质淡，苔薄白，脉弱。

治则：补气摄血，养血调经。

处方：固本止血汤加减。

人参6克，黄芪15克，白术12克，熟地12克，升麻9克，山

药15克，乌贼骨9克，炮姜9克，益母草15克。水煎服。

若兼畏寒肢冷、腰腿酸软者，去熟地、山药、乌贼骨，加鹿

角胶9克(烊化)，菟丝子9克，杜仲9克；若血色淡红，伴头晕、

menstrual blood is reddish accompanied with dizziness, tinnitus, lassitude in loins and legs, omit baked ginger (*Rhizoma Zingiberis*), cimicifuga (*Rhizoma Cimicifugae*), cuttle-bone (*Os Sepiella seu Sepiae*) and Chinese yam (*Rhizoma Dioscoreae*), add 9 grams of glossy privet fruit (*Fructus Ligustri Lucidi*), 9 grams of eclipta (*Herba Ecliptae*) and 9 grams of melted antler glue (*Colla Cornus Cervi*) which is to be melted.

Section 3
Amenorrhea

By amenorrhea it is meant primary amenorrhea and secondary amenorrhea. The former applies to those who have never menstruated until they are 18 years old, while the latter refers to those whose menses have ceased for over three months after the formation of menstrual cycle.

MAIN POINTS OF DIAGNOSIS

1. The diagnosis of the disease is characterized by the absence of menstruation.

2. Women at the age of 18 who have never menstruated are considered to have primary amenorrhea; women whose menses have ceased for over three months after their formation of menstrual cycle are said to have secondary amenorrhea.

3. In physical examination, attention should be paid to the development of the body and reproductive organs.

4. Other examinations: PRL, FSH, LH, E_2, P.T., sex chromosomes examination or X-ray of sella turcica may be considered.

DIFFERENTIATION AND TREATMENT OF COMMON SYNDROMES

1. Insufficiency of the Liver and Kidney

Main Symptoms and Signs: Primary amenorrhea of a girl over 18 years old, or delayed menstrual cycle with scanty menstruation leading gradually to amenorrhea, accompanied with

耳鸣、腰腿酸软者，去炮姜、升麻、乌贼骨、山药，加女贞子 9
克，旱莲草 9 克，鹿角胶 9 克(烊化)。

第三节 闭 经

女子年逾十八岁尚未行经，或月经周期建立后又连续停闭达
三个月以上者称为闭经。前者称"原发性闭经"，后者称"继发性
闭经"。

【诊断要点】

1. 本病诊断以月经不潮为特征。

2. 若年逾十八周岁月经尚未初潮者，称"原发性闭经"；已
行经而又中断达三个月以上者，称"继发性闭经"。

3. 查体注意全身及生殖器官发育情况。

4. 其他检查：如 PRL、FSH、LH、E_2、P.T.、性染色体、
X 线蝶鞍拍片等，可予考虑。

【辨证论治】

1. 肝肾不足型

主证：年逾十八岁尚未行经，或月经后期量少渐至闭经，体

constitutional debility, lassitude in loins and legs, dizziness, tinnitus, reddish tongue with little fur, deep and thready pulse.

Therapeutic Principle: Tonifying both the kidney and liver to regulate menstruation.

Recipe: Modified recipe of Bolus for Invigorating the Kidney.

dodder seed, *Semen Cuscutae*   12g
eucommia bark, *Cortex Eucommiae*   9g
wolfberry fruit, *Fructus Lycii*   12g
glossy privet fruit, *Fructus Ligustri Lucidi*   12g
eclipta, *Herba Ecliptae*   12g
dogwood fruit, *Fructus Corni*   9g
Chinese angelica root, *Radix Angelicae Sinensis*   9g
prepared rehmannia root, *Radix Rehmanniae*   9g
Chinese yam, *Rhizoma Dioscoreae*   15g
poria, *Poria*   9g

All the above drugs are to be decocted in water for oral administration.

2. Deficiency of both *Qi* and Blood

Main Symptoms and Signs: Gradual delay of menstruation with very little blood which is thin and reddish, then leading to amenorrhea, accompanied with dizziness, blurred vision, palpitation, short breath or lusterless hair, emaciation with sallow complexion, pale tongue with very little fur, deep and moderate pulse.

Therapeutic Principle: Invigorating *qi* and nourishing the blood to regulate menstruation

Recipe: Modified Ginseng Nutrition Decoction.

ginseng, *Radix Ginseng*   6g
astragalus root, *Radix Astragali Seu Hedysari*   15g
roasted bighead atractylodes rhizome, *Rhizoma Atractylodis Macrocephalae*   12g
poria, *Poria*   9g
schisandra fruit, *Fructus Schisandrae*   9g

质虚弱，腰酸腿软，头晕耳鸣，舌淡红，苔少，脉沉细。

治则：补肾养肝调经。

处方：归肾丸加减。

菟丝子12克，杜仲9克，枸杞子12克，女贞子12克，旱莲草12克，山萸肉9克，当归9克，熟地9克，山药15克，茯苓9克。水煎服。

2. 气血虚弱型

主证：月经逐渐后延，量少，色淡，质稀渐至闭经，伴头晕眼花、心悸气短，或毛发不泽、羸瘦萎黄，舌质淡，苔少，脉沉缓。

治则：补气养血调经。

处方：人参养荣汤加减。

人参6克，黄芪15克，煨白术12克，茯苓9克，五味子9

Chinese angelica root, *Radix Angelicae Sinensis*   9g

prepared rehmannia root, *Radix Rehmanniae Praeparata*   12g

white peony root, *Radix Paeoniae Alba*   9g

cinnamon bark, *Dortex Cinnamomi*   3g

human placenta, *Placenta Hominis*   12g

All the above drugs are to be decocted in water for oral administration.

For amenorrhea due to profuse uterine bleeding, 6 grams of pilose antler (*Cornu Cervi Pantotrichum*) should be added (ground into fine powder to be swallowed).

3. Blood Stasis due to Stagnation of *Qi*

Main Symptoms and Signs: Amenorrhea for several months, accompanied with fidgets and liability to anger, feeling fullness in the chest and hypochondrium, distending pain in the lower abdomen, ecchymoses on the tongue edges, deep and uneven pulse.

Therapeutic Principle: Regulating the flow of *qi*, promoting the circulation of blood and removing blood stasis to induce menstruation.

Recipe: Modified Decoction for Removing Blood Stasis in the Chest.

peach kernel, *Semen Persicae*   9g

safflower, *Flos Carthami*   9g

Chinese angelica root, *Radix Angelicae Sinensis*   9g

red sage root, *Radix Salviae Miltiorrhizae*   15g

chuanxiong rhizome, *Rhizoma Ligustici Chuanxiong*   9g

red peony root, *Radix Paeoniae Rubra*   12g

cinnamon bark, *Cortex cinnamomi*   3g

cyathula root, *Radix Cyathulae*   12g

bitter orange, *Fructus Aurantii*   9g

lindera root, *Radix Linderae*   9g

prepared nutgrass flatsedge rhizome, *Rhizoma Cyperi*   9g

All the above drugs are to be decocted in water for oral administration.

克，当归9克，熟地12克，白芍9克，桂心3克，紫河车12克。

水煎服。

若产后大出血所致闭经者，加鹿茸0.6克（研末吞服）。

3. 气滞血瘀型

主证：月经数月不行，烦燥易怒，胸胁胀满，少腹胀痛，舌

边有瘀点，脉沉涩。

治则：祛瘀通经。理气活血。

处方：血府逐瘀汤加减。

桃仁9克，红花9克，当归9克，丹参15克，川芎9克，赤

芍12克，桂心3克，川牛膝12克，枳壳9克，乌药9克，制香附

9克。水煎服。

Section 4

Dysmenorrhea

Dysmenorrhea means that women have periodic pain during or prior to or after menstrual period in the lower abdomen or even faint in severe cases. It has been customary to classify cases of dysmenorrhea into two main groups: primary or functional dysmenorrhea referring to the one which is not caused by organic diseases, and secondary dysmenorrhea referring to the one caused by organic diseases in reproductive system.

MAIN POINTS OF DIAGNOSIS

1. The pain in the lower abdomen appears with menstrual cycle.

2. The pain can spread over the whole abdomen, lumbosacral region or there is dragging pain in the vulva and anus. It varies in degrees and can be relieved when the menstrual blood flows smoothly.

3. Gynecological examination: Those without organic diseases in the pelvic cavity are primary dysmenorrhea; those with organic diseases in the pelvic cavity are secondary dysmenorrhea.

DIFFERENTIATION AND TREATMENT OF COMMON SYNDROMES

1. Blood Stasis due to Stagnation of *Qi*

Main Symptoms and Signs: Distending pain and tenderness in the lower abdomen one or two days prior to or during menstruation accompanied with fullness sensation in the chest, hypochondrium and breast, deep-purple blood with clots, relief of pain after discharge of clots, ecchymoses on the tongue edges, string-like pulse.

Therapeutic Principle: Regulating the flow of *qi* and removing blood stasis to alleviate the pain.

第四节　痛　经

妇女正值经期或行经前后，出现周期性小腹疼痛，或痛引腰骶，甚至剧痛昏厥者，称为"痛经"，亦称"经行腹痛"。生殖器官无器质性病变者，称原发性痛经或功能性痛经；因生殖器官器质性病变所引起的痛经，称为继发性痛经。

【诊断要点】

1. 经行小腹疼痛，伴随月经周期而发作。

2. 疼痛可引及全腹或腰骶部，或外阴、肛门坠痛。疼痛程度有轻有重，经血排出流畅时，疼痛常可缓解。

3. 妇科检查：无盆腔器质性病变者多为原发性痛经，有相应盆腔器质性病变者为继发性痛经。

【辨证论治】

1. 气滞血瘀型

主证：经前一、二日或经期小腹胀痛拒按，伴胸 胁 乳 房 作胀、经血紫暗有块、块下痛减，舌边有瘀点，脉弦。

治则：理气化瘀止痛。

Recipe: Modified Decoction for Dissipating Blood Stasis Under Diaphram.

Chinese angelica root, *Radix Angelicae Sinensis*   9g
chuanxiong rhizome, *Rhizoma Ligustici Chuanxiong*   9g
red peony root, *Radix Paeoniae Rubra*   12g
peach kernel, *Semen Persicae*   9g
safflower, *Flos Carthami*   9g
bitter orange, *Fructus Aurantii*   9g
corydalis tuber, *Rhizoma Corydalis*   12g
trogopterus dung, *Faeces Trogopterorum*   9g
Sichuan chinaberry, *Fructus Meliae Toosendan*   12g
lindera root, *Radix Linderae*   12g
nutgrass flatsedge rhizome, *Rhizoma Cyperi*   12g

All the above drugs are to be decocted in water for oral administration.

2. Stagnancy of Cold and Dampness

Main Symptoms and Signs: Distending pain in the lower abdomen several days prior to or during menstruation, which can be relieved by warmth, menstrual flow scanty in amount, dark in colour and with clots, pale tongue with white and greasy fur, deep and tense pulse.

Therapeutic Principle: Warming the channels and expelling dampness to arrest pain.

Recipe: Modified Decoction for Removing Blood Stagnation in the Lower Abdomen.

common fennel fruit, *Fructus Feoniculi*   3g
cinnamon bark, *Cortex Cinnamomi*   6g
red peony root, *Radix Paeoniae Rubra*   12g
Chinese angelica root, *Radix Angelicae Sinensis*   12g
chuanxiong rhizome, *Rhizoma Ligustici Chuanxiong*   9g
corydalis tuber, *Rhizoma Corydalis*   12g
myrrh, *Myrrha*   9g
cat-tail pollen, *Pollen Typhae*   9g
trogopterus dung, *Faeces Trogopterorum*   12g

处方：膈下逐瘀汤加减。

当归9克，川芎9克，赤芍12克，桃仁9克，红花9克，枳壳9克，延胡索12克，五灵脂9克，川楝子12克，乌药12克，香附12克。水煎服。

2. 寒湿凝滞型

主证：经前数日或经期小腹冷痛，得温痛减，月经量少，色暗有块，舌质淡，苔白腻，脉沉紧。

治则：温经祛湿止痛。

处方：少腹逐瘀汤加减。

小茴香3克，肉桂6克，赤芍12克，当归12克，川芎9克，

poria, *Poria*   12g

All the above drugs are to be decocted in water for oral administration.

For those with lassitude in loins and legs and excreting copious clear urine, omit poria (*Poria*) and add 6 grams of prepared aconite root (*Radix Aconiti Praeparata*) and 9 grams of argyi leaf (*Folium Artemisiae Argyi*).

3. Deficiency of Both *Qi* and Blood

Main Symptoms and Signs: Vague pain in the lower abdomen during or 1–2 days after menstruation which can be relieved by pressing, scanty menstruation with reddish and thin blood, accompanied with lack of vitality and asthenia, pale tongue with white and thin fur, thready and weak pluse.

Therapeutic Principle: Invigorating *qi* and enriching the blood to alleviate pain.

Recipe: Modified Dysmenorrhea-curing Decoction.

ginseng, *Radix Ginseng*   3g

astragalus root, *Radix Astragali seu Hedysari*   15g

Chinese angelica root, *Radix Angelicae Sinensis*   9g

chuanxiong rhizome, *Rhizoma Ligustici Chuanxiong*   9g

prepared rehmannia root, *Radix Rehmanniae Praeparata*   9g

white peony root, *Radix Paeoniae Alba*   12g

nutgrass flatsedge rhizome, *Rhizoma Cyperi*   12g

corydalis tuber, *Radix Corydalis*   12g

Decoct the above drugs in water for oral administration.

Section 5
Polycystic Ovary Syndrome

Polycystic ovary syndrome, also named polycystic ovary disease, is a kind of syndrome caused by ovarian dysfunction. Its clinical manifestations are scanty menstruation or infrequent

延胡索12克，没药9克，蒲黄9克，五灵脂12克，茯苓12克。水煎服。

若伴腰腿酸软、小便清长者，去茯苓加附子6克，艾叶9克。

3．气血虚弱型

主证：经后一二日或经期小腹隐隐作痛，喜按，月经量少，色淡质稀，伴神疲乏力，舌质淡，苔薄白，脉细弱。

治则：益气补血止痛。

处方：圣愈汤加减。

人参3克，黄芪15克，当归9克，川芎9克，熟地9克，白芍12克，香附12克，延胡索12克。水煎服。

第五节　多囊卵巢综合征

多囊卵巢综合征或称多囊卵巢病，是由于卵巢功能失调所产

menstruation in occurence, amenorrhea, pilosity, obesity and sterility.

MAIN POINTS OF DIAGNOSIS

1. Patients have menstrual disorders. Most of them have scanty menstruation or infrequent menstruation or amenorrhea, yet some of them may have dysfunctional uterine bleeding.

2. Patients are often fat, hairy and sterile.

3. In some cases ovaries can be found enlarged through gynecological examination.

4. The surfaces of the enlarged ovaries can be found uneven with the capsule thickened and greyish white through ultra sound B and ventroscopy.

5. Hormonal test shows high amount of testosterone, low level of FSH and high level of LH.

DIFFERENTIATION AND TREATMENT OF COMMON SYNDROMES

1. Phlegm-dampness Type

Main Symptoms and Signs: Amenorrhea or infrequent menstruation, obesity, pilosity, pale and enlarged tongue with white and greasy fur, deep and moderate pulse.

Therapeutic Principle: Removing phlegm and dampness and promoting blood circulation to remove stagnation.

Recipe: Modified recipe of Pills of Atractylodes and Nutgrass Flatsedge for Expelling Phlegm.

atractylodes rhizome, *Rhizoma Atractylodis*   9g
nutgrass flatsedge rhizome, *Rhizoma Cyperi*   12g
tangerine peel, *Pericarpium Citri Recticulatae*   9g
prepared pinellia rhizome, *Rhizoma Pinelliae Praeparate*
     9g
Japanese sea tangle, *Thallus Laminariae*   12g
prunella spike, *Spica Prunellae*   15g
fritillary bulb, *Bulbus Fritillariae*   12g
pangolin scales, *Squama Maniitis*   12g

生的一种综合征。临床主要表现为月经稀发、稀少或闭经、多毛、肥胖和不孕。

【诊断要点】

1. 月经失调，多数病人月经稀发、稀少或闭经，部分病人可患功能性子宫出血。

2. 病人多有肥胖、多毛及不孕。

3. 部分患者妇科检查可发现卵巢增大。

4. B超检查、腹腔镜检查可见增大的卵巢凹凸不平，包膜增厚呈灰白色。

5. 激素测定血中睾酮含量增高，FSH 值偏低，LH 值偏高。

【辨证论治】

痰湿型

主证：闭经或月经稀发，肥胖，多毛，舌淡胖，苔白腻，脉沉缓。

治则：豁痰除湿，活血行滞。

处方：苍附导痰丸加减。

苍术 9 克，香附 12 克，陈皮 9 克，法半夏 9 克，昆布 12

pleione rhizome, *Rhizoma Pleionis*　9g
honeylocust thorn, *Spina Gleditsiae*　9g
bitter orange, *Fructus Aurantii*　9g
poria, *Poria*　12g

All the above drugs are to be decocted in water for oral administration.

2. Kidney-deficiency Type

Main Symptoms and Signs: Scanty menstruation or ame-norrhea, magersucht and hairiness, soreness of the waist, dizziness, intolerance of cold, loose stool, pale tongue with white thin fur, deep and thready pulse.

Therapeutic Principle: Warming the kidney, replenishing the vital essence and removing stagnation.

Recipe: Modified recipe of Kidney-*Yin*-Reinforcing Bolus.
prepared rehmannia root, *Radix Rehmanniae Praeparata*
　12g
antler glue, *Colla Cornus Cervi*　9g (melted)
dodder seed, *Semen Cuscutae*　12g
raspberry fruit, *Fructus Rubi*　12g
cibot rhizome, *Rhizoma Cibotii*　9g
fenugreek seed, *Semen Trigonellae*　9g
epimedium, *Herba Epimedii*　12g
siberian solomonseal rhizome, *Rhizoma Polygonati*　15g
prunella spike, *Spica Prunellae*　15g

All the above drugs, except antler glue which is melted with the finished decoction, are to be decocted in water for oral administration.

Section 6
Premenstrual Tension Syndrome

Premenstrual tension syndrome includes a series of symptoms such as distending pain in the breasts, headache and dizziness, restlessness and insomnia, distension in sternocostal

克，夏枯草 15 克，贝母 12 克，山甲 12 克，山慈菇 9 克，皂刺

9 克，枳壳 9 克，茯苓 12 克。水煎服。

2．肾虚型

主证：月经稀少或闭经，体瘦多毛，腰酸头昏，畏寒便溏，

舌质淡，苔薄白，脉沉细。

治则：温肾益精散结。

处方：左归丸加减。

熟地 12 克，鹿角胶 9 克(烊化)，菟丝子 12 克，复盆子 12

克，狗脊 9 克，葫芦巴 9 克，仙灵脾 12 克，黄精 15 克，夏枯草

15 克。水煎服。

第六节　经前期紧张症

经前及经期出现乳房胀痛、头痛头晕、烦躁失眠、胸胁作

region, edema, diarrhea, restless sleep and general malaise which appears before or during menstruation.

MAIN POINTS OF DIAGNOSIS:

1. All the above symptoms or some of them can occur before or during menstruation.

2. Physical examination shows no abnormal findings. Organic diseases are excluded through gynecological examination.

DIFFERENTIATION AND TREATMENT OF COMMON SYNDROMES

1. Stagnation of the Liver-*qi*

Main Symptoms and Signs: Premenstrual distension and fullness in the breasts, thelalgia, dizziness, headache, distending pain in the lower abdomen or involving the chest and hypochondrium, restlessness and tendency to anger, dark coloured tongue with white and thin fur, taut pulse.

Therapeutic Principle: Soothing the depressed liver to regulate the circulation of *qi*, promoting blood circulation to remove obstruction in the channels.

Recipe: Modified recipe of Bupleurum Powder for Relieving Liver-*qi*.

bupleurum root, *Radix Bupleuri*   9g
white peony root, *Radix Paeoniae Alba*   9g
nutgrass flatsedge rhizome, *Rhizoma Cyperi*   12g
Chinese angelica root, *Radix Angelicae Sinensis*   9g
cur uma root, *Radix Curcumae*   9g
Sichuan chinaberry fruit, *Fructus Meliae Toosendan*   12g
tangerine peel, *Pericapium Citri Reciculatae*   9g
bitter orange, *Fructus Aurantii*   9g
chuanxiong rhizome, *Rhizoma Ligustici Chuanxiong*   9g
rose, *Flos Rose Rugosae*   3g

All the above drugs are to be decocted in water for oral administration.

For those with a bitter taste in the mouth, add 9 grams of

胀、浮肿腹泻、夜寐不安、神疲乏力等一系列症状，称为"经前期紧张症"。

【诊断要点】

1. 经前及经期出现上述一系列症状或部分症状。

2. 全身检查无异常发现，妇科检查排除器质性病变。

【辨证论治】

1. 肝郁气滞型

主证：经前乳胀，乳头痛，头晕头痛，小腹胀痛，连及胸胁，烦躁易怒，舌质暗，苔薄白，脉弦。

治则：疏肝理气，活血通络。

处方：柴胡疏肝散加减。

柴胡9克，白芍9克，香附12克，当归9克，郁金9克，川楝子12克，陈皮9克，枳壳9克，川芎9克，玫瑰花3克。水煎服。

both moutan bark (*Cortex Moutan Radicis*) and 9 grams of capejasmine fruit (*Fructus Gardeniae*).

2. Deficiency of *Qi* and Blood in the Heart and Spleen

Main Symptoms and Signs: Premenstrual palpitation, restless sleep, lack of vitality with asthenia, cold extremeties, excessive thin clear leukorrhea, pale tongue with white fur, deep and thready pulse.

Therapeutic Principle: Nourishing the heart to calm the mind and reinforcing the spleen to remove dampness.

Recipe: Modified Decoction for Invigorating the Spleen and Nourishing the Heart.

dangshen, *Radix Codonopsis Pilosulae*　　9g

astragalus root, *Radix Astragali seu Hedysari*　　15g

Chinese angelica root, *Radix Angelicae Sinensis*　　9g

bighead atractylodes rhizome, *Rhizoma Atractylodis Macroce-*
　　phalae　　9g

poria with hostwood, *Poria cum Ligno Hospite*　　9g

polygala root, *Radix Polygalae*　　6g

longan arii, *Arillus Longan*　　9g

aucklandia root, *Radix Aucklandiae*　　3g

parched wild jujuba seed, *Semen Ziziphi Spinosae*　　9g

coix seed, *Semen Coicis*　　15g

alismatis rhizome, *Rhizoma Alismatis*　　9g

All the above drugs are to be decocted in water for oral administration.

3. *Yang* Insufficiency of Both the Spleen and Kidney

Main Symptoms and Signs: Premenstrual edema in the face and limbs, dizziness, bodily languor, drowsiness, loss of appetite, loose stool, abdominal distension, lassitude in the loins and legs, corpulent tongue with teeth marks on its margin, white and moist fur, deep and thready pulse.

Therapeutic Principle: Strengthening the spleen and warming the kidney to promote diuresis.

Recipe: Modified Decoction for Strengthening the Spleen

若口苦咽干者，加丹皮9克，山栀子9克。

2. 心脾两虚型

主证：经前心悸，夜寐不安，神疲乏力，四肢清冷，白带清

稀量多，舌质淡，苔白，脉沉细。

治则：养心安神，健脾利湿。

处方：归脾汤加减。

党参9克，黄芪15克，当归9克，白术9克，茯神9克，

远志6克，龙眼肉9克，木香3克，炒枣仁9克，薏苡仁15克，

泽泻9克。水煎服。

3. 脾肾阳虚型

主证：经前四肢、面目浮肿、头晕体倦，嗜睡，纳少便溏，

脘腹胀满，腰酸腿软，舌胖边有齿印，苔白润，脉沉细。

治则：健脾温肾利水。

and Reinforcing the Kidney.

dangshen, *Radix Codonopsis Pilosulae*   9g

bighead atractylodes rhizome, *Rhizoma Atractylodis Macro-cephalae*   9g

poria, *Poria*   9g

coix seed, *Semen Coicis*   15g

cibot rhizome, *Rhizoma Cibotii*   9g

morinda root, *Radix Morindae Officinalis*   9g

alismatis rhizome, *Rhizoma Alismatis*   9g

All the above drugs are to be decocted in water for oral administration.

Section 7
Climacteric Syndrome

Before or after menopause, women may have some symptoms associated with it, which may be serious or slight; long or short, or irregular. In modern medicine it is called climacteric syndrome, and in TCM it belongs to the category of *"jue jing qian hou zhu zheng"* (syndromes before or after menopause).

MAIN POINTS OF DIAGNOSIS:

1. Women near the time of menopause have delayed menstrual cycle, short in period, scanty in amount and then menopause; sometimes disorder of mentrual cycle, menostaxis, profuse menstruation and metrorrhagia or metrostaxis may occur.

2. There may be tidal fever with flushed face, or paroxysmal feverishness with sweating or tension and depression, or irritability and tendency to anger.

3. Physical examination shows no abnormal findings, atrophic changes of reproductive organs may be found through gynecological examination.

DIFFERENTIATION AND TREATMENT OF

处方：健固汤加减。

党参 9 克，白术 9 克，茯苓 9 克，薏苡仁 15 克，狗脊 9 克，

巴戟天 9 克，泽泻 9 克。水煎服。

第七节　更年期综合征

妇女在绝经前后，出现一些与绝经有关的征候，或轻或重，

或久或暂，参差出现，现代医学称为"更年期综合征"，中医则称

为"绝经前后诸证"。

【诊断要点】

1．妇女在近绝经年龄，月经周期延后，经期缩短，经量减

少，然后绝经；或出现周期紊乱，经期延长，经量增多，甚至崩

漏。

2．潮热面红，或轰热汗出，或紧张抑郁，或烦躁易怒。

3．体格检查无异常发现，妇科检查可见生殖器官有萎缩现

象。

COMMON SYNDROMES

1. Deficiency of the Kidney-*yin*

Main Symptoms and Signs: Dizziness, tinnitus, paroxysmal feverishness with sweating, dysphoria with feverish sensation in the chest, palms and soles, restlessness and tendency to anger, lassitude in loins and legs, preceded menstrual cycle or in irregularity of menstrual cycle with bright red colour and menorrhagia or scanty menstruation, red tongue with very little fur, thready and rapid pulse.

Therapeutic Principle: Nourishing the kidney to suppress the hyperative *yang*.

Recipe: Modified Decoction for Reinforcing Kidney-*yin*.

prepared rehmannia root, *Radix Rehmanniae Praeparata* 24g

Chinese yam, *Rhizoma Dioscoreae* 12g

wolfberry fruit, *Fructus Lycii* 12g

dogwood fruit, *Fructus Corni* 9g

parched white peony root, *Radix Paeoniae Alba* 12g

uncaria stem with hooks, *Ramulus Uncariae cum Uncis* 12g

tortoise plastron, *Plastrum Testudinis* 9g

human placenta, *Placenta Hominis* 12g

glossy privet fruit, *Fructus Ligustri Lucidi* 9g

eclipta, *Herba Ecliptae* 9g

All the above drugs are to be decocted in water for oral administration.

2. Deficiency of the Kidney-*yang*

Main Symptoms and Signs: Darkish complexion, soreness of waist, cold limbs, abdominal distension, loose stool, edema of the face and limbs, profuse menstrual flow with dark colour and clots, pale tongue with tooth marks on its margin.

Therapeutic Principle: Warming up the kidney to support *yang*, warming the middle-*jiao* to strengthen the spleen.

【辨证论治】

1. 肾阴虚型

主证：头晕目眩，耳鸣，轰热汗出，五心烦热，烦躁易怒，腰膝酸软，月经先期或先后不定，经色鲜红，量或多或少，舌质红，苔少，脉细数。

治则：滋肾潜阳。

处方：左归饮加减。

熟地24克，山药12克，枸杞12克，山萸肉9克，炒白芍12克，钩藤12克，龟板9克，紫河车12克，女贞子9克，旱莲草9克。水煎服。

2. 肾阳虚型

主证：面色晦暗，腰酸肢冷，腹胀便溏，面浮肢肿，经行量多，色暗有块，舌质淡，边有齿印，苔薄白，脉沉细。

治则：温肾扶阳，温中健脾。

Recipe: Modified combinative recipe of Kidney-*Yang*-Reinforcing Bolus and Bolus for Regulating the Function of Middle-*jiao*.

prepared rehmannia root, *Radix Rehmanniae Praeparata* 24g

dogwood fruit, *Fructus Corni* 9g

prepared aconite root, *Radix Aconiti Praeparata* 6g

cinnamon bark, *Cortex Cinnamomi* 6g

antler glue, *Colla Cornus Cervi* 9g (melted)

eucommia bark, *Cortex Eucommiae* 9g

dodder seed, *Semen Cuscutae* 9g

epimedium, *Herba Epimedii* 9g

dangshen, *Radix Codonopsis Pilosulae* 12g

bighead atractylodes rhizome, *Rhizoma Atractylodis Marcocephalae* 12g

dried ginger, *Rhizoma Zingiberis* 3g

prepared licorice root, *Radix Glycyrrhizae Praeparata* 12g

All the drugs are to be decocted in water except the antler glue which is melted in the finished decoction for oral administration.

In case of deficiency of both *yin* and *yang* in the kidney, use the modified Docoction of Curculigo and Epimedium together with Pill of Glossy Privet Fruit and Eclipta.

curculigo rhizome, *Rhizoma Curculiginis* 9g

epimedium, *Herba Epimedii* 9g

morinda root, *Radix Morindae Officinalis* 9g

glossy privet fruit, *Fructus Ligustri Lucidi* 9g

eclipta, *Herba Ecliptae* 9g

prepared rehmannia root, *Radix Rehmanniae Praeparata* 9g

Chinese angelica root, *Radix Angelicae Sinensis* 9g

anemarrhena rhizome, *Rhizoma Anemarrhenae* 9g

phellodendron bark, *Cortex Phellodendri* 9g

All the above drugs are to be decocted in water for oral

处方：右归丸合理中丸加减。

熟地24克，山茱肉9克，附子6克，肉桂6克，鹿角胶9

克(溶化服)，杜仲9克，菟丝子9克，仙灵脾9克，党参12克，

白术12克，干姜3克，炙甘草12克。水煎服。

若肾阴阳俱虚者，用二仙汤合二至丸加减：仙茅9克，仙灵

脾9克，巴戟天9克，女贞子9克，旱莲草9克，熟地9克，当

administration.

Section 8
Vulvovaginitis

Colpitis and vulvitis often exist simultaneously in women. Its main symptoms are pruritus vulvae and profuse leukorrhea, and its causes can be the stimulation of forieign bodies, bacterial or viral, trichomonal or mycotic infections; cervicitis or senile atrophic vulvovaginitis can also be the etiological factors.

MAIN POINTS OF DIAGNOSIS

1. There is serious pruritus in the vulva and vagina, even pain in severe cases. Sometimes the pain can spread around the anus, making the patients restless. Burning or stabbing pain may occur in the pudendum after scratching, sometimes accomplanied with the irritation symptoms of the bladder.

2. The leukorrhea is profuse in amount looking like pus in yellow colour, frothy rice-water, bean dregs or in intermixed white-yellow or red-yellow colour.

3. Examination shows hyperemia in the vulva and vaginal membrane. Pin-pointed hemorrhage and submucosal patchy bleeding can be seen, accompanied with local hemorrhage or erosion in severe cases.

4. Causative agents can be discovered by the examination of discharge.

DIFFERENTIATION AND TREATMENT OF COMMON SYNDROMES

1. Dampness and Heat in the Liver Channel

Main Symptoms and Signs: Pudendal pruritus or itching and pain in severe cases, restlessness, profuse leukorrhea with yellow colour looking like pus, or forthy rice-water, vexation and oppression in the chest, bitter taste in the mouth and

归9克，知母9克，黄柏9克。水煎服。

第八节　外阴阴道炎

妇女阴道与外阴炎症常同时存在，主要表现为阴痒及白带增多。其病因可为异物刺激，细菌或病毒、滴虫或霉菌感染，以及宫颈炎或老年萎缩性外阴阴道炎。

【诊断要点】

1. 外阴及阴道瘙痒不堪，甚则疼痛难忍，坐卧不安，有时可波及肛门周围，搔抓后阴部灼痛或刺痛，有时伴有膀胱刺激症状。

2. 带下增多，或色黄如脓，或呈泡沫米泔样，或呈渣样，或黄白、黄赤相间。

3. 检查外阴、阴道粘膜充血，可见针尖样出血点或粘膜下片状充血，严重时伴有局部出血或糜烂。

4. 分泌物检查可找到病原体。

【辨证论治】

1. 肝经湿热型

主证：阴部瘙痒，甚则痒痛，坐卧不安，带下量多，色黄如

anorexia, yellow and greasy fur of the tongue, and taut and rapid pulse.

Therapeutic Principle: Eliminating dampness and heat, and destroying pathogens to relieve itching.

Recipe: Yam Decoction for Removing Dampness with additional ingredients.

seven-lobed yam, *Rhizoma Dioscoreae Septemlobae*   9g
coix seed, *Semen Coicis*   30g
phellodendron bark, *Cortex Phellodendri*   9g
red poria, *Poria Rubra*   9g
moutan bark, *Cortex Moutan Radicis*   9g
oriental water plantain rhizome, *Rhizoma Alismatis*   9g
ricepaper pith, *Tetrapanacis*   9g
tale, *Talcum*   9g
atractylodes rhizome, *Rhizoma Atractylodis*   9g
flavescent sophora root, *Radix Sophorae Flavescentis*   9g
dittany bark, *Cortex Dictamni Radicis*   15g

All the above drugs are to be decocted in water for oral administration.

In cases with distending pain in the chest and hypochondrium, bitter taste and dry mouth, constipation, scanty dark urine, red tongue with yellow and thin fur, taut and rapid pulse, replace the above recipe with the Decoction of Gentian for Purging Liver-fire:

gentian root, *Radix Gentianae*   9g
capejasmine fruit, *Fructus Gardeniae*   9g
scutellaria root, *Radix Scutellariae*   9g
plantain seed, *Semen Plantaginis*   9g (wrapped in a piece of cloth before it is to be decocted)
armend clematis stem, *Caulis Clematidis Armendii*   3g
oriental water plantain rhizome, *Rhizoma Alismatis*   9g
dried rehmannia root, *Radix Rehmanniae*   12g
Chinese angelica root, *Radix Angelicae Sinensis*   9g
buplerum root, *Radix Bupleuri*   9g

脓，或呈泡沫米泔样，心烦胸闷，口苦纳差，苔黄腻，脉弦数。

治则：清热利湿，杀虫止痒。

处方：萆薢渗湿汤加味。

萆薢 9 克，苡仁 30 克，黄柏 9 克，赤茯苓 9 克，丹皮 9 克，

泽泻 9 克，通草 9 克，滑石 9 克，苍术 9 克，苦参 9 克，白藓皮

15 克。水煎服。

若胸胁胀痛、口苦而干、大便秘结、小便短赤、舌质红、苔

薄黄、脉弦数者，改用龙胆泻肝汤：龙胆草 9 克，山栀子 9 克，

黄芩 9 克，车前子 9 克（布包煎），木通 3 克，泽泻 9 克，生地 12

licorice root, *Radix Glycyrrhizae*   6g

The above drugs are to be decocted in water for oral administration.

2. *Yin*-deficiency of Both the Liver and Kidney

Main Symptoms and Signs: Dryness, burning and itching in the pudendal region, yellowish or even blood-like leukorrhea, dysphoria with feverish sensation in the chest, palms and soles, dizziness, reddish tongue with little fur, thready, rapid and weak pulse.

Therapeutic Principle: Nourishing *yin* to reduce pathogenic fire, regulating and tonifying the liver and kidney.

Recipe: Decoction of Anemarrhena, Phellodendren and Rehmannia with additional ingredients.

prepared rehmannia root, *Radix Rehmanniae Praeparata* 12g

dogwood fruit, *Fructus Corni*   9g

Chinese yam, *Rhizoma Dioscoreae*   15g

moutan bark, *Cortex Moutan Radicis*   9g

poria, *Poria*   9g

alismatis rhizome, *Rhizoma Alismatis*   9g

phellodendron bark, *Cortex Phellodendri*   9g

anemarrhena rhizome, *Rhizoma Anemarrhenae*   9g

All the above drugs are to be decocted in water for oral administration.

In addition, attention should be paid to local treatment, for which Cnidium Powder is often employed.

cnidium fruit, *Fructus Cnidii*   15g

flavescent sophora root, *Radix Sophorae Flavescentis*   15g

stemona root, *Radix Stemonae*   15g

pepertree, *Pericarpium Zanthoxyli*   9g

alum, *Alumen*   9g

Decoct the above drugs in water and use the decoction for pudendal fumigation and hip-bath once a day, 7–10 days as a course.

克，当归9克，柴胡9克，甘草6克。水煎服。

2．肝肾阴虚型

主证：阴部干涩，灼热瘙痒，或带下量少色黄，甚则血样，五心烦热，头晕目眩，舌红少苔，脉细数无力。

治则：滋阴降火，调补肝肾。

处方：知柏地黄汤加味。

熟地黄12克，山茱萸9克，山药15克，丹皮9克，茯苓9克，泽泻9克，黄柏9克，知母9克。水煎服。

此外，阴痒还应重视局部治疗，常用蛇床子散。处方：蛇床子15克，苦参15克，百部15克，川椒9克，明矾9克。以上药煎汤熏洗局部并坐浴，每日1次，7～10次为1疗程。

Section 9
Pelvic Inflammation

Pelvic inflammation is an inflammation occurring in internal genital organs (including uterus, fallopian tubes and ovaries), pelvic connective tissues and pelvic peritoneum. Clinically, it is further divided into acute pelvic inflammation and chronic pelvic inflammation. This disease in TCM pertains to the categories *"re ru xueshi"* (invasion of the blood chamber by heat), *"dai xia"* (leukorrhagia), *"Zheng jia"* (mass in the abdomen), etc.

1. Acute Pelvic Inflammation
MAIN POINTS OF DIAGNOSIS:

1) Patients with acute pelvic inflammation often have high fever, aversion to cold, headache, pain in the lower abdomen, and profuse leukorrhea looking like pus with a fetid smell.

2. The body temperature can be high up to 39—40°C, showing the appearance of on acute illness.

3) Patients have tenderness or rebound tenderness in the lower abdomen, sometimes masses can be felt.

4) Vaginal examination reveals the hyperemia in the vagina and uterine cervix, much secretion looking like pus, touching pain in the neck of uterus. The uterus is a bit larger and tender. Two appendage areas are thickened and tender or masses can be felt.

DIFFERENTIATION AND TREATMENT OF COMMON SYNDROMES

1. Damp-heat Excess in Interior
Main Symptoms and Signs: High fever, headache, pain and tenderness in the lower abdomen, profuse and fetid leukorrhea which is yellow in colour or red and white intermin-

第九节　　盆腔炎

盆腔炎是指内生殖器官(包括子宫、输卵管及卵巢)、盆腔结缔组织及盆腔腹膜的炎症，临床上一般分为急性盆腔炎及慢性盆腔炎两种。本病属中医"热入血室"、"带下"、"癥瘕"等范畴。

1. 急性盆腔炎

【诊断要点】

1）急性盆腔炎常有高热，恶寒，头痛，下腹疼痛，带下量多，呈脓性，有秽臭。

2）体温高达 39～40℃，呈急性病容。

3）下腹压痛及反跳痛，有时可触及包块。

4）阴道检查见阴道及子宫颈充血，脓样分泌物多，宫颈举痛，子宫略大，压痛，两附件区增厚，压痛，或可触及包块。

【辨证论治】

1）湿热壅盛型

主证：高热，头痛，下腹痛拒按，带下量多秽臭，**色黄或赤**

gled, dry mouth and desire for drink, nausea and anorexia, red tongue with yellow and greasy fur, slippery and rapid pulse or full and rapid pulse.

Therapeutic Principle: Clearing away heat and toxic material and promoting diuresis and pus discharge.

Recipe: Anti-infective Decoction of Honeysuckle, Forsythia, Sargentgloryvine and Partrinia.

honeysuckle flower, *Flos Lonicerae*	30g
forsythia fruit, *Fructus Forsythiae*	15g
sargentgloryvine, *Caulis Sargentodoxae*	30g
partrinia, *Herba Partriniae*	30g
coix seed, *Semen Coicis*	30g
capejasmine fruit, *Fructus Gardeniae*	9g
moutan bark, *Cortex Moutan Radicis*	9g
red peony root, *Radix Paeoniae Rubra*	12g
Sichuan chinaberry, *Fructus Meliae Toosendan*	9g
corydalis tuber, *Radix Corydalis*	9g
peach kernel, *Semen Persicae*	9g
prepared myrrh, *Myrrha Praeparata*	4.5g
prepared frankincense, *Resian Olibani Praeparata*	4.5g

All the above drugs are to be decocted in water for oral administration twice a day.

In case of constipation, add 3—6 grams of rhubarb (*Radix et Rhizoma Rhei*) to clear away heat and relieve constipation by purgation; 6 grams of aucklandia (*Radix Aucklandiae*) and 6 grams of immature bitter orange (*Fructus Aurantii Immaturus*) are used to relieve the stagnation of *qi* in case of diarrhea but unsmooth defecation. For those with profuse and fetid leukorrhea, 9 grams of each phellodendron bark (*Cortex Phellodendron*) oriental wormwood (*Herba Artemisiae Capillaris*) and poria (*Poria*) should be used to clear away heat and promote diuresis.

2. Accumulation of Stagnant Toxin-heat in Interior

Main Symptoms and Signs: Residual fever or undulating

白相兼，口干喜饮，恶心纳差，舌质红，苔黄腻，脉滑数或洪数。

治则：清热解毒，利湿排脓。

处方：银翘红酱解毒汤。

银花30克，连翘15克，红藤30克，败酱草30克，薏苡仁30克，栀子9克，丹皮9克，赤芍12克，川楝子9克，元胡9克，桃仁9克，制乳没各4.5克。水煎服，每日服2剂。

若大便秘结者，加大黄3～6克，以清热泻下；大便溏而不爽者，加木香、枳实各6克，以行气滞；带下量多、臭秽者，加黄柏9克，茵陈9克，茯苓9克，以清热利湿。

2）瘀毒内结型

主证：余热未去或低热起伏，神疲肢软，下腹胀痛拒按，带

low fever, lack of vitality and myasthenia of limbs, distending pain and tenderness in the lower abdomen, profuse, yellow, thick and foul leukorrhea, red tongue with yellow or greasy fur, thready and rapid pulse.

Therapeutic Principle: Removing blood stasis and lumps, dissipating the accumulation of stagnant toxin-heat.

Recipe: Burreed and Zedoary Decoction for Removing Stagnancy.

burreed tuber, *Rhizoma Sparganii*   9g
zedoary, *Rhizoma Zedoariae*   9g
red sage root, *Radix Salviae NMiltiorrhizae*   15g
corydalis tuber, *Rhizoma Corydalis*   9g
red peony root, *Radix Paeoniae Rubra*   9g
moutan bark, *Cortex Moutan Radicis*   9g
peach kernel, *Semen Persicae*   9g
coix seed, *Semen Coicis*   15g
sargentgloryvine, *Caulis Sargentodoxae*   30g
partinia, *Herba Partiniae*   30g

All the above drugs are to be decocted in water for oral administration.

2. Chronic Pelvic Inflammation

MAIN POINTS OF DIAGNOSIS

1) There is no obvious constitutional symptoms but only a feeling of dragging distending pain in the lower abdomen, lumbosacral aching or sometimes dragging and distending discomfort in the anus.

2) Frequency of micturition, profuse leukorrhea, disorder of menstruation, dysmenorrhea and sterility may be associated.

3) Gynecological examination shows much secretion, retroversion of uterus, adnexal thickening and tenderness, or cystic form masses or lump-like things can be felt.

DIFFERENTIATION AND TREATMENT OF COMMON SYNDROMES

1. Blood Stasis due to Stagnancy of *Qi*

下黄稠有臭味，舌质红，苔黄或腻，脉细数。

治则：破瘀散结，清热解毒。

处方：棱莪消积汤。

三棱9克，莪术9克，丹参15克，延胡索9克，赤芍9克，丹皮9克，桃仁9克，薏苡仁15克，红藤、败酱草各30克。水煎服，每日服2剂。

2. 慢性盆腔炎

【诊断要点】

1）全身症状多不明显，主要表现为下腹坠胀疼痛、腰骶酸痛，有时肛门坠胀不适。

2）可伴有尿频、白带增多、月经异常、痛经及不孕。

3）妇科检查可见阴道分泌物增多、子宫后倾，附件区可有组织增厚、压痛，或触及囊性包块或片块状物。

【辨证论治】

1）气滞血瘀型

Main Symptoms and Signs: Distending and dragging pain in the lower abdomen, pain in the lumbosacral region, dragging and distending sensation in the anus, aggravated by sexual intercourse, defecation and overwork, continuous leukorrhagia, purplish red tongue with thin and greasy fur, taut and thready pulse.

Therapeutic Principle: Promoting blood circulation, removing blood stasis and regulating the flow of *qi* to alleviate pain.

Recipe: Decoction for Chronic Pelvic Inflammation.

safflower, *Flos Carthami*   9g
red sage root, *Radix Salviae Miltiorrhizae*   15g
red peony root, *Radix Paeoniae Rubra*   12g
pueraria root, *Radix Puerariae*   12g
prepared nutgrass flatsedge rhizome, *Rhizoma Cyperi*   12g
lindera root, *Radix Linderae*   6g
aucklandia root, *Radix Aucklandiae*   6g
corydalis tuber, *Rhizoma Corydalis*   12g
common fennel fruit, *Fructus Feoniculi*   3g
cinnamon twig, *Ramulus Cinnamomi*   9g
moutan bark, *Cortex Moutan Radicis*   9g
alismatis rhizome, *Rhizoma Alismatis*   9g

All the above drugs are to be decocted in water for oral administration.

2. Blood Stasis due to Accumulation of Cold

Main Symptoms and Signs: Distending and dragging pain in the lower abdomen and lumbosacral region aggravated by cold, clear and cold leukorrhagia, normal tongue with thin white fur, deep and thready or deep and uneven pulse.

Therapeutic Principle: Dispersing cold to relieve pain and promoting blood circulation to remove blood stasis.

Recipe: Modified Cinnamon Twig and Poria Pill.

cinnamon twig, *Ramulus Cinnamomi*   9g

主证：下腹坠胀疼痛，腰骶疼痛，肛门坠胀感，性生活、大便及过劳时加重，白带连绵不断，舌紫暗，脉弦细。

治则：活血化瘀，理气止痛。

处方：慢盆汤。

红花9克，丹参15克，赤芍12克，葛根12克，制香附12克，乌药6克，木香6克，延胡索12克，小茴香3克，桂枝9克，丹皮9克，泽泻9克。水煎服。

2）寒凝血滞型

主证：下腹腰骶坠胀疼痛，遇寒则重，白带清冷，舌质正常，苔薄白，脉沉细或沉涩。

治则：散寒止痛，活血化瘀。

poria, *Poria*   **9g**

peach kernel, *Semen Persicae*   9g

moutan bark, *Cortex Moutan Radicis*   9g

nutgrass flatsedge rhizome, *Rhizoma Cyperi*   9g

red sage root, *Radix Salviae Miltiorrhizae*   15g

red peony root, *Radix Paeoniae Rubra*   9g

white peony root, *Radix Paeoniae Alba*   9g

corydalis tuber, *Rhizoma Corydalis*   9g

forsythia fruit, *Fructus Forsythiae*   9g

myrrh, *Myrrha*   9g

chicken's gizzard-membrane, *Endothelium Corneum Gigeriae Galli*   9g

All the above drugs are to be decocted in water for oral administration.

Section 10
Endometriosis

Endometriosis refers to the presence of endometrial tissue in sites outside the endometrium. When this tissue is found in the myometrium, it is called endometriosis interna, while endometriosis externa is the term used when the condition occurs in other sites which include the rectovaginal pouches, ovaries, the uterotsacral ligaments, etc. Its clinical manifestations are mainly represented by progressive periodical lower abdominal pain. This term is not employed in TCM, pertaining mainly to the categories of *"tong jing"* (dysmenorrhea), *"bu yun"* (sterility), *"yue jing butiao"* (menoxenia), *"zheng jia"* (mass in the abdomen), etc.

MAIN POINTS OF DIAGNOSIS

1. Dysmenorrhea: It is secondary or progressive dysmenorrhea and gradually gets worse year after year, sometimes accompanied with periodical irritation symptoms of blad-

处方：桂枝茯苓丸化裁。

桂枝 9 克，茯苓 9 克，桃仁 9 克，丹皮 9 克，香附 9 克，丹参 15 克，赤白芍各 9 克，元胡 9 克，连翘 9 克，没药 9 克，鸡内金 9 克。水煎服。

第十节　子宫内膜异位症

当子宫内膜组织出现在子宫腔面以外部位时，称子宫内膜异位症。如子宫内膜异位至子宫肌层时，称内在性子宫内膜异位症或子宫肌腺病；异位至宫体以外部位，称外在性子宫内膜异位症，常见于直肠阴道陷凹、卵巢、子宫骶骨韧带等部位。临床以周期下腹痛且进行性加重为主要表现。中医文献中无子宫内膜异位症这一病名，多属"痛经"、"不孕"、"月经不调"、"癥瘕"等范畴。

【诊断要点】

1. 痛经：为继发性和进行性痛经，逐年加重，或伴有周期

der and rectum.

2. Menoxenia: Profuse menstruation and menostaxis are common.

3. Sterility: It is caused by endocrinous disorder and limitation of oviductal peristalsis resulting from adhesion.

4. Gynecological examination shows the uterine enlargement, fixation, adnexal masses, and nodular thickening of the utero-sarcal ligaments and rectovaginal pouch which are tender when touched.

5. Under peritoneoscope, the focus is an implanted one which is purplish blue, brown or black in color, pathologic changes often occur in utero-sacral ligaments, ovaries, rectovaginal pouches and reflected peritoneum of bladder. Adhesion is often found in pelvis. Chocolate coloured mucus is drawn from the ovaries.

DIFFERENTIATION AND TREATMENT OF COMMON SYNDROMES

1. Blood Stasis due to Stagnancy of *Qi*

Main Symptoms and Signs: Severe pain in the lower abdomen before, during or after menstruation accompanied with dragging pain in the lumbosacral region and anus, tenderness and nodules in the posterior fronix or isthmus of uterus, purplish red tongue with white and thin fur, taut and thready pulse.

Therapeutic Principle: Promoting blood circulation to remove blood stasis and regulating the flow of *qi* to alleviate pain.

Recipe: Dysmenorrhea Recipe.

stir-fried Chinese angelica root, *Radix Angelicae Sinensis* 9g

chuanxiong rhizome, *Rhizoma Ligustici Chuanxiong*   4.5g

red sage root, *Radix Salviae Miltiorrhizae*   9g

cyathula root, *Radix Cyathulae*   9g

red peony root, *Radix Paeoniae Rubra*   9g

性膀胱刺激症状和周期性直肠刺激症状。

2．月经失调：以月经增多及经期延长为多见。

3．不孕：由于内分泌失调及粘连所致的输卵管蠕动受限而不孕。

4．妇科检查时可有子宫增大、固定，附件区有包块感，骶韧带及后凹陷处有大小不等小硬结节，触痛明显。

5．在腹腔镜直观下，内异病灶通常呈紫兰色、棕色或黑色的种植灶，病变多累及子宫骶韧带、卵巢、子宫直肠凹及膀胱反褶腹膜，盆腔内常见粘连，卵巢内抽出巧克力样粘稠的液体。

【辨证论治】

1．气滞血瘀型

主证：经期或行经前后下腹痛重，常伴腰骶及肛门坠痛，阴道后穹窿或子宫峡部触痛结节，舌紫暗，苔薄白，脉弦细。

治则：活血化瘀，理气止痛。

处方：痛经方。

炒当归9克，川芎4.5克，丹参9克，川牛膝9克，赤芍9

cinnamon twig, *Ramulus Cinnamomi*　4.5g

prepared nutgrass flatsedge rhizome, *Rhizoma Cyperi*　9g

corydalis tuber, *Radix Corydalis*　9g

dragon's blood, *Resina Draconis*　3g

myrrh, *Myrrha*　4.5g

Wonderful Powder for Relieving Blood Stagnation (wrapped in a piece of cloth before it is decocted)　15g

All the above drugs are to be decocted in water for oral administration.

2. Deficiency of the Kidney with Blood Stasis

Main Symptoms and Signs: Pain in the lower abdomen before, during or after menstruation, menorrhagia, tenderness and nodules in the posterior fornix or isthmus of uterus, dark and pale tongue with thin and white fur, taut and thready or deep and uneven pulse.

Therapeutic Principle: Promoting blood circulation to remove blood stasis and reinforcing the kidney to arrest hemorrhage.

Recipe: Metrorrhagia Recipe.

stir-fried Chinese angelica root, *Radix Angelicae Sinensis*　9g

cat-tail pollen, *Pollen Typhae*　15g (wrapped in a piece of cloth before it is decocted)

achyranthes root, *Radix Achyranthis Bidentatae*　9g

red sage root, *Radix Salviae Miltiorrhizae*　6g

red peony root, *Radix Paeoniae Rubra*　9g

white peony root, *Radix Paeoniae Alba*　9g

prepared nutgrass flatsedge rhizome, *Rhizoma Cyperi Praeparata*　9g

ophicalcite, *Ophicalcitum*　15g

carbonized rhubarb, *Radix et Rhizoma Rhei Praeparata*　9g

dragon's blood, *Resina Draconis*　3g

All the above drugs are to be decocted in water for oral administration.

3. Blood Stasis due to Accumulation of Cold

克，桂枝4.5克，制香附9克，延胡索9克，血竭3克，没药4.5克，失笑散（布包煎）15克。水煎服。

2．肾虚血瘀型

主证：经期或行经前后下腹痛，月经过多，阴道后穹窿或子宫峡部触痛结节，舌暗淡，苔薄白，脉弦细或沉涩。

治则：活血化瘀，补肾止血。

处方：血崩方。

炒当归9克，生蒲黄（包）15克，怀牛膝9克，丹参6克，赤白芍各9克，制香附9克，花蕊石15克，熟军炭9克，血竭3克。水煎服。

3．寒凝血瘀型

Main Symptoms and Signs: Cold-pain in the lower abdomen during, before or after menstruation, aversion to cold, cold limbs, soreness of the waist and asthenia, tenderness and nodules in the posterior fornix and isthmus of uterus, dark tongue with thin white fur, deep and slow pluse.

Therapeutic Principle: Promoting blood circulation to remove blood stasis, dispersing cold to resolve lumps.

Recipe: Recipe for Resolving Lumps.

stir-fried Chinese angelica root, *Radix Angelicae Sinensis* 9g

red sage root, *Radix Salviae Miltiorrhizae*   12g

red peony root, *Radix Paeoniae Rubra*   9g

cyathula root, *Radix Cyathulae*   9g

prepared nutgrass flatsedge rhizome, *Rhizoma Cyperi Praeparata*   9g

cinnamon twig, *Ramulus Cinnamomi*   3g

seaweed, *Sargassum*   9g

stir-fried pangolin scales, *Squama Manitis*   9g

honeylocust thorn, *Sprina Gleditsiae*   12g

dragon's blood, *Resina Draconis*   3g

zedoary, *Rhizoma Zedoariae*   12g

All the above drugs are to be decocted in water for oral administration.

Section 11
Leukorrhagia

Leukorrhagia refers to profuse leukorrhea with abnormal colour, quality and smell, accompanied with constitutional or local symptoms.

MAIN POINTS OF DIAGNOSIS

1. Profuse and continuous discharge of leukorrhea.

2. Abnormality in the colour, quality and smell of leukorrhea.

主证：经期或行经前后下腹冷痛，畏寒肢冷，腰酸乏力，阴道后穹窿或子宫峡部触痛结节，舌质暗，苔薄白，脉沉迟。

治则：活血化瘀，散寒消结。

处方：散结方。

炒当归9克，丹参12克，赤芍9克，川牛膝9克，制香附9克，桂枝3克，海藻9克，炙穿山甲片9克，皂角刺12克，血竭3克，莪术12克。水煎服。

第十一节 带 下 病

带下量多，色、质、臭气异常，伴全身或局部症状者，称带下病。

【诊断要点】

1. 妇女阴道内流出的白带量多，绵绵不断。

2. 带下之色、质、气味异常。

3. Accompanied with constitutional or local symptoms.

DIFFERENTIATION AND TREATMENT OF COMMON SYNDROMES

1. Leukorrhagia due to Deficiency of the Spleen

Main Symptoms and Signs: Whitish or yellowish, continuous sticky leukorrhagia, but without foul smell, pale or sallow complexion, lack of vitality, lack of appetite, pale tongue with white or greasy fur, moderate and weak pulse.

Therapeutic Principle: Strengthening the spleen and replenishing qi, lifting yang and removing dampness.

Recipe: Decoction for Curing Leukorrhagia.

bighead atractylodes rhizome, *Rhizoma Atractylodis Macrocephalae* 9g

Chinese yam, *Rhizoma Dioscoreae* 15g

ginseng, *Radix Ginseng* 6g

white peony root, *Radix Paeoniae Alba* 9g

atractylodes rhizome, *Rhizoma Atractylodis* 9g

tangerine peel, *Pericarpium Citri Reticulatae* 9g

carbonized schizonepeta, *Herba Schizonepetae* 6g

bupleurum root, *Radix Bupleuri* 9g

plantain seed, *Semen Plantaginis* (wrapped in a piece of cloth before it is decocted) 9g

licorice root, *Radix Glycyrrhizae* 6g

All the above drugs are to be decocted in water for oral administration.

2. Leukorrhagia due to Deficiency of the Kidney

Main Symptoms and Signs: Leukorrhea which is lucid, cold, thin and profuse, and is discharged continuously, soreness in the waist and coldness in the abdomen, pale tongue with white and thin fur, deep and slow pulse.

Therapeutic Principle: Warming yang and tonifying the kidney to stop leukorrhagia with astringents.

Recipe: Tonifying Interior Pill.

pilose antler, *Cornu Cervi Pantotrichum* 1.5g

3. 伴有全身或局部症**状。**

【辨证论治】

1. 脾虚带下

主证：带下色白或淡黄，质粘稠，无臭气，绵绵不断，面色㿠白或萎黄，神疲纳少，舌质淡，苔白或腻，脉缓弱。

治则：健脾益气，升阳除湿。

处方：完带汤。

白术9克，山药15克，人参6克，白芍9克，苍术9克，陈皮9克，芥穗炭6克，柴胡9克，车前子9克(布包煎)，甘草6克。水煎服。

2. 肾虚带下

主证：白带清冷，量多，质稀薄，淋漓不断，腰酸腹冷，舌质淡，苔薄白，脉沉迟。

治则：温阳益肾，固涩止带。

处方：内补丸。

dodder seed, *Semen Cuscutae*   9g

flatstem milkvetch seed, *Semen Astragali Complnaati*   9g

astragalus root, *Radix Astragali seu Hedysari*   15g

cinnamon bark, *Cortex Cinnamomi*   4.5g

mantis egg-case, *Oötheca Mnatidis*   9g

desertliving cistanche, *Herba Cistanchis*   9g

prepared aconite root, *Radix Aconiti Praeparata*   6g

tribulus fruit, *Fructus Tribuli*   9g

aster root, *Radix Asteris*   6g

All the above drugs, except the first one which should be prepared into powder and mixed with the finished decoction, are to be decocted in water for oral administration.

3. Leukorrhagia due to Dampness-toxin

Main Symptoms and Signs: Excessive pus-like leukorrhea yellow or green in colour, or mixed with blood, or turbid like rice-water, with fetid smell, or like bean-curd dregs, vaginal itching, bitter mouth and dry throat, scanty dark urine, red tongue with yellow and greasy fur, rapid or slippery rapid pulse.

Therapeutic Principle: Clearing away heat and toxic material and removing dampness to stop leukorrhagia.

Recipe: Recipe for Stopping Leukorrhagia.

umbellate pore fungus, *Polyporus Umbellatus*   9g

poria, *Poria*   9g

plantain seed, *Semen Plantaginis*   9g (wrapped in a piece of cloth)

alismatis rhizome, *Rhizoma Alismatis*   9g

oriental wormwood, *Herba Artemisiae Capillaris*   9g

red peony root, *Radix Paeoniae Rubra*   9g

moutan bark, *Cortex Moutan Radicis*   9g

phellodendron bark, *Cortex Phellodendri*   9g

capejasmine fruit, *Fructus Gardeniae*   9g

achyranthes root, *Radix Achyranthis Bidentatae*   9g

All the above drugs are to be decocted for oral administration.

鹿茸 1.5 克(冲)，菟丝子 9 克，潼蒺藜 9 克，黄芪 15 克，肉

桂 4.5 克，桑螵蛸 9 克，肉苁蓉 9 克，制附子 6 克，白蒺藜 9 克，

紫菀 6 克。水煎服。

3. 湿毒带下

主证：带下量多，色黄绿如脓，或夹血液，或浑浊如米泔，

有秽臭气，或如豆腐渣样，阴中瘙痒，口苦咽干，小便短赤，舌

质红，苔黄腻，脉数或滑数。

治则：清热解毒，除湿止带。

处方：止带方。

猪苓 9 克，茯苓 9 克，车前子 9 克(布包煎)，泽泻 9 克，茵

陈 9 克，赤芍 9 克，丹皮 9 克，黄柏 9 克，栀子 9 克，牛膝 9 克。

水煎服。

Section 12
Sterility

Primary sterility means that married women, who live together with their spouse with normal genital functions for over two years, fail to be pregnant without contraception. And secondary sterility refers to the fact that women fail to be pregnant over two years after previous delivery or miscarriage, without contraception.

MAIN POINTS OF DIAGNOSIS

Women who are unable to be pregnant for 2 years after marriage, or after the previous pregnancy, with normal intercourses and without contraception, can be considered to have sterility provided that her husband has normal genital function.

DIFFERENTIATION AND TREATMENT OF COMMON SYNDROMES

1. Deficiency of the Kidney

Main Symptoms and Signs: Sterility long after marriage, delayed menstruation, little and pale menstrual blood, dark and gloomy complexion, lassitude in loins and legs, sexual hypoesthesia, pale tongue with white fur, deep and thready or deep and slow pulse.

Therapeutic Principle: Warming the kidney and nourishing the liver, regulating and tonifying the *chong* and *ren* channels.

Recipe: Conceptive Pill with additional ingredients.

ginseng, *Radix Ginseng*   6g

bighead atractylodes rhizome, *Rhizoma Atractylodis Macrocephalae*   9g

poria, *Poria*   9g

第十二节 不孕症

女子结婚后，夫妇同居两年以上，配偶生殖功能正常，未避孕而不受孕者，称"原发性不孕"。如曾生育或流产后，未避孕而又两年以上不再受孕者，称"继发性不孕"。

【诊断要点】

结婚两年以上，或曾孕育后二年以上，夫妇同居，配偶生殖功能正常，未避孕而不受孕者，可诊为不孕症。

【辨证论治】

1. 肾虚型

主证：婚久不孕，月经后期，量少色淡，面色晦暗，腰酸腿软，性欲淡漠，舌淡苔白，脉沉细或沉迟。

治则：温肾养肝，调补冲任。

处方：毓麟珠加味。

人参6克，白术9克，茯苓9克，白芍9克，川芎9克，熟

white peony root, *Radix Paeoniae Alba*   9g

chuanxiong rhizome, *Rhizoma Ligustici Chuanxiong*   9g

prepared rehmannia root, *Radix Rehmanniae Praeparata* 12g

Chinese angelica root, *Radix Angelicae Sinensis*   9g

prepared licorice root, *Radix Glycyrrhizae Praeparata*   6g

dodder seed, *Semen Cuscutae*   9g

eucommia bark, *Cortex Eucommiae*   9g

deglued antler powder, *Cornu Cervi Pantotrichum*   9g

pricklyash peel, *Pericarpium Zanthoxyli*   1.5g

human placenta, *Placenta Hominis*   12g

red sage root, *Radix Salviae Miltiorrhizae*   15g

nutgrass flatsedge rhizome, *Rhizoma Cyperi*   9g

All the above drugs are to be decocted in water for oral administration.

2. Stagnation of the Liver-*qi*

Main Symptoms and Signs: Sterility long after marriage, irregular menstrual cycle, abdominal pain before menstruation, impeded menstrual flow, scanty menstrual blood with dark colour, fullness sensation in the breast prior to menstruation, irritability and tendency to anger, normal or dark red tongue with white and thin tongue coating, and taut pulse.

Therapeutic Principle: Soothing the liver to regulate the circulation of liver-*qi*

Recipe: Conceptive Decoction by Soothing the Liver.

Chinese angelica root, *Radix Angelicae Sinensis*   9g

bighead atractylodes rhizome, *Rhizoma Atractylodis Macrocephalae*   9g

white peony root, *Radix Paeoniae Alba*   15g

poria, *Poria*   9g

moutan bark, *Cortex Moutan Radicis*   9g

nutgrass flatsedge rhizome, *Rhizoma Cyperi*   9g

trichosanthes root, *Radix Trichosanthis*   9g

All the above drugs are to be decocted in water for oral

地 12 克，当归 9 克，炙甘草 6 克，菟丝子 9 克，杜仲 9 克，鹿

角霜 9 克，川椒 1.5 克，紫河车 12 克，丹参 15 克，香附 9 克。

水煎服。

2. 肝郁型

主证：婚久不孕，经期先后不定，经前腹痛，行而不畅，量

少色暗，经前乳胀，烦躁易怒，舌质正常或暗红，苔薄白，脉

弦。

治则：疏肝解郁。

处方：开郁种玉汤。

当归 9 克，白术 9 克，白芍 15 克，茯苓 9 克，丹皮 9 克，香

administration.

3. Phlegm-dampness

Main Symptoms and Signs: Sterility long after marriage, obesity, delayed menstrual cycle, or even amenorrhea in severe cases, excessive and sticky leukorrhea, pallor, dizziness, palpitation, fullness in the chest, nausea, white and greasy tongue coating, and slippery pulse.

Therapeutic Principle: Eliminating dampness and resolving phlegm.

Recipe: Modified recipe of Pill for Opening the Uterus.

prepared pinellia tuber, *Rhizoma Pinelliae Praeparata* 9g

atractylodes rhizome, *Rhizoma Atractylodis* 9g

nutgrass flatsedge rhizome, *Rhizoma Cyperi* 9g

medicated leaven, *Massa Fermentata Medicinalis* 9g

poria, *Poria* 9g

tangerine peel, *Pericarpium Citri Reticulatae* 9g

chuanxiong rhizome, *Rhizoma Ligustici Chuanxiong* 9g

seaweed *Sargassum* 9g

Japanese sea tangle, *Thallus Laminariae* 9g

grass-leaved sweetflag rhizome, *Rhizoma Acori Graminei* 9g

All the above drugs are to be decocted in water for oral administration.

Section 13
Colporrhagia During Pregnancy and
Threatened Abortion

The condition in which there is a small amount of vaginal bleeding during pregnancy without lumbar soreness and abdominal pain is described as *"tai lou"* (colporrhagia during pregnancy); while the condition in which there are lumbar soreness, abdominal pain or distension in the lower abdomen with a small amount of vaginal bleeding is referred to as *"tai*

附9克，花粉9克。水煎服。

3．痰湿型

主证：婚久不孕，形体肥胖，经行延后，甚或闭经，带下量多，质粘稠，面色㿠白，头晕心悸，胸闷泛恶，苔白腻，脉滑。

治则：燥湿化痰。

处方：启宫丸加味。

制半夏9克，苍术9克，香附9克，神曲9克，茯苓9克，陈皮9克，川芎9克，海藻9克，昆布9克，石菖蒲9克。水煎服。

第十三节　胎漏、胎动不安

妊娠期阴道少量出血，时下时止而无腰酸、腹痛者，称为"胎漏"。若妊娠期仅有腰酸、腹痛或下腹坠胀，或伴有少量阴道

dong bu an" (threatened abortion). Both of the two conditions are the premonition of fetal abortion or miscarriage.

MAIN POINTS OF DIAGNOSIS:

1. The clinical manifestations of colporrhagia during pregnancy are a small amount of vaginal bleeding without lumbar soreness and abdominal pain. Pregnancy test shows positive.

2. Clinically threatened abortion manifests lumbar soreness, abdominal pain or dragging distension in the lower abdomen, but not severe; occasionally accompanied with a small amount of vaginal bleeding. Pregnancy test shows positive.

DIFFERENTIATION AND TREATMENT OF COMMON SYNDROMES

1. Deficiency of the Kidney

Main Symptoms and Signs: Vaginal bleeding with the blood darkish in colour during pregnancy, soreness in the waist, dragging pain in the abdomen, or accompanied with dizziness, tinnitus, or with history of several abortions, pale tongue with white fur, deep and slippery pulse especially weak at *chi* site.

Therapeutic Principle: Reinforcing the kidney to prevent abortion and invigorating *qi* as subsidiary treatment.

Recipe: Miscarriage Prevention Bolus with additional ingredients.

　　　dodder seed, *Semen Cuscutae*　　15g
　　　loranthus mulberry mistletoe, *Ramulus Loranthi*　　18g
　　　dipsacus root, *Radix Dipsaci*　　15g
　　　donkey-hide gelatin, *Colla Corii Asini*　　12g (melted)
　　　dangshen, *Radix Codonopsis Pilosulae*　　12g
　　　bighead atractylodes rhizome, *Rhizoma Atractylodis Macrocephalae*　　9g

All the above drugs are to be decocted in water, except the donkey-hide gelatin which is to be melted and mixed

出血者，称为"胎动不安"。胎漏与胎动不安常是堕胎、小产的先兆，西医称之为"先兆流产"。

【诊断要点】

1. 胎漏临床表现为出血量少，不伴腰酸、小腹坠胀作痛，妊娠试验阳性。

2. 胎动不安的临床表现为腰酸、腹痛或下腹坠胀，但不甚重，或同时有少量阴道出血，妊娠试验阳性。

【辨证论治】

1. 肾虚型

主证：妊娠期阴道少量下血，色淡暗，腰酸坠痛，或伴头晕耳鸣，或曾屡次坠胎，舌淡苔白，脉沉滑尺弱。

治则：固肾安胎，佐以益气。

处方：寿胎丸加味。

菟丝子15克，桑寄生18克，川断15克，阿胶12克（烊

with the finished decoction, for oral administration.

2. Insufficiency of both *Qi* and Blood

Main Symptoms and Signs: A modicum of vaginal bleeding during pregnancy with reddish and thin blood, dragging and distension in the waist and abdomen accompanied with spiritlessness and lassitude in the limbs, pale complexion, palpitation, shortness of breath, pale tongue with white and thin fur, thready and slippery pulse.

Therapeutic Principle: Invigorating *qi* and enriching the blood, and reinforcing the kidney to prevent abortion.

Recipe: Modified Decoction for Preventing Abortion.

ginseng, *Radix Ginseng*   6g

eucommia bark, *Cortex Eucommiae*   9g

white peony root, *Radix Paeoniae Alba*   9g

prepared rehmannia root, *Radix Rehmanniae Praeparata* 12g

bighead atractylodes rhizome, *Rhizoma Atractylodis Macrocephalae*   9g

tangerine peel, *Pericarpium Citri Reticulatae*   9g

prepared licorice root, *Radix Glycyrrhizae Praeparata*   6g

astragalus root, *Radix Astragali seu Hedysari*   15g

donkey-hide gelatin, *Colla Corii Asini*   30g (melted)

All the above drugs are to be decocted in water, except the donkey-hide gelatin which is to be melted with the finished decoction, for oral administration.

3. Heat in the Blood

Main Symptoms and Signs: Vaginal bleeding with the blood bright red in colour during pregnancy, or dragging and distending pain in the waist and abdomen accompanied with vexation and restlessness with feverish sensaion in the palms, dry mouth and throat, red tongue with yellow and dry fur, slippery and rapid or taut and slippery pulse.

Therapeutic Principle: Nourishing *yin*, clearing away heat and enriching the blood to prevent abortion.

化），党参 12 克，白术 9 克。水煎服。

2. 气血虚弱型

主证：妊娠期阴道少量流血，色淡红，质稀薄；或腰腹坠胀，伴神疲肢倦、面色㿠白、心悸气短，舌质淡，苔薄白，脉细滑。

治则：补气养血，固肾安胎。

处方：胎元饮加减。

人参 6 克，杜仲 9 克，白芍 9 克，熟地 12 克，白术 9 克，陈皮 9 克，炙甘草 6 克，黄芪 15 克，阿胶 30 克（烊化）。水煎服。

3. 血热型

主证：妊娠期阴道下血，色鲜红，或腰腹坠胀作痛，伴心烦不安、手心烦热、口干咽燥，舌质红，苔黄而干，脉滑数或弦滑。

治则：滋阴清热，养血安胎。

Recipe: Modified Decoction for Protecting *Yin*.

dried rehmannia root, *Radix Rehmanniae*   12g

prepared rehmannia root, *Radix Rehmanniae Praeparata*   12g

white peony root, *Radix Paeoniae Alba*   9g

scutellaria root, *Radix Scutellariae*   9g

phellodendron bark, *Cortex Phellodendri*   9g

dipsacus root, *Radix Dipsaci*   15g

Chinese yam, *Rhizoma Dioscoreae*   15g

boehmeria root, *Radix Boehmeriae*   12g

All the above drugs are to be decocted in water for oral administration.

4. Trauma Involving the Intrauterine Fetus

Main Symptoms and Signs.   Trauma during pregnancy, soreness of the waist, dragging distension in the abdomen, or vaginal bleeding, normal tongue, slippery and weak pulse.

Therapeutic Principle: Supplementing *qi* and regulating blood flow to prevent abortion.

Recipe: *Sheng Yu* Decoction with additional ingredients.

ginseng, *Radix Ginseng*   6g

astragalus root, *Radix Astragali seu Hedysari*   **18g**

Chinese angelica root, *Radix Angelicae Sinensis*   9g

chuanxiong rhizome, *Rhizoma Ligustici Chuanxiong*   9g

prepared rehmannia root, *Radix Rehmanniae Praeparata*   12g

dried rehmannia root, *Radix Rehmanniae*   12g

dodder seed, *Semen Cuscutae*   9g

loranthus mulberry mistletoe, *Ramulus Loranthi*   15g

dipsacus root, *Radic Dipsaci*   15g

All the above drugs are to be decocted in water for oral administration.

处方：保阴煎加味。

生地 12 克，熟地 12 克，白芍 9 克，黄芩 9 克，黄柏 9 克，

川断 15 克，山药 15 克，苧麻根 12 克。水煎服。

4. 跌打伤胎

主证：妊娠外伤，腰酸，腹胀坠，或阴道下血，舌质正常，

脉滑无力。

治则：补气、和血、安胎。

处方：圣愈汤加味。

人参 6 克，黄芪 18 克，当归 9 克，川芎 9 克，熟地 12 克，

生地 12 克，菟丝子 9 克，桑寄生 15 克，川断 15 克。水煎服。

Section 14

Heterotopic Pregnancy

When the fertilized ovum embeds and develops in some other sites outside the uterine cavity, the pregnancy is described as heterotopic pregnancy. Among the cases tubal pregnancy is the most common. The rupture of the tube can result in acute internal hemorrhage in adbominal cavity. As its onset is sudden and the condition severe, emergency measures must be taken.

MAIN POINTS OF DIAGNOSIS:

1. Patients often have the history of menolipsis, and the attack usually occurs around the sixth week of pregnancy.

2. Serious tearing pain suddenly occurs in the lower abdomen and spreads over the whole abdomen when the bleeding is excessive.

3. Irregular colporrhagia may be slight, occurring in drops, intermittently or continuously.

4. In patient with severe abdominal pain and internal hemorrhage, faint and shock may occur.

5. There are prominent tenderness and rebound tenderness over the abdomen. On gynecological examination lifting pain of uterine cervix, slightly enlarged and soft uterus, fullness and prominent tenderness over the posterior fornix may be found. Sometimes an irregular mass of various sizes may be felt on one side of uterus or at the posterior fornix.

6. With paracentesis of posterior fornix incoagulable blood may be obtained.

7. Ultrasound B may show the picture of accumulated blood in rectovaginal pouch or abdominal cavity. Sometimes sac of heterotopic pregnancy or early heart pulsation may be demonstrated.

8. Peritoneoscopy or diagnostic uterine curettage may be

第十四节　　异位妊娠

受精卵在子宫腔以外的任何部位种植并发育者，为异位妊娠，亦称宫外孕。其中以输卵管妊娠为多见。输卵管妊娠破裂后，可造成急性腹腔内出血，发病急，病情重，需紧急处理。

【诊断要点】

1．发病前患者常有停经史，多发生在妊娠第六周左右。

2．突然发生剧烈下腹撕裂样疼痛，疼痛开始多起于下腹一侧，出血多时呈全腹疼痛。

3．不规则阴道出血，呈点滴状、间断性或持续不止。

4．剧烈腹痛和急性内出血，患者可发生晕厥与休克。

5．腹部有明显压痛及反跳痛，妇科检查宫颈有举痛，子宫稍大且软，后穹窿饱满，触痛明显，有时在子宫的一侧或后穹窿处可触及大小不等、形状不规则的包块。

6．后穹窿穿刺可抽出不凝集血液。

7．B超显示子宫直肠凹处及腹腔内积血图象。有时可见子宫外妊娠囊或早期胎心跳动。

8．腹腔镜检查与诊断性刮宫，对不典型宫外孕或有所帮

helpful in atypical cases.

DIFFERENTIATION AND TREATMENT OF COMMON SYNDROMES

1. Un-ruptured Type

Main Symptoms and Signs: Un-ruptured oviductal pregnancy with morning sickness, or vague pain, discomfort and dragging distension on one side of the lower abdomen. Slight tubal dilatation or soft mass in which tenderness can be found in one side of oviduct through gynecological examination. Urine pregnancy test is positive.

Therapeutic Principle: Promoting blood circulation and removing blood stasis, eliminating mass and destroying the embryo.

Recipe: Recipe No. 2 for Treating Heterotopic Pregnancy.

red peony root, *Radix Paeoniae Rubra*   15g
red sage root, *Radix Salviae Miltiorrhizae*   15g
peach kernel, *Semen Persicae*   9g
zedoary, *Rhizoma Zedoariae*   9g
burreed tuber, *Rhizoma Sparganii*   9g

All the above drugs are to be decocted in water for oral administration.

2. Ruptured Type

1) Shock Type

Main Symptoms and Signs: Abrupt pain in the lower abdomen, tenderness, pallor, cold limbs, profuse cold sweat, vexation, lowered blood pressure, pale tongue, pulse as faint as none or thready, or rapid and weak pulse.

Therapeutic Principle: Promoting blood circulation to remove blood stasis, recuperating depleted *yang* to rescue the patient from collapse.

Recipe: Recipe No. 1 for Treating Heterotopic Pregnancy with additional ingredients.

red peony root, *Radix Paeoniae Rubra*   15g

助。

【辨证论治】

1. 未破损型

主证：输卵管妊娠尚未破损，有早孕反应，或下腹一侧有隐痛和坠胀不适感。妇科检查发现一侧输卵管略有膨大或有软性包块，压痛。尿妊娠试验可为阳性。

治则：活血化瘀，消癥杀胚。

处方：宫外孕Ⅱ号。

赤芍15克，丹参15克，桃仁9克，莪术9克，三棱9克。水煎服。

2. 已破损型

1）休克型

主证：突发下腹剧痛、拒按，面色苍白，四肢厥逆，冷汗淋漓，烦躁不安，血压下降，舌质淡，脉微欲绝或细数无力。

治则：活血祛瘀，回阳救脱。

处方：宫外孕Ⅰ号加味。

red sage root, *Radix Salviae Miltiorrhizae*   15g
peach kernel, *Semen Persicae*   9g
prepared aconite root, *Radix Aconiti Praeparata*   6g
ginseng, *Radix Ginseng*   6g
ophiopogon root, *Radix Ophiopogonis*   9g
schisandra fruit, *Fructus Schisandrae*   9g

All the above drugs are to be decocted in water for oral administration.

2) Unstable Type

Main Symptoms and Signs: Abdominal pain with **tenderness** gradually alleviated, palpable mass with unclear margins, or a small amount of vaginal bleeding, stable blood pressure, thready and moderate pulse.

Therapeutic Principle: Promoting blood circulation and resolving mass.

Recipe: Recipe No. 1 for Treating Heterotopic Pregnancy.
red peony root, *Radix Paeoniae Rubra*   15g
red sage root, *Radix Salviae Miltiorrhizae*   15g
peach kernel, *Semen Persicae*   9g

All the above drugs are to be decocted in water for oral administration.

3) Mass Type

Main Symptoms and Signs: Formation of hematomole, gradual disappearance of abdominal pain, sometimes dragging distension in the lower abdomen, thready and unsmooth pulse.

Therapeutic Principle: Resolving mass.

Recipe: Recipe No. 2 for Treating Heterotopic **Pregnancy** with additional ingredients.

red peony root, *Radix Paeoniae Rubra*   15g
red sage root, *Radix Salviae Miltiorrhizae*   15g
peach kernel, *Semen Persicae*   9g
zedoary, *Rhizoma Zedoariae*   9g
burreed tuber, *Rhizoma Sparganii*   9g
dangshen, *Radix Codonopsis Pilosulae*   15g

赤芍 15 克，丹参 15 克，桃仁 9 克，附子 6 克，人参 6 克，

麦冬 9 克，五味子 9 克。水煎服。

2）不稳定型

主证：腹痛拒按逐渐减轻，可触及界限不清之包块，或有少

量阴道出血，血压较稳定，脉细缓。

治则：活血消癥。

处方：宫外孕Ⅰ号。

赤芍 15 克，丹参 15 克，桃仁 9 克。水煎服。

3）包块型

主证：血肿包块形成，腹痛逐渐消失，有时可有下腹坠胀，

脉细涩。

治则：消癥散结。

astragalus root, *Radix Astragali seu Hedysari*　　18g

All the above drugs are to be decocted in water for oral administration.

Section 15
Pernicious Vomiting

The condition in which nausea, vomiting, dizziness, anorexia or prompt vomiting after eating appear during pregnancy is referred to as pernicious vomiting.

MAIN POINTS OF DIAGNOSIS

1. There is a history of menolipsis with the regular menstrual cycle in the past. The symptoms occur usually around 40 days after menolipsis.

2. In mild cases, there may be recurrence of vomiting, disgust of food, food preference, tiredness with normal temperature and pulse. In severe cases, repeated episodes of vomiting, inability to eat and drink with vomitus containing bile or chocolate coloured blood residue, severe tiredness, emaciation and dehydration may occur.

3. Laboratory examination: Test of ketone in urine is positive

DIFFERETIATION AND TREATMENT OF COMMON SYNDROMES

1) Deficiency of the Spleen and Stomach

Main Symptoms and Signs: Nausea, vomiting, anorexia after conception, accompanied with tastelessness or vomiting of saliva, spiritlessness, drowsiness, pale tongue with white and moist fur, moderate, slippery and weak pulse.

Therapeutic Principle: Strengthening the spleen, regulating the stomach and lowering the adverse flow of *qi* to stop vomiting.

Recipe: Decoction of Costus and Amomum with Six Noble

处方：宫外Ⅱ孕号方，另加党参 15 克，黄芪 18 克。水煎服。

第十五节　　妊娠恶阻

妊娠后出现恶心呕吐、头晕厌食，或食入即吐者，称为"恶阻"。

【诊断要点】

1. 有停经史，以往月经周期规律，一般在停经40天前后出现。

2. 轻者可有反复呕吐、厌食、择食、软弱无力，但体温、脉搏正常。重者呕吐发作频繁，不能进食、进水，呕吐物可能有胆汁和咖啡色血渣，全身无力，消瘦，脱水状态。

3. 实验室检查：尿酮体阳性。

【辨证论治】

1. 脾胃虚弱型

主证：孕后恶心、呕吐、不食，口淡或呕吐清涎，神疲思睡，舌质淡，苔白润，脉缓滑无力。

治则：健脾和胃，降逆止呕。

处方：香砂六君子汤。

Ingredients.

dangshen, *Radix Codonopsis Pilasulae*   12g

bighead atractylodes rhizome, *Rhizoma Atractylodis Macrocephalae*   9g

poria, *Poria*   9g

licorice root, *Radix Glycyrrhizae*   6g

pinellia, *Rhizoma Pinelliae*   9g

tangerine peel, *Pericarpium Citri Reticulatae*   9g

aucklandia root, *Radix Aucklandiae*   9g

amomum fruit, *Fructus Amomi*   6g

fresh ginger, *Rhizoma Zingiberis*   3 slices

Chinese-date, *Fructus Ziziphi Jujubae*   10 pieces

All the above drugs are to be decocted in water for oral
administration.

2. Incoordination between the Liver and Spleen

Main Symptoms and Signs: Vomiting of sour or bitter (bi-
lious) fluid after conception, distension and pain in the chest
and hypochondrium, eructation and sigh, distension of the
head, dizziness, excessive thirst and bitter taste, light red tongue
with yellowish fur, taut and slippery pulse.

Therapeutic Principle: Checking hyperfunction of the liver
and regulating the stomach, lowering the adverse flow of *qi* to
stop vomiting.

Recipe: Decoction of Perilla and Coptis with additional
ingredients.

perilla leaf, *Folium Perillae*   9g

coptis root, *Rhizoma Coptidis*   1.5g

pinellia, *Rhizoma Pinelliae*   9g

tangerine peel, *Pericarpium Citri Reticulatae*   9g

bamboo shavings, *Caulis Bambusae in Taenis*   9g

black plum, *Fructus Mume*   9g

All the above drugs are to be decocted in water for oral
administration.

党参 12 克，白术 9 克，茯苓 9 克，甘草 6 克，半夏 9 克，

陈皮 9 克，木香 9 克，砂仁 6 克，生姜三片，大枣 10 枚。水煎服。

2. 肝胃不和型

主证：孕后呕吐酸水或苦水，胸胁满痛，嗳气叹息，头胀而晕，烦渴口苦，舌淡红，苔微黄，脉弦滑。

治则：抑肝和胃，降逆止呕。

处方：苏叶黄连汤加味。

苏叶 9 克，黄连 1.5 克，半夏 9 克，陈皮 9 克，竹茹 9 克，

乌梅 9 克。水煎服。

Section 16
Edema During Pregnancy

Edema of the limbs and face after conception is termed "edema during pregnancy".

MAIN POINTS OF DIAGNOSIS

The disease is characterized by edema of the limbs and face after conception and is common in the second or third trimester of pregnancy. Clinically, it is divided into three degrees: mild, moderate and severe, according to the severity of edema. In mild cases, obvious edema appears in the legs and feet but can disappear after rest. In moderate cases, edema extends to the thighs and vulva or even involving the abdomen. General edema sometimes accompanied with ascites is seen in severe cases.

DIFFERENTIATION AND TREATMENT OF COMMON SYNDROMES

1. Insufficiency of the Spleen

Main Symptoms and Signs: Edema in the limbs and face, or all over the body some months after conception, slight yellowish or pale complexion, thin and shiny skin, chest tightness and shortness of breath, lack of appetite, loose stool, thick and tender tongue with thin and white fur and also tooth prints on the margins, moderate slippery and weak pulse.

Therapeutic Principle: Strengthening the spleen to induce diuresis.

Recipe: Atractylodes Powder with additional ingredients.
bighead atractylodes rhizome, *Rhizoma Atractylodis Macrocephalae* 9g (stir-fried with honey)
poria, *Poria* 9g
shell of areca nut, *Pericarpium Arecae* 9g
ginger peel, *Cortex Zingiberis* 9g

第十六节　妊娠肿胀

妊娠后，肢体面目发生肿胀者，称"妊娠肿胀"。

【诊断要点】

本病以孕后出现肢体、面目浮肿为特点，多发于妊娠中、后期。临床根据水肿程度，一般分为轻、中、重三级。轻者，小腿及足部明显浮肿，经休息能自消，中者，水肿延及大腿、外阴，甚至涉及腹部；重者，全身浮肿，有时伴有腹水。

【辨证论治】

1．脾虚型

主证：妊娠数月，面目四肢浮肿，或遍及全身，肤色淡黄或㿠白，皮薄而光亮，胸闷气短，纳差便溏，舌胖嫩，苔薄白，边有齿痕，脉缓滑无力。

治则：健脾行水。

处方：白术散加味。

白术9克（蜜炙），茯苓9克，大腹皮9克，生姜皮9克，橘

tangerine peel, *Pericarpium Citri Reticulatae*   9g

amomum fruit, *Fructus Amomi*   6g

All the above drugs are to be decocted in water for oral administration.

2. Deficiency of the Kidney

Main Symptoms and Signs: Edema in the limbs and face which develops several months after conception and is especially severe in the legs where a deep pitting appears when pressing with a finger, palpitation, shortness of breath, cold legs, lassitude in the waist, pale tongue with white moist fur, deep and thready pulse.

Therapeutic Principle: Promoting the activities of *qi* to induce diuresis.

Recipe: Diuretic Decoction by Strengthening the *Yang* of the Spleen and Kidney.

prepared aconite root, *Radix Aconiti Praeparata*   9g

fresh ginger, *Rhizoma Zingiberis Recens*   9g

poria, *Poria*   9g

bighead atractylodes rhizome, *Rhizoma Atractylodis Macro-cephalae*   6g

white peony root, *Radix Paeoniae Alba*   9g

All the above drugs are to be decocted in water for oral administration.

3. Stagnation of *Qi*

Main Symptoms and Signs: Edema which develops three or four months after conception and starts first from feet then up to the legs, elastic edema at pressing without pitting and change of skin colour, dizziness, distending pain in the head, distension and fullness in the chest and hypochondrium, thin and greasy tongue fur, taut and slippery pulse.

Therapeutic Principle: Regulating the flow of *qi* to remove stagnation, reinforcing the function of the spleen to remove dampness.

Recipe: Powder of Birth Wort Vine combined with

皮9克，砂仁6克。水煎服。

2. 肾虚型

主证：孕后数月，面浮肢肿，下肢尤甚，按之没指，心悸气

短，下肢逆冷，腰酸无力，舌质淡，苔白润，脉沉细。

治则：化气行水。

处方：真武汤。

附子9克，生姜9克，茯苓9克，白术6克，白芍9克。水

煎服。

3. 气滞型

主证：妊娠三四月后，先为脚肿，渐及于腿，皮色不变，随

按随起，头晕胀痛，胁胀，苔薄腻，脉弦滑。

治则：理气行滞，健脾化湿。

Powder of Four Diuretic Drugs.

    birth wort vine, *Caulis Aristolochiae*   9g

    nutgrass flatsedge rhizome, *Rhizoma Cyperi*   9g

    tangerine peel, *Pericarpium Citri Reticulatae*   9g

    licorice root, *Radix Glycyrrhizae*   6g

    lindera root, *Radix Linderae*   9g

    fresh ginger, *Rhizoma Zingiberis Recens*   9g

    chaenomeles fruit, *Fructus Chaenomelis*   9g

    perilla leaf, *Folium Perillae*   9g

    poria, *Poria*   9g

    bighead atractylodes rhizome, *Rhizoma Atractylodis Macrocephalae*   9g

    alismatis rhizome, *Rhizoma Alismatis*   9g

All the above drugs are to be decocted in water for oral administration.

Section 17
Eclampsia Gravidarum

If a woman, during the third trimester, before or after delivery, has vertigo, syncope, tetany and general rigidity with superduction, regaining and then losing consciousness repeatedly or even falling into coma for long duration, she is said to suffer from eclampsia gravidarum. The disease pertains to the categories of *"ren shen xian zheng"* or *"zi xian"* (eclampsia) in TCM.

MAIN POINTS OF DIAGNOSIS

1. The condition may occur before, during or after delivery, but clinically it is commonest before delivery and commoner during delivery.

2. The condition is often preceded by headache, blurred vision, oppressed feeling in the chest, giddiness, etc. The blood pressure is remarkably elevated, edema and proteinuria are aggravated. The patient may develop oliguria or even anure-

处方：天仙藤散合四苓散。

天仙藤9克，香附9克，陈皮9克，甘草6克，乌药9克，生姜9克，木瓜9克，紫苏叶9克，茯苓9克，白术9克，泽泻9克。水煎服。

第十七节　妊娠痫证

妊娠晚期或正值临产或新产后，发生眩晕倒仆，昏不知人，手足搐搦，全身强直，双目上视，须臾醒，醒复发，甚或昏迷不醒者，称为"妊娠痫证"，亦称"子痫"。

【诊断要点】

1．妊娠痫证在产前、产时或产后均可发生，临床以产前子痫为常见，其次为产时子痫。

2．本病在抽搐发作前常有头痛、眼花、胸闷、眩晕等症，

sis.

DIFFERENTIATION AND TREATMENT OF COMMON SYNDROMES

1. Up-stirring of Liver

Main Symptoms and Signs: During the third trimester of pregnancy, flush in the face, palpitation, irritability, sudden oneset of convulsion or coma in severe cases, red tongue with thin yellow fur, taut, slippery and rapid pulse.

Therapeutic Principle: Calming the liver to stop convulsion.

Recipe: Decoction of Antelope's Horn and Uncaria Stem.

powder of antelope's horn, *Cornu Saigae Tataricae*   0.3g
  (infused alone)

uncaria stem with hooks, *Ramulus Uncariae cum Uncis*   9g
  (added later)

mulberry leaf, *Folium Mori*   9g

chrysanthemum flower, *Flos Chrysanthemi*   9g

fritillary bulb, *Bulbus Fritillariae*   9g

fresh bamboo shavings, *Caulis Bambusae in Taeniam*   9g

dried rehmannia root, *Radix Rehmanniae*   12g

white peony root, *Radix Paeoniae Alba*   9g

poria with hostwood, *Poria cum Ligno Hospite*   9g

licorice root, *Radix Glycyrrhizae*   6g

All the above drugs are to be decocted in water, with the uncaria stem with hooks put in later than others and the powder of antelope's horn (*Cornu Saigae Tataricae*) mixed with the finished decoction, for oral administration.

2. Upper Body Disturbed by Phlegm-fire

Main Symptoms and Signs: In the third trimester of pregnancy or during delivery, sudden coma, convulsion, coarse breathing with rale, red tongue with yellow and greasy fur, taut and slippery pulse.

Therapeutic Principle: Clearing away heat and eliminating phlegm to induce resuscitation.

Recipe: Bezoar Sedative Bolus with additional ingredients.

血压显著升高，水肿和蛋白尿加重，小便短少，甚或尿闭。

【辨证论治】

1. 肝风内动型

主证：妊娠后期，颜面潮红，心悸烦躁，突发四肢抽搐，甚则昏不知人，舌质红，苔薄黄，脉弦滑数。

治则：平肝熄风。

处方：羚羊钩藤汤。

羚羊角粉 0.3 克(冲服)，钩藤 9 克(后入)，桑叶 9 克，菊花 9 克，贝母 9 克，鲜竹茹 9 克，生地 12 克，白芍 9 克，茯神 9 克，甘草 6 克。水煎服。

2. 痰火上扰型

主证：妊娠晚期，或正值分娩时，卒然昏不知人，四肢抽搐，气粗痰鸣，舌质红，苔黄腻，脉弦滑。

治则：清热，豁痰，开窍。

cow-bezoar, *Calculus Bovis*   30g
cinnabar, *Cinnabaris*   30g
coptis root, *Rhizoma Coptidis*   30g
scutellaria root, *Radix Scutellariae*   30g
capejasmine seed, *Semen Gardeniae*   30g
curcuma root, *Radix Curcumae*   30g
bamboo juice, *Succus Bambusae*   30ml

Make all the drugs into fine powder and mix the powder with honey to make boluses of 3g each. Taken orally, one bolus each time, two or three times a day.

Section 18
Hypogalactia or Agalactia

Hypogalactia or agalactia refers to very little or no milk secreted from the puerpera breasts. Other terms for the condition are *"ruzhi buzu"* (hypogalactia) or *"ruzhi buxing"* (agalactia).

MAIN POINTS OF DIAGNOSIS

The condition is characterized by very small amount of breast milk insufficient to feed the baby, or even no milk at all after delivery.

DIFFERENTIATION AND TREATMENT OF COMMON SYNDROMES

1. Deficiency of Both *Qi* and Blood

Main Symptoms and Signs: Postpartum hypogalactia or agalactia, thin and clear milk, soft breasts without feeling of fullness, dim complexion, lack of vitality, poor appetite, pale tongue with little fur, feeble and thready pulse.

Therapeutic Principle: Reinforcing *qi* and nourishing the blood and promoting lactation as a subsidiary treatment.

Recipe: Pill for Promoting Lactation with additional ingredients.

处方：牛黄清心丸加味。

牛黄 30 克，朱砂 30 克，黄连 30 克，黄芩 30 克，栀子仁 30 克，郁金 30 克，竹沥 30 毫升。共为极细末，炼蜜为丸，每丸 3 克，每服 1 丸，1 日 2～3 次。

第十八节　缺乳

产后乳汁甚少或全无，称为"缺乳"。亦称"乳汁不足"或"乳汁不行"。

【诊断要点】

本病的特点是产后排出的乳汁量少，甚或全无，不足喂养婴儿。

【辨证论治】

1．气血虚弱型

主证：产后乳少，甚或全无，乳汁清稀，乳房柔软，无胀感，面色少华，神疲食少，舌淡少苔，脉虚细。

治则：补气养血，佐以通乳。

处方：通乳丹加味。

ginseng, *Radix Ginseng*   9g
astragalus root, *Radix Astragali seu Hedysari*   30g
Chinese angelica root, *Radix Angelicae Sinensis*   12g
ophiopogon root, *Radix Ophiopogonis*   9g
ricepaper pith, *Medulla Tetrapanacis*   9g
platycodon root, *Radix Platycodi*   9g
prepared rehmannia root, *Radix Rehmanniae Praeparata*   12g
tricosanthes root, *Radix Tricosanthis*   9g

All the above drugs are to be decocted in pig trotter broth for oral administration.

2. Stagnation of the Liver-*qi*

Main Symptoms and Signs: Postpartum hypogalactia or agalactia in severe cases, fullness and oppressed feeling in the chest and hypochondrium, emotional depression, or mild fever, anorexia, normal tongue with thin and yellow fur, taut and thready or rapid pulse.

Therapeutic Principle: Soothing the liver and regulating the flow of *qi*, activating the channels and collaterals to promote lactation.

Recipe: Powder for Promoting Lactation Like Bubbling Spring.

Chinese angelica root, *Radix Angelicae Sinensis*   9g
white peony root, *Radix Paeoniae Alba*   9g
chuanxiong rhizome, *Rhizoma Ligusti Chuanxiong*   6g
dried rehmannia root, *Radix Rehmanniae*   15g
bupleurum root, *Radix Bupleuri*   6g
green tangerine peel, *Pericarpium Citri Reticulatae Viride*   6g
tricosanthes root, *Radix Tricosanthis*   9g
globethistle, *Radix Rhapontici seu Echinopsis*   6g
ricepaper pith, *Medulla Tetrapanacis*   9g
platycodon root, *Radix Platycodi*   9g
dahurian angelica root, *Radix Angelicae Dahuricae*   6g
pangolin scales, *Squama Manitis*   9g
vaccaria seed, *Semen Vaccariae*   12g

人参 9 克，黄芪 30 克，当归 12 克，麦冬 9 克，通草 9 克，

桔梗 9 克，熟地 12 克，花粉 9 克。用猪蹄汤煎药服之。

2. 肝郁气滞型

主证：产后乳汁分泌少，甚或全无，胸胁胀闷，情志抑郁，

或有微热，食欲减退，舌质正常，苔薄黄，脉弦细或数。

治则：疏肝解郁，通络下乳。

处方：下乳涌泉散。

当归 9 克，白芍 9 克，川芎 6 克，生地 15 克，柴胡 6 克，青

皮 6 克，花粉 9 克，漏芦 6 克，通草 9 克，桔梗 9 克，白芷 6 克，

Licorice root, *Radix Glycyrrhizae*   6g

All the above drugs are to be decocted in water for oral administration.

穿山甲9克，王不留行12克，甘草6克。水煎服。

Chaper Three

COMMON PEDIATRIC DISEASES

Section 1
Neonatal Jaundice Syndrome

Neonatal jaundice syndrome is characterized by persistent jaundice with hepatosplenomegaly and elevation of serum conjugated bilirubin, occurring from several days to 1—3 months after birth. The main cause is infection by viruses, such as hepatitis B virus, cytomegalovirus, coxsackie virus, herpes simplex virus and rubella virus. Neonatal septicemia caused by bacterial infection is also a common factor. This disease belongs to the category of *"tai huang"* (neonatal jaundice) in TCM.

MAIN POINTS OF DIAGNOSIS

1. The most noticeable symptoms are jaundice and dark tea-coloured urine. The jaundice may last for 2—3 months, and there is intermittent loss of pigment from stools. The other symptoms, such as mild anemia, fever, vomiting or diarrhea and poor appetite are occasionally encountered.

2. Englarged liver and spleen, mainly hepatomegaly, are usually present.

3. Lab findings include elevated total serum bilirubin ranging from 8—12 mg/dl, positive direct-reacting of van den Bergh's test, slightly elevated SGPT and AKP, and positive AFP which usually exceeds 2000 ng/ml. Bacterial culture, HBsAg and other virological antigen-antibody assay might help ascertain the etiology.

4. The jaundice can be reduced when phenobarbitone or

第 三 章
儿科常见疾病

第一节　新生儿肝炎综合征

新生儿肝炎综合征是以持续性黄疸、肝脾肿大及血清直接胆红素升高为主要特点的临床综合征，好发于生后数日和1～3个月的婴儿。病因多为病毒感染，如乙型肝炎病毒、巨细胞病毒、柯萨奇病毒、单纯疱疹和风疹病毒等。细菌感染引起的败血症也可引起本病。本病属中医"胎黄"范畴。

【诊断要点】

1. 主要症状是黄疸、黑茶色尿，可持续2～3个月，大便颜色转白或时黄时白，可伴有轻度贫血、发热、呕吐或腹泻、食欲低下。

2. 肝脾明显增大，以肝大为主。

3. 实验室检查　血清胆红素升高，可达8～12毫克/分升，凡登白试验直接反应阳性，血清谷丙转氨酶和硷性磷酸酶可轻度升高，甲种胎儿球蛋白大于2000纳克/毫升。细菌培养和病毒学抗原体检查可帮助病因学诊断。

4. 应用苯巴比妥或消胆胺能使黄疸减轻。应用^{131}碘-孟加

cholestyramine is given in neonatal jaundice syndrome, and ^{131}I-rose bengal excretion test or 99m Tc hepatoscintiscanning could help to exclude biliary atresia in most cases.

DIFFERENTIATION AND TREATMENT OF COMMON SYNDROMES

1. Neonatal Jaundice due to Damp-heat

Main Symptoms and Signs: Yellowish complexion which turns bright sometime later, fever, restlessness, thirst, scanty dark urine, sucking rejection, vomiting, constipation, abdominal distention, red tongue with yellow and greasy fur, and red superficial venule of the index finger.

Therapeutic Principle: Clearing away pathogenic heat and dampness.

Recipe: Modified Oriental Wormwood Decoction.

oriental wormwood, *Herba Artemisiae Capillaris*   9g
capejasmine fruit, *Fructus Gardeniae*   3g
rhubarb, *Radix et Rhizoma Rhei* 3g (to be decocted later)

All the above drugs are to be decocted in water for oral administration.

In case of high fever, 6 grams of scutellaria root (*Radix Scutellariae*), 3 grams of coptis root (*Rhizoma Coptidis*) should be added; for those with heavy dampness, 9 grams of poria (*Poria*) and 9 grams of coix seed (*Semen Coicis*) should be included; in case of vomiting, add 6 grams of bamboo shavings (*Caulis Bambusae*) and 3 grams of pinellia tuber (*Rhizoma Pinelliae*), 3 grams of magnolia bark (*Cortex Magnoliae Officialis*) added in case of abdominal distention.

2. Neonatal Jaundice Caused by Cold-dampness

Main Symptoms and Signs: Lasting yellowish and blackish complexion and skin, mental fatigue, cold extremities, greyish and whitish loose stool, pale tongue with white and greasy fur, pale superficial venule of the index finger.

Therapeutic Principle: Invigorating the spleen, warming

拉玫瑰红排泄试验或锝99m肝闪烁扫描大部分病例能与胆道闭锁区别。

【辨证论治】

1. 湿热胎黄

主证：面目、皮肤色黄而转鲜明，发热，烦躁不安，口渴，尿少短赤，拒乳，呕吐，便秘，腹胀，舌质红，苔黄腻，指纹红。

治则：清热利湿。

处方：茵陈蒿汤加减。

茵陈9克，栀子3克，大黄3克（后下）。水煎服。

若热重者，加黄芩6克，黄连3克；湿重者，加茯苓9克，苡仁9克；呕吐者，加竹茹6克，半夏3克；腹胀者，加厚朴3克。

2. 寒湿胎黄

主证：面目、皮肤色黄而晦暗，日久不退，精神疲乏，手足不温，大便灰白，稀薄，舌质淡，苔白腻，指纹淡。

the middle-*jiao* and eliminating dampness.

Recipe: Oriental Wormwood Decoction for Regulating the Function of Middle-*jiao* with additional ingredients.

oriental wormwood, *Herba Arhmisae Capillaris*   9g

dried ginger, *Rhizoma Zingiberis*   1.5g

ginseng, *Radix Ginseng*   3g

white atractylodes rhizome, *Rhizoma Atractylodis Macrocephalae*   9g

poria, *Poria*   9g

liquorice, *Radix Glycyrrhizae*   3g

All the above drugs are to be decocted in water for oral administration.

3. Neonatal Jaundice Caused by Blood Stasis

Main Symptoms and Signs: Abnormal yellowish complexion and skin which worsen gradually and turn darkish and dim, magersucht, poor appetite, easy vomiting after sucking, hepatomegaly or splenomegaly, greyish-white stool tinged with kaolin colour, dark red lips and tongue with yellowish fur, and dark purple superficial venule of the index finger.

Therapeutic Principle: Promoting blood circulation and removing blood stasis to treat hepatomegaly or splenomegaly, soften and remove food stagnancy.

Recipe: Modified prescriptions of Decoction for Removing Blood Stasis in the Chest and Decocted Turtle Shell Pill.

peach kernel, *Semen Persicae*   6g

safflower, *Flos Carthami*   3g

Chinese angelica, *Radix Angelicae Sinensis*   6g

red peony root, *Radix Paeoniae Rubra*   6g

poria, *Poria*   6g

bupleurum root, *Radix Bupleuri*   6g

fresh-water turtle shell, *Carapax Trionycis*   9g

All the above drugs are to be decocted in water for oral administration.

治则：健脾温中化湿。

处方：茵陈理中汤加味。

茵陈9克，干姜1.5克，人参3克，白术9克，茯苓9克，

甘草3克。水煎服。

3. 瘀血胎黄

主证：面目、皮肤发黄，日益加重，色暗滞，消瘦，纳呆，

吸乳后易呕逆，腹部膨隆有痞块，大便灰白呈陶土色，唇舌暗红，

舌苔黄，指纹紫暗。

治则：活血化瘀，软坚消积。

处方：血府逐瘀汤合鳖甲煎丸加减。

桃仁6克，红花3克，当归6克，赤芍6克，茯苓6克，柴

胡6克，鳖甲9克。水煎服。

Section 2
Scleroderma Neonatorum

Scleroderma neonatorum is a common neonatal disease characterized by subcutaneous fat sclerosis and edema. The pathogenic factors may include cold, premature birth, bacterial infection and defective thermoregulation, inadequate brown fat and unsaturated fatty acid, etc. In TCM, this disease belongs to the categories of *"wu ying"* (five types of stiffness) and *"tai han"* (cold-syndrome of newborn), etc.

MAIN POINTS OF DIAGNOSIS

1. It usually occurs in cold seasons. The patient often has histories of premature birth and infection.

2. The clinical manifestations may include lower temperature without tendency to rise, inability to cry and suck milk, inaction, redness of skin or jaundice, and pale skin or cyanosis in severe cases. Coldness, hardness and edema of the extremities (especially, of the lower) may present. In severe cases, the upper extremeties and the face may be involved. Other symptoms and signs include irregular respiration, scanty urine and hemorrhagic tendency such as hematemesis and pneumorrhagia.

3. Lab findings may include leukocytosis, prolongated bleeding time and coagulation time, fibrinogenopenia, delayed prothrombin time and other DIC features. Blood culture may reveal the pathogen.

DIFFERENTIATION AND TREATMENT OF COMMON SYNDROMES

1. Insufficiency of *Yang-qi*

Main Symptoms and Signs: The whole body as cold as ice within 3—5 days after birth, lying stiff with little movement, grey and dark complexion, soporous state, weak breath,

第二节 新生儿硬肿症

新生儿硬肿症是以皮下脂肪硬化和水肿为特点的常见新生儿疾病。其致病因素有受寒、早产、细菌感染、新生儿体温调节功能不全、棕色脂肪少和不饱和脂肪酸少等。本症属中医"五硬"、"胎寒"等范畴。

【诊断要点】

1．多在寒冷季节发病，有早产及感染史。

2．临床表现有体温不升、不哭、不吃、不动，皮肤红色或黄疸，重者苍白或青紫；四肢皮肤凉、硬和水肿，下肢更明显，重者累及上肢和面颊部。往往有呼吸不均、尿少，可有吐血或肺出血等出血倾向。

3．实验室检查可有白细胞增高、出凝血时间延长、纤维蛋白元减少、凝血酶元时间延长等弥漫性血管内凝血 (DIC) 的特点。血培养可能发现感染的病原体。

【辨证论治】

1．阳气虚衰

主证：生后3～5天全身冰冷，僵卧少动，面色灰暗，昏昏多

strengthless sucking, low crying, local skin hardness as board with paleness and brightness due to swelling, skin pitting upon finger-pressing, hard swelling to quite a large extent, pale lips and tongue with white fur, reddish or invisible superficial venule of the index finger.

Therapeutic Principle: Invigorating *qi* and warming *yang*.

Recipe: Flavoured Decoction of Ginseng and Prepared Aconite.

ginseng, *Radix Genseng*   1.5g

prepared aconite root, *Radix Aconiti Praeparata*   1g

astragalus root, *Radix Astragali seu Hedysari*   3g

cinammon twig, *Ramulus Cinnamomi*   1g

poria, *Poria*   3g

white atractylodes rhizome, *Rhizoma Atractylodis Macrocephalae*   3g

safflower, *Flos Carthami*   1g

All the above drugs are to be decocted in water and then concentrated into small quantity to be dropped frequently into the mouth of the sick baby.

2. Blood Stagnation Caused by Cold

Main Symptoms and Signs: After birth, having purple and dark complexion, general low temperature, cold extremities, and stiff skin without normal state of softness which is unable to be pinched up; the hard swelling occurring more often in the calves, buttocks, arms, face and other regions where there is more fat and blood circulation is poorer. Or the red swelling looks like injury due to cold, dark red lips and tongue, red stagnant or invisible superficial venule of the index finger.

Therapeutic Principle: Invigorating *qi* and warming the channels to promote blood circulation.

Recipe: Modified Chinese Angelica Decoction for Restoring *Yang*.

Chinese angelica root, *Radix Angelicae Sinensis*   1.5g

white peony root, *Radix Paeoniae Alba*   6g

睡，气息微弱，吸吮无力，哭声低弱。局部皮肤板硬如木，苍白肿亮，按之凹陷，硬肿范围较广。唇舌淡白，舌苔白，指纹淡红或隐伏不显。

治则：益气温阳。

处方：参附汤加味。

人参 1.5 克，附子 1 克，黄芪 3 克，桂枝 1 克，茯苓 3 克，白术 3 克，红花 1 克。水煎服。浓缩少量频滴入患儿口内。

2. 寒凝血滞

主证：初生后面色紫暗，全身欠温，四肢发凉，皮肤失去柔软之常态，僵硬不能捏起。硬肿多发生于脂肪较多、血运较差的小腿、臀、臂、面颊等部位，或红肿如冻伤。唇舌暗红，指纹红滞或不显。

治则：益气温经，活血通脉。

处方：当归四逆汤加减。

当归 1.5 克，白芍 6 克，桂枝 1.5 克，羌活 1.5 克，独活 1.5

cinammon twig, *Ramulus Cinnamomi*   1.5g

notopterygium root, *Rhizome seu Radix Notopterygii*   1.5g

pubescent angelica root, *Radix Angelicae Pubescentis*   1.5g

liquorice, *Radix Glycyrrhizae*   1.5g

antler glue, *Colla Cornus Cervi*   3g (melted alone)

astraglus root, *Radix Astragali*   9g

spatholobus stem, *Caulis Spatholobi*   3g

Chinese date, *Fructus Ziziphi Jujubae*   3 pieces

All the above drugs are to be decocted in water for oral administration.

3. Retention of Cold and Dampness in the Spleen

Main Symptoms and Signs: Besides low temperature, inaction, lassitude, hardness and edema of the skin, it is also manifested as productive cough or vomiting sometimes, loose stool, abdominal distention, oliguria, light pale lips and tongue with white or greasy fur, darkish and invisible superficial venule of the index finger.

Therapeutic Principle: Strengthening the spleen and eliminating dampness, regulating the flow of *qi* and resolving phlegm.

Recipe: Modified Aconite Decoction for Regulating the Function of Middle-*jiao*.

prepared aconite root, *Radix Aconiti Praeparata*   1.5g

dried ginger, *Rhizoma Zingiberis*   0.6g

ginseng, *Radix Ginseng*   1.5g

white atractylodes rhizome, *Rhizoma Atractylodis Macroce-phalea*   3g

liquorice, *Radix Glycyrrhizae*   3g

All the above drugs are to be decocted in water for oral administration.

克，甘草 1.5 克，鹿角胶 3 克，黄芪 9 克，鸡血藤 3 克，大枣 3

枚。水煎服。

3. 寒湿困脾

主证：除体温不升、身倦不动、肌肤硬肿外，尚见咳嗽痰多，

或时有呕吐，大便清稀，腹胀尿少。唇舌偏淡，苔白或腻，指纹

晦暗不显。

治则：健脾燥湿，理气化痰。

处方：附子理中汤加减。

制附子 1.5 克，干姜 0.6 克，人参 1.5 克，白术 3 克，甘草

3 克。水煎服。

Section 3
Anorexia

Anorexia in children is characterized by loss of or regressive appetite associated with general or digestive diseases, psychic factors and bad feeding habit. This disease, in TCM, is called *"yan shi"* (anorexia).

MAIN POINTS OF DIAGNOSIS

1. The clinical manifestation is dislike or refusal of feeding. Delayed treatment may result in emaciation, malnutrition and mild anemia.

2. The causes of anorexia, such as primary disorders, psychic factors and bad feeding habit can be found.

3. Besides the evidence of primary disorders that cause anorexia, hypoproteinemia, mild anemia and deficiency of vitamins or mineral substances may be discovered through laboratory examinations.

DIFFERENTIATION AND TREATMENT OF COMMON SYNDROMES

1. Infantile Dyspepsia

Main Symptoms and Signs: Continued food refusal after dyspepsia due to improper feeding, accompanied with vexation, insomnia, mental fatigue, frequent vomiting, abdominal distention and uncomfortable feeling, sour and fetid stool, red tongue with white and thick fur, taut and slippery pulse, purple and stagnant superficial venule of the index finger.

Therapeutic Principle: Promoting digestion to relieve dyspepsia.

Recipe: Modified Lenitive Pill.

hawthorn fruit, *Fructus Crataegi*   15g
germinated barley, *Fructus Hordei Germinatus*   9g
medicated leaven, *Massa Fermentata Medicinalis*   9g

第三节　厌食症

小儿厌食症是指小儿较长时间的食欲减退或消失，多与全身性疾病、消化系统疾病、精神因素及不良饮食习惯等因素有关。中医文献中亦有"厌食"的记载。

【诊断要点】

1．临床特点是不思饮食或拒食，日久可表现消瘦、营养欠佳或轻度贫血。

2．可检查出引起厌食的原发病、精神因素和不良生活习惯。

3．除有引起厌食的原发病特点外，实验室检查可发现低蛋白血症、轻度贫血或维生素、矿物质缺乏的证据。

【辨证论治】

1．乳食壅滞

主证：伤食伤乳后，小儿较长时间拒食，伴有心烦不眠、精神疲惫、时有呕吐、腹胀不舒、大便酸臭，舌质红，苔白厚，脉弦滑，指纹紫滞。

治则：消食导滞。

处方：保和丸加减。

山楂15克，麦芽9克，神曲9克，莱菔子9克，厚朴6克，

radish seed, *Semen Raphani*   9g
magnolia bark, *Cortex Magnoliae Officianlis*   6g
tangerine peel, *Pericarpium Citri Reticulatae*   6g
immature fruit, *Fructus Aurantii Immaturus*   6g
pinellia tuber, *Rhizoma Pinelliae*   6g
aucklandia root, *Radix Aucklandiae*   3g
liquorice, *Radix Glycyrrhizae*   3g

All the above drugs are to be decocted in water for oral administration.

2. Weakness of the Spleen and Stomach

Main Symptoms and Signs: Prolonged poor appetite or food refusal, accompanied with physical leanness, pale complexion, mental fatigue, general weakness, loose stool or that with milk remains, pale tongue with white fur, thready and weak pulse, and reddish superficial venule of the index finger.

Therapeutic Principle: Strengthening the spleen and regulating the stomach.

Recipe: Modified Decoction of Costus and Amomum with Six Noble Ingredients.

dangshen, *Radix Codonopsis Pilosulae*   9g
white atractylodes rhizome, *Rhizoma Atractylodis Macrocephalae*   9g
poria, *Poria*   9g
tangerine peel, *Pericarpium Citri Reticulatae*   9g
amomum fruit, *Fructus Amomi*   6g
aucklandia root, *Radix Aucklandiae*   3g
pinellia tuber, *Rhizoma Pinelliae*   3g
liquorice, *Radix Glycyrrhizae*   3g

All the above drugs are to be decocted in water for oral administration.

3. Deficiency of the Stomach-*yin*

Main Symptoms and Signs: Continued poor appetite or food refusal, accompanied with thirst, dryness of the mouth and tongue, vexation and restlessness, red and dry tongue or that

陈皮 6 克，枳实 6 克，半夏 6 克，木香 3 克，甘草 3 克。水煎服。

2. 脾胃虚弱

主证：较长时间的食欲不振或拒食，伴形体消瘦、面色㿠白、

精神疲惫、全身乏力、大便溏薄或夹有乳食残渣，舌质淡，苔白，

脉细弱，指纹淡红。

治则：健脾和胃。

处方：香砂六君子汤加减。

党参 9 克，白术 9 克，茯苓 9 克，陈皮 9 克，砂仁 6 克，木

香 3 克，半夏 3 克，甘草 3 克。水煎服。

3. 胃阴不足

主证：较长时间的食欲不振或拒食，伴口渴欲饮、口干舌燥、

with lacerated marks, thready and rapid pulse, and dark and purple superficial venule of the index finger.

Therapeutic Principle: Promoting the production of body fluid and nourishing the stomach.

Recipe: Modified Decoction for Nourishing the Stomach.
aderophora root, *Radix Aderophorae*   9g
ophiopogon root, *Radix Ophiopogonis*   9g
dried rehmannia root, *Radix Rehmanniae*   9g
fragrant solomonseal rhizome, *Rhizoma Polygonati Odorati*   9g
dendrobium, *Herba Dendrobii*   9g
Chinese Yam, *Rhizoma Dioscoreae*   15g
hyacinth bean, *Semen Dolichoris*   15g

All the above drugs are to be decocted in water for oral administration.

Section 4
Acute Upper Respiratory Tract Infection

Acute upper respiratory tract infection is one of the common infectious diseases caused by bacteria or viruses. The nose, nasopharynx and tonsils are mainly involved. The disease, in TCM, belongs to the categories of *"gan mao"* or *"shang feng"* (the common cold), *"ru e"* (tonsillitis), etc.

MAIN POINTS OF DIAGNOSIS

1. Clinical manifestations usually include rhinorrhea, rhinocleisis, sneezing, lacrimation and mild cough. Fever, sore throat, headache, fatigue, poor appetite or vomiting can also be present.

2. Physical examinations may reveal redness of the pharynx with herpes or ulcer in the mouth. Patients with acute tonsillitis may have excessive purulent discharge on the surface of the tonsils and swelling of tonsils. Submaxillary lymphnodes are usually swollen and tender.

3. Laboratory examinations may reveal normal leukocyte

烦躁不安，舌红而干或有裂纹，脉细数，指纹青紫。

治则：生津养胃。

处方：养胃汤加减。

沙参9克，麦冬9克，生地9克，玉竹9克，石斛9克，山药15克，扁豆15克。水煎服。

第四节　急性上呼吸道感染

急性上呼吸道感染是由细菌或病毒引起的常见感染性疾病。主要侵及鼻、鼻咽部和扁桃体等器官。本病属中医"感冒"、"伤风"、"乳蛾"等范畴。

【诊断要点】

1．临床表现有流涕、鼻塞、喷嚏、流泪和微咳，也可有发热、咽痛、头痛、乏力、食欲减退或呕吐。

2．体格检查可发现咽红、口内疱疹或溃疡。有扁桃体炎时，扁桃体表面有脓性分泌物和扁桃体肿大，颌下淋巴结肿大及压痛。

3．实验室检查：因病毒感染所致者白细胞计数正常，因细

count in patients with viral infection, and higher one in those with bacterial infection. X-ray examination of the chest is usually normal.

DIFFERENTIATION AND TREATMENT OF COMMON SYNDROMES

1. Wind-cold Type

Main Symptoms and Signs: Aversion to cold, fever, absence of sweat, stuffy nose, thin nasal discharge, sneezing, mild cough, thin sputum, absence of thirst, headache, iching throat, reddish tongue with thin and white fur, floating and tight pulse, and shallow red superficial venule of the index finger.

Therapeutic Principle: Relieving exterior syndrome with drugs pungent in flavor and warm in property, ventilating the lung and expelling pathogenic cold.

Recipe: Modified Antiphlogistic Powder of Schizonepeta and Ledebouriella.

schizonepeta, *Herba Schizonepetae*   6g
ledebouriella root, *Radix Ledebouriellae*   6g
notopterygium root, *Rhizoma seu Radix Notopterygii*   9g
peucedanum root, *Radix Peucedani*   9g
platycodon root, *Radix Platycodi*   9g
liquorice, *Radix Glycyrrhizae*   3g

All the above drugs are to be decocted in water for oral administration.

Besides, in case of headache, 6 grams of dahurian angelica root (*Radix Angelica Dahuricae*) should be included; for those with serious cough, add 6 grams of apricot kernel (*Semen Armeniacae*) and 9 grams of white swallowwort rhizome (*Rhizoma Cynanchi Stauntonii*).

2. Wind-heat Type

Main Symptoms and Signs: Higher fever and milder aversion to cold, headache, stuffy nose, purulent nasal discharge, sneezing, cough with yellowish thick sputum, painful red and swollen throat, dry mouth and thirst, red tongue with thin and

菌感染白细胞计数升高。胸部X线检查正常。

【辨证论治】

1. 风寒型

主证：恶寒，发热，无汗，鼻塞，流清涕，喷嚏，微咳嗽，吐痰清稀，口不渴，头痛，喉痒，舌淡红，苔薄白，脉浮紧，指纹浮红。

治则：辛温解表，宣肺散寒。

处方：荆防败毒散加减。

荆芥6克，防风6克，羌活9克，前胡9克，桔梗9克，甘草3克。水煎服。

若头痛者，加白芷6克；咳嗽甚者，加杏仁6克，白前6克。

2. 风热型

主证：发热重，恶寒轻，头痛，鼻塞，流脓涕，喷嚏，咳嗽，吐痰黄稠，咽部红肿疼痛，口干而渴，舌质红，苔薄白或薄黄，

white or thin and yellow fur, floating and rapid pulse, and shallow and clear superficial venule of the index finger with red colour.

Therapeutic Principle: Expelling exopathogens from the body surface with drugs of acrid flavour and cool nature, ventilating the lung and clearing away pathogenic heat.

Recipe: Modified Powder of Lonicera and Forsythia.

honeysuckle flower, *Flos Lonicerae*   9g

forsythia fruit, *Fructus Forsythiae*   9g

schizonepeta, *Herba Schizonepetae*   6g

prepared soybean, *Semen Sojae Praeparatum*   6g

arctium fruit, *Fructus Arctii*   9g

peppermint herb, *Herba Menthae*   6g (to be decocted later)

lophatherum, *Herba Lophatheri*   6g

reel rhizome, *Rhizoma Phragmitis*   15g

liquorice, *Radix Glycyrrhizae*   3g

All the above drugs are to be decocted in water for oral administration.

Besides, in case of high fever, 9 grams of bupleurum root (*Radix Bupleuri*), 15 grams of pueraria root (*Radix Puerariae*) and 9 grams of capejasmine fruit (*Fructus Gardeniae*) should be added. In case of bad headache, 9 grams of chastetree fruit (*Fructus Viticis*) should be added. For those with sore throat, add 9 grams of puffball (*Lasiosphaera seu Calvatia*), wrapped in a piece of cloth before it is to be decocted, 9 grams of belamcanda rhizome (*Rhizoma Belamcandae*) and 12 grams of isatis root (*Radix Isatidis*). In case of yellow and greasy fur on the tongue, 9 grams of coix seed (*Semen Coicis*) and 12 grams of tale (*Talcum*) should be included. For those with severe thirst, 9 grams of trichosanthes root (*Radix Tricosanthis*) should be added. In case of constipation, add 6 grams of rhubarb (*Radix et Rhizoma Rhei*) which is to be decocted later, 9 grams of scrophularia root (*Radix Scrophulariae*) and 9 grams of snakegourd fruit (*Fructus Polygalae Japonica*).

3. Summer-heat-dampness Type

Main Symptoms and Signs: High fever, aversion to cold,

脉浮数，指纹浮露，色较红赤。

治则：辛凉解表，宣肺清热。

处方：银翘散加减。

银花9克，连翘9克，荆芥6克，淡豆豉6克，牛蒡子9克，

薄荷6克(后入)，竹叶6克，芦根15克，甘草3克。水煎服。

若高热者，加柴胡9克，葛根15克，栀子9克；头痛重者，

加蔓荆子9克；咽喉痛者，加马勃9克(布包煎)，射干9克，板

蓝根12克；舌苔黄腻者，加苡仁9克，滑石12克；口渴甚者，加

天花粉9克；大便秘结者，加大黄6克(后入)，玄参9克，瓜蒌

9克。

3．暑湿型

主证：高热，恶寒，身重困倦，呕吐，腹痛，腹泻，心烦口

heaviness sensation in the limbs, fatigue, vomiting, abdominal pain, diarrhea, restlessness, thirst, scanty dark urine, thick and greasy fur on the tongue, and soft and rapid pulse.

Therapeutic Principle: Clearing away summer-heat to relieve the exterior syndrome and removing pathogenic dampness to regulate the stomach.

Recipe: Modified Elsholtzia Decoction.

elscholtzia, *Herba Elscholziae seu Moslae*   9g
white hyaciath bean, *Semen Dolichoris Album*   15g
magnolia bark, *Cortex Magnoliae Officinalis*   9g

All the above drugs are to be decocted in water for oral administration.

Besides, for those with more heat than dampness, instead of elscholtzia (*Herba Elscholtziae seu Moslae*), add 6 grams of coptis (*Rhizoma Coptidis*), 12 grams of honeysuckle flower (*Flos Lonicerae*), 12 grams of tale (*Talcum*) and 3 grams of liquorice (*Radix Glycyrrhizae*). In case of more dampness than heat, add 15 grams of fresh lotus leaf (*Folium Nelumbinis*), 9 grams of fresh elscholtzia (*Herba Elscholtziae seu Moslae*), 9 grams of eupatorium (*Herba Eupatorii*) and 15 grams of watermelon peel (*Exocarpium Citrulli*).

Section 5
Acute Bronchitis

Acute bronchitis is an acute inflammation of bronchi. It is a common disease in children, usually preceded by viral or bacterial infection of upper respiratory tract. This disease belongs to the category of *"waigan kesou"* (cough due to the exo-pathogen) in TCM.

MAIN POINTS OF DIAGNOSIS

1. Clinical manifestations include fever, unproductive cough, tachypnea, restlessness and poor sleep. Vomiting may occur when coughing is severe with discomfort or pain in the

渴，小便短赤，舌苔厚腻，脉濡数。

治则：清暑解表，化湿和中。

处方：**香薷饮加减。**

香薷9克，白扁豆15克，厚朴9克。水煎服。

若热重于湿者，去香薷，加黄连6克，银花12克，滑石12

克，甘草3克；若湿重于热者，加鲜荷叶15克，鲜香薷9克，**佩**

兰9克，西瓜翠衣15克。

第五节　急性支气管炎

急性支气管炎是小儿常见的支气管的急性炎症，常继发于病

毒性或细菌性上呼吸道感染。本病属中医"外感咳嗽"的范畴。

【诊断要点】

1. 临床表现特点有发热、无分泌物的咳嗽、呼吸短促、烦

chest. After several days, the cough becomes productive and the sputum changes from clear to purulent. There are malaise and loss of appetite in the course of the disease.

2. Results of physical examinations vary with the age of the patients and the stage of the disease. There are signs of nasopharyngitis and conjunctivitis. Auscultation of the chest reveals respiratory harshness, coarse moist rales and high-pitched dry rales.

3. Laboratory examinations show normal or high peripheral blood picture. X-ray examination of the chest is normal or with increased lung-markings.

DIFFERENTIATION AND TREATMENT OF COMMON SYNDROMES

1. Cough due to Pathogenic Wind-cold

Main Symptoms and Signs: Frequent cough with clear and thin sputum, aversion to cold with anhidrosis, fever, headache, stuffy nose with nasal discharge, itching in the throat, hoarseness or general pantalgia with soreness, thin and white fur of the tongue, floating and tight pulse and shallow red superficial venule of the index finger.

Therapeutic Principle: Expelling pathogenic wind-cold and relieving cough by promoting the dispersing function of the lung.

Recipe: Flavoured Decoction of Three Grude Drugs.

ephedra, *Herba Ephedrae*   6g

apricot kernel, *Semen Armeniacae Amarum*   6g

liquorice, *Radix Glycyrrhizae*   3g

schizonepeta, *Herba Schizonepetae*   6g

peucedanum root, *Radix Peucedani*   9g

pinellia tuber, *Rhizoma Pinelliae*   6g

platycodon root, *Radix Platycodi*   6g

Sichuan fritillary bulb, *Bulbus Fritillariae Cirrhosae*   9g

All the above drugs are to be decocted in water for oral administration.

躁、睡眠不安，咳嗽重者可有呕吐，胸前不适或胸痛等。几天后咳嗽变为有清痰或脓痰，然后逐渐恢复。常伴有乏力和食欲下降。

2. 体格检查发现随年龄和病程而异。可有鼻咽炎、结合膜炎。听诊可闻及呼吸音粗糙、粗湿罗音和高调干性罗音。

3. 实验室检查周围血象可以升高或正常。胸部X线检查正常或肺纹理增强。

【辨证论治】

1. 风寒咳嗽

主证：咳嗽频作，痰白清稀，恶寒无汗，发热头痛，鼻塞流涕，喉痒声重，或全身酸痛，舌苔薄白，脉浮紧，指纹浮红。

治则：疏风散寒，宣肺止咳。

处方：三拗汤加味。

麻黄6克，杏仁6克，甘草3克，荆芥6克，前胡9克，半夏6克，桔梗6克，川贝9克。水煎服。

In addition to the above ingredients, 1.5 grams of asarum herb (*Herbar Asari*) and 9 grams of stemona root (*Radix Stemonae*) are added for those with severe cough. For the case with much sputum, 6 grams of red tangerine peel (*Exocarpium Citri Reticulatae*) should be included.

2. Cough due to Pathogenic Wind-heat

Main Symptoms and Signs: Cough with unclear throat, yellow and thick sputum which is not easy to be coughed up, sore throat, stuffy nose with turbid nasal discharge, accompanied with fever, headache, slight sweating, red lips and tongue with thin and yellow fur, floating and rapid pulse and shallow purple superficial venule of the index finger.

Therapeutic Principle: Expelling pathogenic wind-heat, relieving cough by promoting the dispersing function of the lung.

Recipe: Modified Decoction of Mulberry Leaf and Chrysanthemum.

mulberry leaf, *Folium Mori*   9g
chrysanthemum flower, *Flos Chrysanthemi*   9g
forsythia fruit, *Fructus Forsythiae*   9g
pepermint, *Herba Menthae*   9g
platycodon root, *Radix Platycodi*   9g
reel rhizome, *Rhizoma Phragmitis*   15g
liquorice, *Radix Glycyrrhizae*   3g
apricot kernel, *Semen Armeniacae Amarum*   6g

All the above drugs are to be decocted in water for oral administration.

Besides, in case of severe lung-heat with yellow fur of the tongue, 9 grams of scutellaria root (*Radix Scutellariae*) should be added. For those with severe heat in the lung and stomach manifested as strong dyspnea, add 18 grams of gypsum (*Gypsum Fibrosum*), 9 grams of anemarrhena rhizome (*Rhizoma Anemarrhenae*) and 9 grams of lepidium seed (*Semen Lepidii seu Descuraniae*). For those with swollen and sore throat, add 9

若咳重者，加细辛 1.5 克，百部 9 克；若痰多者，加橘红 6 克。

2. 风热咳嗽

主证：咳嗽不爽，痰黄稠，不易咯出，咽痛、鼻塞流浊涕，

伴有发热、头痛、微汗出，唇红，舌质红，苔薄黄，脉浮数，指

纹浮紫。

治则：疏风清热，宣肺止咳。

处方：桑菊饮加减。

桑叶 9 克，菊花 9 克，连翘 9 克，薄荷 9 克，桔梗 9 克，芦

根15克，甘草 3 克，杏仁 6 克。水煎服。

若肺热盛、舌苔黄者，加黄芩 9 克；肺胃热盛、气喘而粗者，

grams of ophiopogon root (*Radix Ophiopogonis*), 9 grams of arctium (*Fructus Arctii*) and 9 grams of belamcanda rhizome (*Rhizoma Belamcandae*). In case of much yellow and thick sputum, add 15 grams of waxgourd seed (*Semen Benincasae*), 6 grams of fritillary bulb (*Blubus Fritillariae*) and 9 grams of trichosanthes (*Fructus Trichosanthis*). 9 grams of peucedanum root (*Radix Peucedani*) and 9 grams of prepared loquat leaf (*Folium Eriobotryae Praeparatae*) are included for severe cough.

3. Cough due to Pathogenic Wind-dryness

Main Symptoms and Signs: Dry cough without any sputum or with little and mucoid sputum difficult to be coughed up, dry mouth and throat, dry nose, persistent cough with unclear throat, dull pain in both sides of the chest and hypochondrium, constipation, reddened lips and tongue with thin and yellowish or white and dry fur, rapid pulse, and blue and purple superficial venule of the index finger.

Therapeutic Principle: Clearing away lung-heat and moisturizing dryness.

Recipe: Modified Decoction for Relieving Dryness of the Lung.

gypsum, *Gypsum Fibrosum*   18g
trichosanthes, *Fructus Trichosanthis*   12g
adenophora root, *Radix Adenophorae*   9g
ophiopogon root, *Radix Ophiopogonis*   9g
prepared loquat leaf, *Folium Eriobotryae Praeparatae*   9g
mulberry leaf, *Folium Mori*   9g
apricot kernel, *Semen Armeniacae Amarum*   6g
anemarrhena rhizome, *Rhizoma Anemarrhenae*   6g

All the above drugs are to be decocted in water for oral administration.

Besides, for those with continued cough, add 9 grams of stemona root (*Radix Stemonae*) and 9 grams of wolfberry bark (*Cortex Lycii Radicis*). For those with epistaxis or hemoptysis, add 9 grams of rubia root (*Radix Rubiae*), 9 grams of dried reh-

加生石膏18克，知母9克，葶苈子9克；咽喉肿痛甚者，加麦冬9克，牛蒡子9克，射干9克；痰多黄稠者，加冬瓜仁15克，贝母6克，瓜蒌9克；咳重者，加前胡9克，炙枇杷叶9克。

3. 风燥咳嗽

主证：干咳无痰，或痰少而粘难以咳出，口燥咽干，鼻燥呛咳不爽，胸胁引痛，便难，唇红舌红，苔薄黄或薄白而干，脉数，指纹青紫。

治则：清肺润燥。

处方：清燥救肺汤加减。

生石膏18克，瓜蒌12克，沙参9克，麦冬9克，炙杷叶9克，桑叶9克，杏仁6克，知母6克。水煎服。

若久咳不止者，加百部9克，地骨皮9克；伴衄血、咯血者，

mannia root (*Radix Rehmanniae*), 9 grams of scutellaria root (*Radix Scutellariae*) and 15 grams of cogongrass rhizome (*Rhizoma Imperatae*).

Section 6
Infantile Pneumonia

Pneumonia is a very common disease in infants, usualy defined as acute inflammation of the lung caused by bacteria, viruses, *Mycoplasma pneumoniae*, etc. Clinically it can be classified as pneumococcal pneumonia, staphylococcal pneumonia, adenoviral pneumonia and so on, and pathogenically, as lobar pneumonia, lobular pneumonia, interstitial pneumonia and bronchopneumonia. This disease belongs to the categories of "*mapi feng*" (acute infantile pneumonia), "*bao chuan*" (sudden attack of asthma) in TCM.

MAIN POINTS OF DIAGNOSIS

1. Upper respiratory tract infection, characterized by fever, cough and nasal discharge, is followed by symptoms and signs of pneumonia, such as tachypnea, dyspnea, cyanosis, pallor, nares flaring, 3 concave signs and restlessness which may be accompanied with vomiting, abdominal distention, tachycardia and hepatomegaly.

2. Physical examinations may reveal dullness in the affected area through percussion, and diminished breathing sound, fine cracking rales or crepitus and moist rales on the affected side through auscultation.

3. Laboratory examinations may show elevated leukocyte count in the cases with bacterial pneumonia. Bacteriological evidence may be found by culture and isolation of bacteria from the sputum, tracheal aspirates, and pleural fluid obtained through thoracentesis.

4. Pneumonographic changes in early pneumonia include consolidation, pleural reaction with the presence of fluid,

加茜草9克，生地9克，黄芩9克，白茅根15克。

第六节　婴幼儿肺炎

肺炎是婴幼儿的常见病，多为细菌、病毒、肺炎支原体等引起的肺的急性炎性病变。临床上按病原体可分为肺炎球菌肺炎、葡萄球菌肺炎和腺病毒肺炎等；按病理可分为大叶性肺炎、小叶性肺炎、间质性肺炎和支气管肺炎等。本病属中医"马脾风"、"暴喘"等范畴。

【诊断要点】

1．发病前往往有上呼吸道感染，如发热、咳嗽、流涕。继之出现肺炎的表现，如呼吸增快、呼吸困难、发绀、苍白、鼻翼煽动和三凹征阳性、烦躁不安，可伴有呕吐、腹胀、心率快和肝肿大。

2．体格检查可发现病变区叩诊变浊，听诊有呼吸音减弱、细小劈啪罗音或捻发音和细小水泡音。

3．实验室检查在细菌性肺炎常有白细胞升高，痰或气管吸出物、胸腔穿刺液培养能发现细菌学证据。

4．X线检查在肺炎早期可有肺实质病变、胸膜反应、肺纹理

roughened lung-marking and sporadic mottlings on the lower field of the lung. It is very important that roentgenographic demonstration of complete resolution should be obtained 3–4 weeks after disappearance of symptoms.

DIFFERENTIATION AND TREATMENT OF COMMON SYNDROMES

1. Wind-cold Pathogen Tightening the Lung

Main Symptoms and Signs: Aversion to cold, fever, anhidrosis, absence of thirst, cough with unclear throat, white and thin sputum, normal tongue proper with thin and white or white and greasy fur, floating, tight and rapid pulse, and blue red superficial venule of the index finger existing more often on the wind pass.

Therapeutic Principle: Relieving exterior syndrome with drugs pungent in flavor and warm in property, ventilating the lung and eliminating sputum.

Recipe: Modified *Huagai* Powder

ephedra, *Herba Ephedrae*   6g

apricot kernel, *Semen Armeniacae Amarum*   6g

perilla fruit, *Fructus Perillae*   6g

tangerine peel, *Pericarpium Citri Reticulatae*   6g

pinellia tuber, *Rhizoma Pinelliae*   6g

tatarian aster root, *Radix Asteris*   9g

coltsfoot flower, *Flos Farfarae*   9g

fresh ginger, *Rhizoma Zingiberis Recens*   1 slice

Chinese-date, *Fructus Ziziphi Jujubae*   5 pieces

All the above drugs are to be decocted in water for oral administration.

Besides, in case of abundant expectoration, 6 grams of radish seed (*Semen Raphani*) and 6 grams of white mustard seed (*Semen Sinapis Albae*) should be included. For those with cold-syndrome in both exterior and interior, 1.5 grams of asarum herb (*Herba Asari*) should be added.

2. Wind-heat Pathogen Tightening the Lung

增强，可见斑点状散在的阴影，且以两肺下野居多。在症状消失后3～4周X线检查证明病变完全吸收很重要。

【辨证论治】

1. 风寒闭肺

主证：恶寒发热，无汗，不渴，咳嗽不爽，痰白且稀，舌质不红，苔薄白或白腻，脉浮紧而数，指纹青红多在风关。

治则：辛温解表，宣肺化痰。

处方：华盖散加减。

麻黄6克，杏仁6克，苏子6克，陈皮6克，半夏6克，紫菀9克，冬花9克，生姜1片，大枣5枚。水煎服。

若痰多者，加莱菔子6克，白芥子6克；表里俱寒者，加细辛1.5克。

2. 风热闭肺

Main Symptoms and Signs: Fever with sweat, thirst, cough with thick sputum, rapid breath with nares flaring, red face and lips, reddish throat, yellow urine, constipation or mucous stool, red tongue with yellowish fur, floating and rapid or smooth and rapid pulse, and blue purple superficial venule of the index finger existing more often on the *qi* pass.

Therapeutic Principle: Relieving exterior syndrome with drugs pungent in flavor and cool in property, ventilating the lung and eliminating sputum.

Recipe: Decoction of Ephedra, Apricot Kernel, Gypsum and Licorice with additional ingredients.

ephedra, *Herba, Ephedrae*   6g
apricot kernel, *Semen Armeniacae Amarum*   6g
gypsum, *Gypsum Fibrosum*   18g
liquorice, *Radix Glycyrrhizae*   3g
honeysuckle flower, *Flos Loniceerae*   12g
scutellaria root, *Radix Scutellariae*   9g
houttuynia, *Herba Houttuyniae*   9g
isatis root, *Radix Isatidis*   9g
platycodon root, *Radix Platycodi*   9g

All the above drugs are to be decocted in water for oral administration.

Besides, in case of severe cough, add 12 grams of white mulberry bark (*Cortes Mori Radicis*) and 9 grams of honeysuckle flower (*Flos Lonicerae*). For those with high fever and constipation, add 15 grams of reed rhizome (*Rhizoma Phragmitis*) and 20 ml of bamboo juice (*Succus Bambusae*) which is to be mixed up with the finished decoction.

3. Stagnation of Phlegm-heat in the Lung

Main Symptoms ane Signs: High fever, vexation, accumulation of phlegm in throat, polypnea, dyspnea, nares flaring even flaring of the hypochondria, abnormal protrusion of the chest and elevation of the shoulders, shaking of the body and plucking of the abdomen in severe cases, constipation, olguria

主证：发热有汗，口渴，咳嗽痰稠，气促鼻煽，面赤唇红，咽红，小便黄，大便不畅或有粘液，舌质红，舌苔黄，脉浮数或滑数，指纹青紫多在气关。

治则：辛凉解表，宣肺化痰。

处方：麻杏石甘汤加味。

麻黄 6 克，杏仁 6 克，生石膏 18 克，甘草 3 克，银花12克，黄芩 9 克，鱼腥草 9 克，板蓝根 9 克，桔梗 9 克。水煎服。

若咳甚者，加桑白皮12克，冬花 9 克；热重便秘者，加鲜芦根 15 克，鲜竹沥水20毫升（冲服）。

3．痰热闭肺

主证：壮热烦躁，喉间痰壅，气促喘憋，呼吸困难，鼻煽，

with yellow urine, red tongue with yellow and dry fur, full, slippery and rapid pulse, and blue purple superficial venule of the index finger existing more often on the *qi* pass.

Therapeutic Principle: Clearing away pathogenic heat, ventilating the lung and eliminating phlegm to relieve asthma.

Recipe: Modified prescription of Five-tiger Decoction and Decoction of Lepidium Seed and Chinese-date for Removing Phlegm from the Lung.

ephedra, *Herba Ephedrae*   6g

apricot kernel, *Semen Armeniacae Amarum*   9g

gypsum, *Gypsum Fibrosum*   30g (To be decocted first)

asarum herb, *Herba Asari*   6g

liquorice, *Radix Glycyrrhizae*   3g

lepidium seed, *Semen Lepidii Seu Descurainiae*   9g

Chinese-date, *Fructus Ziziphi Jujubae*   5 pieces

tabasheer, *Concretio Silicea Bambusae*   9g

scutellaria root, *Radix Scutellariae*   9g

arisaema with bile, *Arisaema cum Bile*   9g

houttuynia, *Herba Houttuyniae*   12g

fresh bamboo juice, *Succus Bambosae*   20 ml (To be taken
after being infused in the finished decoction)

All the above drugs except fresh bamboo juice are to be decocted in water for oral administration.

Besides, 3 grams of rhubarb (*Radix et Rhizoma Rhei*)which is to be decocted later should be added in case of constipation and abdominal distention. For those with severe cyanosis, remove apricot kernel, add 12 grams of red sage root (*Radix Salviae Miltiorrhizae*), 9 grams of red peony root (*Radix Peoniae Rubra*), 6 grams of safflower (*Flos Carthami*) and 9 grams of Chinese angelica root (*Radix Angelicae Sinensis*). In case of invasion of *ying* system by heat marked by coma, delirium, deep-red tongue, absence of nasal discharge and tears, the above prescription and Decoction for Clearing Away Heat in *Ying* System should include curcuma root (*Radix Curcumae*) and

甚则两肋煽动，胸高抬肩，摇身撷肚，大便干结，小便黄少，舌

质红，苔黄燥，**脉洪滑数**，指纹青紫多在气关以上。

治则：清热宣肺，豁痰平喘。

处方：五虎汤合葶苈大枣泻肺汤加减。

麻黄6克，杏仁9克，生石膏30克（先煎），细辛6克，甘草

3克，葶苈子9克，大枣5枚，天竺黄9克，黄芩9克，胆南星

9克，鱼腥草12克，鲜竹沥水20毫升（冲）。水煎服。

若便秘、腹胀者，加生大黄（后下）；紫绀严重者，去杏仁，

加丹参12克，赤芍9克，红花6克，当归9克；如热入营分出现

神昏谵语、舌质红绛、涕泪俱无者，可用上方合清营汤加郁金、

grassleaved sweetflag rhizome (*Rhizoma Acori Graminei*) which are to be decocted for oral administration. Simultaneously, Purple Snowy Powder should be taken after being infused in the finished decoction of the above ingredients.

Section 7
Infantile Diarrhea

This diarrhea refers to increased frequency and volume of defecation. Acute diarrhea may be associated with improper intake, bacterial infection or affection by its toxin, or viral infection. The course of diarrhea of persisting type is usually over 4 weeks and it is often caused by uncontrolled intestinal infections or induced by flora imbalance resulting from abused antibiotics. In TCM, this disease is categorized as *"xie xie"* (diarrhea).

MAIN POINTS OF DIAGNOSIS

1. A chief complaint of diarrhea is the increase in frequency and volume of stools. In mild cases, there are 5–10 episodes of defecation a day and in severe cases over 10 episodes. The stools are usually yellow or yellow-greenish watery and mucous with a sour or stinking smell.

2. In severe patients, vomiting, loss of appetite, abdominal distension and pain, tenesmus, fever, restlessness, and listlessness usually occur. There may be symptoms or signs of dehydration such as weight loss, emaciation, pitting of anterior fontanel and socket of eye ball, rapid pulse, hypotension and oliguria, and manifestations of acidosis such as somnolence, hyperpnea, cherrylike lips and respiration with acetone smell. Patients with diarrhea of persisting type often have malnutrition, marasmus, anorexia and anemia.

3. Laboratory microscopic examinations may show leukocytes and fat globules in stools. Pathogens may be found in cul-

菖蒲，并冲服紫雪丹。

第七节　婴儿腹泻

婴儿腹泻是指婴儿大便次数和量的增加。引起急性腹泻的原因可能与饮食因素、细菌感染或其毒素作用或病毒感染有关。婴儿迁延性腹泻病程可在 1 个月以上，常与肠道感染未获控制或滥用各种抗生素引起菌群失调有关。本病属中医"泄泻"范畴。

【诊断要点】

1. 主要表现为大便次数和量的增多。轻症每天大 便 5～10 次，重症10次以上，大便呈黄水样或黄绿水样，含有粘液，有酸臭味或腥臭味。

2. 重症除腹泻外尚有呕吐、食欲下降、腹胀、腹痛、里急后重、发热、烦躁不安、精神萎靡等。可出现体重丢失、憔悴、前囟和眼窝凹陷、脉快、血压低、尿量少等脱水症状和嗜睡、呼吸深快、口唇樱桃红样、呼吸有酸味等酸中毒的特点。迁延性腹泻患儿常有营养不良、消瘦、食欲低下和贫血等。

3. 实验室大便镜检可有白细胞和脂肪球，大便培养可能发

tured stools. CO_2-combining power is usually diminshed and electrolyte disturbance may usually be present in severe cases.

DIFFERENTIATION AND TREATMENT OF COMMON SYNDROMES

1. Diarrhea due to Pathogenic Damp-heat

Main Symptoms and Signs: Fever or absence of fever, thirst, greenish or yellowish watery stools with indigested food and mucus, ten or more diarrhea episodes a day, burning and reddened anus, scanty dark urine, yellow and greasy fur of the tongue, slippery and rapid pulse, and blue purple surperficial venule of the index finger.

Therapeutic Principle: Clearing away pathogenic heat and dampness.

Recipe: Decoction of Pueraria, Scutellaria and Coptis with additional ingredients.

pueraria root, *Radix Puerariae*   9g
scutellaria root, *Radix Scutellariae*   9g
coptis root, *Rhizoma Coptidis*   3g
honeysuckle flower, *Flos Lonicerae*   9g
asiatic plantain seed, *Semen Plantaginis*   9g (wrapped in a piece of cloth before it is to be decocted)
tale, *Talcum*   12g
liquorice, *Radix Glycyrrhizae*   3g

All the above drugs are to be decocted in water for oral administration.

Besides, for those with severe symptoms of dampness, add 12 grams of poria (*Poria*), 9 grams of umbellate pore-fungue, (*Polyporus Umbellatus*), 9 grams of white atractylodes rhizome, (*Rhizoma Atractylodis Macrocephalae*) and 9 grams of orienta lwater plantain (*Rhizoma Alismatis*); in case of *yin* damage due to sudden diarrhea resulting from summer-heat, add 12 grams of caryophyllaceous ginseng (*Radix Pseudostellariae*), 18 grams of gypsum (*Gypasum Fibrosum*), 6 grams of black plum (*Fructus Mume*) and 6 grams of schisandra fruit (*Fructus Schisandrae*).

现致病菌。重症患儿常有血二氧化碳结合力下降和电解质紊乱。

【辨证论治】

1. 湿热泄泻

主证：发热或不发热，口渴，大便如水样，色绿或黄，内含不消化食物，或有少许粘液，日十余次，肛门灼热发红，小便短赤，舌苔黄腻，脉滑数，指纹青紫。

治则：清热利湿。

处方：葛根芩连汤加味。

葛根9克，黄芩9克，黄连3克，金银花9克，车前子9克（布包煎），滑石12克，甘草3克。水煎服。

若湿盛者，加茯苓12克，猪苓9克，白术9克，泽泻9克，如为暑热暴泄伤阴者，加孩儿参12克，生石膏18克，乌梅6克五味子6克。

2. 伤食泄泻

2. Diarrhea due to Impairment by Overeating

Main Symptoms and Signs: History of impairment by overeating, abdominal distention and pain, crying and restlessness before diarrhea, pain relief after diarrhea, stools with an odour as sour as that of putrid eggs, wind from bowels, halitosis, anorexia with frequent vomiting, thick and greasy or yellowish fur of the tongue, smooth pulse, deep and stagnated superficial venule of the index finger.

Therapeutic Principle: Promoting digestion, removing stagnated food and regulating the stomach to treat diarrhea.

Recipe: Modified Lenitive Pill.

hawthorn fruit, *Fructus Crataegi*   12g

medicated leaven, *Massa Fermentata Madicinalis*   9g

pinellia tuber, *Rhizoma Pinelliae*   6g

poria, *Poria*   9g

radish seed, *Semen Raphani*   9g

bitter orange immature, *Fructus Aurantii Immaturus*   6g

tangerine peel, *Pericarpium Citri Reticulatae*   6g

chicken's gizzard-skin, *Endothelium Corneum Gigeriae Galli*   6g

aucklandia root, *Radix Aucklandiae*   3g

All the above drugs are to be decocted in water for oral administration.

Besides, in case of fever, 9 grams of scutellaria root (*Radix Scutellariae*) should be added; for those with severe abdominal distention, 6 grams of magnolia bark (*Cortex Magnoliae Officinalis*) is included. In case of anorexia, 9 grams of white atractylodes rhizome (*Rhizoma Atractylodis Macrocephalae*) is added; and for those with vomiting, add 9 grams of agastache, (*Herba Agastachis*) and 6 grams of amomum fruit (*Fructus Amomi*).

3. Diarrhea due to Insufficiency of the Spleen

Main Symptoms and Signs: Intermittent or lingering diarrhea, loose stools, or indigested food in stools with white milky mass or food residues. diarrhea right after food

主证：有伤食史，腹胀腹痛，泻前哭闹，泻后痛减，大便酸臭如败卵，矢气，口臭，纳呆，常伴呕吐，舌苔厚腻或黄，脉滑，指纹沉滞。

治则：消食化积，和中止泻。

处方：保和丸加减。

山楂12克，神曲9克，半夏6克，茯苓9克，莱菔子9克，枳实6克，陈皮6克，鸡内金6克，木香3克。水煎服。

若发热者，加黄芩9克6克；腹胀重者，加厚朴6克；纳呆者，加白术9克；伴呕吐者，加藿香9克，砂仁6克。

3．脾虚泄泻

主证：时泻时止或久泻不愈，便稀或水谷不化，带有白色奶

intake, pale face, sleeping with eyes open, pale tongue with thin and white fur, deep and weak pulse, and pale and superficial venule of the index finger.

Therapeutic Principle: Strengthening the spleen to treat · diarrhea.

Recipe: Powder of Seven Ingredients Including White Atractylodes with additional ingredients.

dangshen, *Radix Codonopsis Pilosulae*   9g

white atractylodes rhizome, *Rhizoma Atractylodis Macrocephalae*   9g

poria, *Poria*   9g

pueraria root, *Radix Puerariae*   12g

agastache, *Herba Agastachis*   9g

hyacinth bean, *Semen Dolichoris*   12g

aucklandia root, *Radix Aucklandia*   3g

baked ginger, *Rhizoma Zingiberis Praeparatae*   3g

All the above drugs are to be decocted in water for oral administration.

For those with insufficiency of the spleen-*yin* marked by red tongue without fur, add 15 grams of Chinese yam. (*Rhizoma Dioscoreae*) and 6 grams of black plum (*Fructus Mume*) instead of baked ginger. In case of insufficiency of the spleen due to fright with dark green stool, 9 grams of white peony root (*Radix Paeoniae Alba*) and 9 grams of hooked uncaria (*Ramulus Uncariae cum Uncis*) should be included.

Section 8
Viral Myocarditis

Viral myocarditis is defined as circumscribed or disseminated lesions of cardiac parenchyma or mesenchyma after viral infections, marked by retrograde degeneration and necrosis occurring in cardiac fibers. This disease belongs to the category

块或食物残渣，每凋食后作泻，面色苍白，睡时露睛，舌质淡，

苔薄白，脉沉无力，指纹淡红。

治则：健脾止泻。

处方：七味白术散加味。

党参9克，白术9克，茯苓9克，葛根12克，藿香9克，扁

豆12克，木香3克，炮姜3克。水煎服。

若脾阴虚、舌红无苔者，去炮姜，加山药15克，乌梅6克，

若脾虚受惊、大便青绿者，可加白芍9克，钩藤9克。

第八节　病毒性心肌炎

病毒性心肌炎是病毒感染后引起的心脏实质或间质局限或弥

of "*xin ji*" (palpitation) in TCM.

MAIN POINTS OF DIAGNOSIS

1. Clinical manifestations of viral myocarditis vary. There are prodromal symptoms preceding to the onset of myocarditis, such as fever, cough, nausea, vomiting, abdominal pain or diarrhea. Myalgia and arthralgia may be present.

2. The symptoms of myocarditis include listlessness, pallor, fatigue, hyperhidrosis, dizziness, palpitation, discomfort of the precordial area and loss of appetite. Heart failure and cardiogenic shock may occur in severe cases.

3. Physical examinations may reveal cardiac enlargement, diminution of heart sound, gallop rhythm and other arrhythmia. Usually murmur can not be obtained, or I-II degree systolic murmur may be heard. If the patients have pericarditis, the pericardial friction sound can be heard. Symptoms and signs of pneumonedema and heart failure may appear in severe cases.

4. Laboratory examinations may show elevated serum creatine phosphokinase (CPK) and its isoenzyme as well as serum glutamic oxalacetic transaminase (SGOT). Viral isolates may be obtained from pericardial effusion or feces, and the specific antibody to the virus will rise obviously 2-3 weeks later.

5. Electrocardiogram usually shows depressed S-T segment lower or inverted, T-waves in most leads, prolonged Q-T interval, myocardial hypertrophy, arrhythmia, etc. X-ray examination of heart can reveal general occurrence of cardiomegaly and diminution of heart beat. Pulmonary congestion and pneumonedema will be present in serious cases.

DIFFERENTIATION AND TREATMENT OF COMMON SYNDROMES

1. Heart Disturbed by Pathogenic Fire-heat

Main Symptoms and Signs: Palpitation, much crying and tendency to be frightened, vexation, thirst, flushed face,

漫性病变，心肌纤维发生退行性改变与坏死。本病属中医"心悸"范畴。

【诊断要点】

1．临床表现不一。起病前有前驱症状，如发热、咳嗽、恶心、呕吐、腹痛或腹泻，常伴有肌痛和关节痛。

2．心肌炎的表现常有精神萎靡、苍白、乏力、多汗、头晕、心悸、心前区不适和食欲下降，严重病例易出现心力衰竭或心源性休克。

3．体格检查可发现心脏增大，心音减弱，奔马律等心律失常，可无心脏杂音或有Ⅰ～Ⅱ级收缩期杂音。有心包炎时可听到心包摩擦音。严重病例可有肺水肿及心力衰竭症状和体征。

4．实验室检查有血清肌酸磷酸激酶及其同功酶升高，血清谷-草转氨酶升高。心包液或粪便可分离出病毒，2～3周后血清中病毒的特异性抗体明显升高。

5．心电图检查大多数导联可见 S—T 段压低，T波低平或倒置，Q—T 间期延长，心肌肥厚，心律失常等。X线检查示心脏普遍性增大，搏动减弱，重者有肺瘀血和肺水肿的表现。

【辨证论治】

1．火热扰心

主证：心悸，多啼善惊，心烦而渴，面红，尿黄赤，舌尖干

dark urine, dry and deep-red tongue apex, smooth and rapid pulse and deep-red superficial venule of the index finger.

Therapeutic Principle: Clearing away heart-fire and tranquilizing the mind.

Recipe: Modified prescriptions of Decoction for Clearing Heart-fire and Sedative Bolus of Cinnabar.

lophatherum, *Herba Lophatheri*   9g

forsythia fruit, *Fructus Forsythiae*   9g

lotus plumule, *Plumula Nelumbinis*   6g

scrophularia root, *Radix Scrophulariae*   9g

wild jujuba seed, *Semen Ziziphi Spinosae*   15g

Chinese angelica root, *Radix Angelicae Sinensis*   9g

dried rehmannia root, *Radix Rehmanniae*   9g

amber, *Succinum*   9g

rhinoceros horn, *Cornu Rhinoceri*   1.5g (To be taken after being infused with the finished decoction)

liquorice, *Radix Glycyrrhizae*   3g

All the above drugs are to be decocted in water for oral administration.

2. Deficiency of the Heart-blood

Main Symptoms and Signs: Palpitation and fidgets, dim complexion, pale lips, dizziness, general lassitude and weakness, anorexia, pale tongue, thready, rapid and weak or knotted pulse with irregular intervals, and pale superficial venule of the index finger.

Therapeutic Principle: Enriching the heart-blood.

Recipe: Decoction for Invigorating the Spleen and Nourishing the Heart.

dangshen, *Radix Codonopsis Pilosulae*   15g

astragalus root, *Radix Asrtagali seu Hedysari*   15g

Chinese angelica root, *Radix Angelicae Sinensis*   6g

white atractylodes rhizome, *Rhizoma Atractylidis Macrocephalae*   9g

poria with hostwood, *Poria cum Ligno Hospite*   9g

绛，脉滑数，指纹深红。

治则：清心安神。

处方：清宫汤合朱砂安神丸加减。

竹叶9克，连翘9克，莲子心6克，元参9克，酸枣仁15克，

当归9克，生地9克，琥珀9克，犀角1.5克(冲)，生甘草3克。

水煎服。

2．心血不足

主证：心悸不安，面色无华，口唇苍白，头晕目眩，体倦乏

力，纳呆，舌质淡，脉细数而弱或结代，指纹淡。

治则：补养心血。

处方：归脾汤加减。

党参15克，黄芪15克，当归6克，白术9克，茯神9克，

fried wild jujuba seed, *Semen Ziziphi Spinosae*   15g
longan pulp, *Arillus Longan*   9g
polygala root, *Radix Polygalae*   9g
prepared liquorice, *Radix Glycyrrhizae Praeparata*   6g
fresh ginger, *Rhizoma Zingiberis Recens*   1 slice
Chinese-date, *Fructus Ziziphi Jujubae*   5 pieces

All the above drugs are to be decocted in water for oral administration.

Besides, those with severe palpitation, slow pulse with irregular intervals should be treated by regulating both *yin* and *yang*, for whom modified Decoction of Prepared Licorice can be used (Refer to relevant part of **Prescriptions of TCM** in this Library).

3. Blood Stasis in the Heart

Main Symptoms and Signs: Palpitation or severe palpitation, oppressed uncomfortable feeling in the chest, or paroxysmal chest pain, dark purple tongue or with ecchymoses, and uneven or knotted pulse.

Therapeutic Principle: Promoting blood circulation to remove blood stasis.

Recipe: Modified Decoction for Removing Blood Stasis in the Chest.

peach kernel, *Semen Persicae*   6g
safflower, *Flos Carthami*   6g
chuanxiong rhizome, *Rhizoma Ligustici Chuanxiong*   6g
red peony root, *Radix Paeoniae Rubra*   9g
achyranthes root, *Radix Achyranthis Bidentatae*   9g
bitter orange, *Fructus Aurantii*   9g
bupleurum root, *Radix Bupleuri*   9g
platycodon root, *Radix Platycodi*   9g
trichosanthes fruit, *Fruit Trichosanthis*   9g
macrostem onion, *Bulbus Allii Macrostemi*   9g
pinellia tuber, *Rhizoma Pinelliae*   9g
Chinese angelica root, *Radix Angelicae Sinensis*   9g

炒酸枣仁15克，桂圆肉9克，远志9克，炙甘草6克，生姜1片，大枣5枚。水煎服。

若心悸动、脉结代者，当阴阳兼调，可用炙甘草汤加减（见本文库《方剂学》有关部分）。

3. 瘀血内阻

主证：心悸怔忡，胸闷不舒，或胸痛阵作，舌质紫暗或有瘀斑、瘀点，脉涩或结代。

治则：活血祛瘀。

处方：血府逐瘀汤加减。

桃仁6克，红花6克，川芎6克，赤芍9克，牛膝9克，枳

dried rehmannia root, *Radix Rehmanniae*   9g

liquorice, *Radix Glycyrrhizae*   3g

All the above drugs are to be decocted in water for oral administration.

Section 9

Urinary Infection

Urinary infection of children is defined as bacterial infections of the urethra, bladder, pelves and renal parenchyma, of which pyelitis is the most common. Acute urinary infection refers to infection lasting for less than 6 months after the onset; and chronic, more than 6 months. This disease belongs to the category of *"lin zheng"* (stranguria) in TCM.

MAIN POINTS OF DIAGNOSIS

1. Clinical manifestations are characterized by symptoms of infection such as fever, vomiting, diarrhea, pallor and loss of appetite. In infants, jaundice may be present.

2. The typical symptoms of urinary infection may include urodynia, urgency and frequency of urination, dysuria, dripping urine, pain in the lumbar region, occasionally with transient hematuria and enuresis. Infants may have irritated cry when urinating and obstinate diaper rash which are liable to be accompanied with inflammation of mucous membrane of the external genital organs.

3. Chronic recurrent infection may be accompanied with intermittent fever, lumbar soreness, fatigue and anemia, or with renal failure in severe cases.

4. In laboratory examinations, urinary sediment after centrifugation usually shows white cells and casts. In urine culture, bacterial colony counts over 100,000 / ml may permit a tentative diagnosis of urinary infection.

5. Ultrasonography of kidney, and nephropyelo-

壳9克，柴胡9克，桔梗9克，瓜蒌9克，薤白9克，半夏9克，当归9克，生地9克，甘草3克。水煎服。

第九节　泌尿系感染

小儿泌尿系感染是指尿道、膀胱、肾盂及肾实质的细菌感染，其中以肾盂炎为最常见。病程在6个月以内者为急性，6个月以上为慢性。本病属中医"淋证"范畴。

【诊断要点】

1. 临床表现是以感染症状为特点，如发热、呕吐、腹泻、苍白、食欲下降。在婴儿，可见黄疸。

2. 泌尿系统症状可有尿痛、尿急、尿频、排尿困难、滴尿、肾区疼痛，偶有一过性血尿或遗尿。在婴儿可有激惹性排尿哭闹、顽固性尿布疹。另外，易伴有外生殖器粘膜炎症。

3. 慢性反复性感染可有间歇性发热、腰酸、乏力和贫血，重者可致肾功能衰竭。

4. 实验室尿沉渣镜检有白细胞、白细胞管型。尿培养菌落计数10万个/毫升以上可以确诊。

5. 肾超声图、肾盂X线造影可发现易引起感染的原因，

graphy may help to find the causes of urinary infection, such as deformity of urinary tract, kidney stone, obstruction, backflow of urine and hydronephrosis.

DIFFERENTIATION AND TREATMENT OF COMMON SYNDROMES

1. Damp-heat in the Urinary Bladder

Main Symptoms and Signs: Aversion to cold, fever, marked by persistent fever after sweating, urgent and frequent micturition, dripping discharge of urine with burning sensation and stabbing pain, nausea, vomiting, distending pain in the lower abdomen, restlessness with frequent crying in infants, urgency of urination with dark urine, red tongue with yellow or white and greasy fur, and rapid pulse.

Therapeutic Principle: Clearing away and purging pathogenic heat-fire, and inducing diuresis to treat stranguria.

Recipe: Modified Eight Health Restoring Powder.

prostrate knotweed, *Herba Polygoni Avicularis*   9g

Chinese pink herb, *Herba Dianthi*   9g

armed clematis stem, *Caulis Clematidis Armandii*   3g

plantain seed, *Semen Plantaginis*   9g (wrapped in a piece of cloth before it is to be decocted)

capejasmine fruit, *Fructus Gardeniae*   9g

tale, *Talcum*   12g

liquorice, *Radix Glycyrrhizae*   3g

lophatherum, *Herba Lophatheri*   9g

honeysuckle flower, *Flos Lonicerae*   15g

cogongrass rhizome, *Rhizoma Imperatae*   15g

All the above drugs are to be decocted in water for oral administration.

2. Stagnated Heat in the Liver and Gallbladder

Main Symptoms and Signs: Fever, aversion to cold, bitter taste in the mouth, anorexia or vomiting, restlesseness, frequent and precipitant urination with scanty dark urine, difficulty and pain in micturition, yellow and greasy fur of

如泌尿道畸型、结石、梗阻、尿反流及肾盂积水等。

【辨证论治】

1．膀胱湿热

主证：恶寒发热，汗出热不退，尿频尿急，淋沥不畅，热涩刺痛，恶心呕吐，少腹胀痛，婴幼儿常时时啼哭不安，尿急黄赤，舌质红，苔黄或白腻，脉数。

治则：清热泻火，利水通淋。

处方：八正散加减。

萹蓄 9 克，瞿麦 9 克，木通 3 克，车前子 9 克（布包煎），栀子 9 克、滑石 12 克，甘草 3 克，淡竹叶 9 克，银花 15 克，白茅根 15 克。水煎服。

2．肝胆郁热

主证：发热，恶寒，口苦纳呆，或有呕吐，烦躁不安，小便

the tongue, taut and rapid pulse.

Therapeutic Principle: Purging pathogenic fire and toxin, removing pathogenic heat from the liver and gall-bladder.

Recipe: Modified Decoction of Gantian for Purging Liver-fire.

capejasmine fruit, *Fructus Gardeniae*   9g

scutellaria root, *Radix Scutellariae*   9g

bupleurum root, *Radix Bupleuri*   9g

dried rhemannia root, *Radix Rhemanniae*   9g

plantain seed, *Semen Plantaginis*   9g (wrapped in a piece of cloth before it is to be decocted)

alismatis rhizome, *Rhizoma Alimatis*   9g

armed clematis stem, *Caulis Clematidis Armandii*   3g

phellodendron bark, *Cortes Phellodendri*   9g

cogongrass rhizome, *Rhizoma Imperatae*   15g

smilax glabra rhizome, *Rhizoma Smilacis Glabrae*   9g

liquorice, *Radix Glycyrrhizae*   3g

All the above drugs are to be decocted in water for oral administration.

3. Deficiency of Both the Spleen and the Kidney

Main Symptoms and Signs: Difficulty and pain in micturition and dripping urination, short breath, disinclination to speak, pale complexion, anorexia and abdominal distention, loose stool, sore waist, fatigue, weakness, pale tongue with thin and white fur, and deep, thready and weak pulse.

Therapeutic Principle: Strengthening the spleen and tonifying the kidney to eliminate dampness.

Recipe: Modified Decoction of Four Noble Drugs with Life Preserving Pill for Replenishing the Kidney *Qi*.

dangshen, *Radix Codonopsis Pilosulae*   9g

poria, *Poria*   9g

white atractylodes rhizome, *Rhizoma Atractylodis Macroce-*

频急短赤，溺时涩痛，苔黄腻，脉弦数。

治则：泻火解毒，清利肝胆。

处方：龙胆泻肝汤加减。

栀子9克，黄芩9g，柴胡9克，生地9克，车前子9克（布包煎），泽泻9克，木通3克，黄柏9克，白茅根15克，土茯苓9克，甘草3克。水煎服。

3. 脾肾两虚

主证：小便艰涩疼痛，淋沥不已，时作时止，气短懒言，面色苍白，纳呆腹胀，便溏，腰酸，倦怠无力，舌质淡，苔薄白，脉沉细无力。

治则：健脾补肾，佐以渗湿。

处方：四君子汤合济生肾气丸加减。

党参9克，茯苓9克，白术9克，山药9克，山萸肉9克，

phalae   9g

Chinese yam, *Rhizoma Dioscoreae*   9g

dogwood fruit, *Fructus Corni*   9g

plantain seed, *Semen Plantaginis*   9g (wrapped in a piece of cloth before it is to be decocted)

achyranthes root, *Radix Achydranthis Bidentatae*   9g

coix seed, *Semen Coicis*   12g

All the above drugs are to be decocted in water for oral administration.

For those with sore waist, add 9 grams of loranthus mulberry mistleloe (*Ramulus Loranthi*); in case of edema, add 15 grams of waxgourd peel (*Exocarpium Benincase*) and 9 grams of alismatis rhizome (*Rhizoma Alismantis*).

Section 10

Enuresis

Enuresis of children is defined as involuntary emptying of the bladder during the daytime or at night when the children are above the age of 3. This disease is categorized as "*yi niao*" (bed wetting) in TCM.

MAIN POINTS OF DIAGNOSIS

1. Clinical features are uncontrolled diurnal or nocturnal enuresis without dysuria.

2. Careful examination should be made on the life habit and mental status of the children to make sure if there are infections of the urinary tract or organic disorders.

3. In laboratory examinations, routine urine examination and culture may help to find out urinary tract infection. Roentgenography and pyelography may show recessive spinal bifida and other deformities of the urinary tract.

DIFFERENTIATION AND TREATMENT OF COMMON SYNDROMES

车前子9克(布包煎)，牛膝9克，生苡仁12克。水煎服。

若腰酸而痛者，加桑寄生9克；水肿者，加冬瓜皮15克，泽泻9克。

第十节　遗　尿　症

小儿遗尿症是指小儿在3岁以后仍有白天或夜间不自主的排尿。本病属中医"遗溺"范畴。

【诊断要点】

1. 临床特点是白天或夜间遗尿，不能自己控制，无排尿困难。

2. 应仔细检查生活习惯、精神状态以及有无泌尿系感染和器质性病变。

3. 实验室检查、尿常规和尿培养可证明泌尿道感染，X线照相术和肾盂造影术可发现隐性脊柱裂和其他泌尿道畸形。

【辨证论治】

1. Deficiency-cold of the Kidney

Main Symptoms and Signs: Frequent enuresis during sleeping, difficulty in being waken up from sound sleep, frequent light-coloured urine, pallor, cold limbs, fear of cold, weakness of the lower extremities, lassitude of the loins and legs, mental retardation, pale tongue with thin and white fur, and deep, slow and weak pulse.

Therapeutic Principle: Warming and recuperating the kidney-*yang* to treat enuresis.

Recipe: Modified prescriptions of Mantis Egg-case Powder and Enuresis Powder.

mantis egg-case, *Ootheca Mantidis*   15g
dodder seed, *Semen Cuscutae*   9g
bitter cardamon, *Fructus Alpiniae Oxyphyllae*   15g
psoralea fruit, *Fructus Psoraleae*   15g
raspberry, *Fructus Rubi*   15 g
prepared aconite root, *Radix Aconiti Praeparata*   6g
cinnamon bark, *Cortex Cinnamomi*   4.5g
astragalus root, *Radix Astragali*   15g
dangshen, *Radix Codonopsis Pilosulae*   15g

All the above drugs are to be decocted in water for oral administration.

2. Deficiency of the Spleen-*qi* and Lung-*qi*

Main Symptoms and Signs: Enuresis during sleeping, frequent and scanty urination, short breath, disinclination to speak, lassitude and weakness, sallow complexion, poor appetite, loose stool, frequent spontaneous perspiration or night sweat, pale and tender tongue with thin and white fur, and moderate pulse.

Therapeutic Principle: Building up the primordial energy and supplementing the kidney-*qi* to arrest enuresis.

Recipe: Modified prescriptions of Decoction for Reinforcing Middle-*jiao* and Replenishing *Qi* and Pill for Treating

1. 下元虚寒

主证：睡中经常遗尿，酣睡不易叫醒，小便清长而频数，面色苍白，肢凉怕冷，下肢无力，腰腿酸软，智力迟钝，舌质淡，苔薄白，脉沉迟无力。

治则：温补肾阳，固摄下元。

处方：桑螵蛸散合巩堤丸加减。

桑螵蛸15克，菟丝子9克，益智仁15克，补骨脂15克，覆盆子15克，熟附子6克，肉桂4.5克，黄氏15克，党参15克。水煎服。

2. 脾肺气虚

主证：睡中遗尿，尿频而尿量不多，少气懒言，神倦乏力，面色苍黄，食欲不振，大便溏，常自汗或盗汗，舌质淡嫩，苔薄白，脉缓。

治则：培元益气，佐以固涩。

Enuresis.

    dangshen, *Radix Codonopsis Pilosulae*   15g

    astragalus root, *Radix Astragali*   15g

    white atractylodes rhizome, *Rhizoma Atractylodis Macrocephalae*   9g

    Chinese yam, *Rhizoma Dioscoreae*   9g

    Chinese angelica root, *Radix Angelicae Sinensis*   9g

    cimicifuga rhizome, *Rhizoma Cimicifugae*   6g

    bupleurum root, *Radix Bupleuri*   6g

    tangerine peel, *Pericaripium Citri Reticulatae*   6g

    bitter cardamon, *Fructus Alpiniae Oxyphyllae*   15g

    schisandra fruit, *Fructus Schisandrae*   9g

    prepared liquorice, *Radix Glycyrrhizae Praeparata*   3g

All the above drugs are to be decocted in water for oral administration.

3. Damp-heat Accumulated in the Liver Channel

Main Symptoms and Signs: Enuresis during sleeping, scanty urine with fish-stink odour and yellow colour, irascible temperament or feverish sensation in the palms and soles, nocturnal muttering and teeth grinding, flushed face and lips, thin and yellowish fur, and taut and smooth pulse.

Therapeutic Principle: Removing pathogenic damp-heat from the liver channel.

Recipe: Modified Decoction of Gentian for Purging Liver-fire.

    gentian root, *Radix Gentianae*   3g

    capejasmine fruit, *Fructus Gardeniae*   9g

    armed clematis stem, *Caulis Clematidis Armandii*   3g

    bupleurum root, *Radix Bupleuri*   6g

    Chinese angelica root, *Radix Angelicae Sinensis*,   9g

    scutellaria root, *Radix Scutellariae*   9g

    alismatis rhizome, *Rhizoma Alismatis*   9g

    plantain seed, *Semen Plantaginis*   9g (wrapped in a piece of cloth before it is to be decocted)

处方：补中益气汤合缩泉丸加减。

党参15克，黄芪15克，白术9克，山药9克，当归9克，

升麻6克，柴胡6克，陈皮6克，益智仁15克，五味子9克，

炙甘草3克。水煎服。

3．肝经湿热

主证：睡中遗尿，尿量不多，但尿味腥臊，尿色黄，平时性情

急躁，或手足灼热，夜间梦语，龀齿，面赤唇红，舌苔薄黄，脉

弦滑。

治则：清利肝经湿热。

处方：龙胆泻肝汤加减。

龙胆草3克，栀子9克，木通3克，柴胡6克，当归9克，

pyrrosia leaf, *Folium Pyrrosiae*   9g
liquorice, *Radix Glycyrrhizae Praeparata*   3g
All the above drugs are to be decocted in water for oral administration.

Section 11

Mixed Nutritional Anemia

Mixed nutritional anemia is defined as megaloblastic and iron-deficiency anemia resulting from deficiency of iron, vitamin B_{12} and folic acid in food. The disease usually occurs in the courses of denutrition and certain chronic disorders. It belongs to the categories of *"xue xu"* (deficiency of blood), *"xu lao"* (consumptive diseases) and others in TCM.

MAIN POINTS OF DIAGNOSIS

1. It usually occurs in infants and children aged from 6 months to 3 years with the history of malnutrition or improper feeding. The main manifestations are anemia, pallor, waxy-yellow face, loss of appetite, delayed development, and thin and discrete hair. In some cases, facial edema may appear.

2. The patients may have symptoms of the nervous system, such as irregular thrill, involuntary motion of the hands and feet, or general shaking which may result in difficult feeding.

3. Mild enlarged liver, spleen and lymph nodes and a few of petechiae may be present.

4. Laboratory examinations may show normal or decreased leukocyte count, thrombocytopenia and different-sized and shaped red blood cells. Serum iron is less than 50 μg / dl, ferroprotein less than 10 ng / ml (normal 35 ng / ml), and serum vitamin B_{12} less than 100 pg / ml. The examination of bone marrow may also show vigorous regeneration of red blood cells and thrombocytopenia.

黄芩9克，泽泻9克，车前子9克(布包煎)，石苇9克，甘草3克。水煎服。

第十一节　营养性混合性贫血

营养性混合性贫血是指饮食中缺铁、维生素B₁₂或叶酸等造血物质而引起的巨幼细胞性和缺铁性贫血，往往在营养缺乏或某些慢性疾病中发生。本病属中医"血虚"、"虚劳"等范畴。

【诊断要点】

1. 好发于6个月～3岁的婴幼儿，多有营养不良和喂养不当史。主要表现为贫血，面色苍白或腊黄，食欲低下，发育迟缓，头发稀疏而细，面部可有浮肿。

2. 可伴有神经系统症状，如不规则性震颤，手足无意识运动或全身发抖而造成喂养困难。

3. 常有轻度的肝、脾、淋巴结肿大和皮肤少许出血点。

4. 实验室检查可见白细胞计数正常或低下，血小板减少，红细胞大小形态不一。血清铁低于50微克/分升，血清铁蛋白低于10纳克/毫升，血清维生素B₁₂可低于100皮克/毫升。骨髓检查示红细胞再生旺盛及血小板减少。

DIFFERENTIATION AND TREATMENT OF COMMON SYNDROMES

1. Blood Deficiency

Main Symptoms and Signs: Pallor, pale lips and nails, pale tongue with white fur, and soft pulse.

Therapeutic Principle: Replenishing *qi* and enriching blood.

Recipe: Flavoured Decoction of Four Ingredients.

prepared rehmannia root, *Radix Rehmanniae Praeparata* 9g

Chinese angelica root, *Radix Angelicae Sinensis* 9g

chuanxiong rhizome, *Rhizoma Ligustici Chuanxiong* 4.5g

white peony root, *Radix Paeoniae Alba* 9g

dangshen, *Radix Codonopsis Pilosulae* 9g

astragalus root, *Radix Astragali seu Hedysari* 15g

All the above drugs are to be decocted in water for oral administration.

In case of constipation, add 9 grams of fleece-flower root (*Radix Polygoni Multiflori*) and 9 grams of desertliving cistanche (*Herba Cistanchis*).

2. Deficiency of Both the Heart and Spleen

Main Symptoms and Signs: Sallow or pale and dim complexion, lack of vitality, lassitude, weak voice, dizziness, palpitation and short breath, aggravated by movement, lack of appetite, loose stool, pale lips and tongue with thin and white fur, and thready and weak pulse.

Therapeutic Principle: Strengthening the spleen, reinforcing the heart, invigorating *qi* and nourishing blood.

Recipe: Modified Decoction for Invigorating the Spleen and Nourishing the Heart.

Prepared astragalus root, *Radix Astragali Praeparata* 15g

dangshen, *Radix Codonopsis Pilosulae* 9g

parched white atractylodes rhizome, *Rhizoma Atractylodis Macrocephalae* 6g

【辨证论治】

1. 血虚

主证：面色苍白，唇、甲色淡，舌质淡，苔白，脉软。

治则：益气养血。

处方：四物汤加味。

熟地9克，当归9克，川芎4.5克，白芍9克，党参9克，黄芪15克。水煎服。

若便秘者，加何首乌9克，肉苁蓉9克。

2. 心脾两虚

主证：面色萎黄或苍白不泽，神疲倦怠，语言……头目眩晕，心悸气短，动则尤甚，纳少便溏……苔薄白，脉细弱。

治则……9克，炒白术6克，当归9克，炒酸枣

Chinese angelica root, *Radix Angelicae Sinensis*   9g
parched wild jujuba seed, *Semen Ziziphi Spinosae*   15g
polygala root, *Radix Polygalae*   6g
longan aril, *Arillus Longan*   9g
red sage root, *Radix Salviae Miltiorrhizae*   15g
prepared rehmannia root, *Radix Rehmanniae Praeparata*
9g
aucklandia root, *Radix Aucklandiae*   3g
prepared licorice root, *Radix Glycyrrhizae Praeparata*   3g
Chinese-date, *Fructus Ziziphi Jujubae*   5 pieces
All the above drugs are to be decocted in water for oral administration.

For patients with edema due to *yang*-deficiency, 9 grams of prepared aconite root (*Radix Aconiti Praeparata*) and 3 grams of dried ginger (*Rhizoma Zingiberis*) should be added; in case of tremor due to deficiency of the spleen and hyperactivity of the liver, add 12 grams of parched white peony root (*Radix Paeoniae Alba*) and 12 grams of uncaria stem with hooks (*Ramulus Uncariae cum Uncis*) which is to be decocted later; in case of ecchymoses on the tongue, add 6 grams of safflower (*Flos Carthami*), 15 gram of spatholobus stem (*Caulis Spatholobi*) and 9 grams of chuanxiong rhizome (*Rhizoma Ligustici Chuanxiong*); for those with abdominal tension of deficiency type and aversion to greasy food, add 12 grams of magnolia bark(*Cortex Magnoliae Officinalis*) and 12 grams of hawthorn fruit (*Fructus Crataegi*).

3. Deficiency of Liver and Kidney

Main Symptoms and Signs: Pale or sallow skin, mucous membranes and uncomfortable feeling in throat, lassitude in tinnitus and deafness, dryness and umbilicate and brittle of the head and limbs, dryness of the mouth and tongue, and thready and night sweat, blighted hair, pulse. retardation, tremor or red and dry and rapid

仁 15 克，远志肉 6 克，桂圆肉 9 克，紫丹参 15 克，熟地 9 克，

木香 3 克，炙甘草 3 克，大枣 5 枚。水煎服。

若阳虚水泛、浮肿者，加附子 9 克，干姜 3 克；脾虚肝旺而

震颤者，加炒白芍 12 克，钩藤 12 克（后下）；若舌有瘀点、瘀斑

者，加红花 6 克，鸡血藤 15 克，川芎 9 克；若虚胀、厌油者，

加厚朴 9 克，山楂 12 克。

3. 肝肾不足

主证：皮肤、粘膜、指甲苍白萎黄，头昏目眩，耳鸣，耳

聋，两目干涩，口燥咽干，腰膝酸软，盗汗，毛发枯槁，爪甲凹

陷易脆，有的可见发育迟缓，甚至头及肢体不时颤抖，舌质淡或

红干，脉细数或弦数。

Therapeutic Principle: Tonifying the liver and kidney, and supplementing the essence and blood.

Recipe: Modified Kidney-*yin*-reinforcing Bolus.

prepared rehmannia root, *Radix Rehmanniae Praeparata*   15g

Chinese yam, *Rhizoma Dioscoreae*   15g

wolfberry fruit, *Fructus Lycii*   9g

achyranthes root, *Radix Achyranthis Bidentatae*   9g

dogwood fruit, *Fructus Corni*   9g

dodder seed, *Semen Cuscutae*   9g

antler glue, *Colla Cornus Cervi*   6g   (melted alone)

tortoise-plastron glue, *Colla Plastri Testudinis*   9g (melted alone)

prepared fleece-flower root, *Radix Polygoni Multiflori Praeparata*   9g

Chinese angelica root, *Radix Angelicae Sinensis*   9g

All the above drugs are to be decocted in water for oral administration.

For those with developmental retardation, 3 grams of powder of human placenta (*Placenta Hominis*) should be added; in case of tremor of the head and limbs due to liver-wind stirring inside, add 12 grams of uncaria stem with hooks (*Ramulus Uncariae cum Uncis*) and 9grams of white peony root (*Radix Paeoniae Alba*); for those with low-grade fever in the afternoon, add 9 grams of each of the following: anemarrhena rhizome (*Rhizoma Anemarrhenae*), stir-fried fresh-water turtle shell (*Carapax Trionycis*) and wolfberry bark (*Cortex Lycii Radicis*.)

Section 12

Allergic Purpura

Allergic purpura, also called Schönlein-Henoch disease, is one of the diseases of the connective tissues associated with allergic reaction of capillaries. It is characterized mainly by exten-

治则：滋补肝肾，补益精血。

处方：左归丸加减。

熟地 15 克，山药 15 克，枸杞 9 克，怀牛膝 9 克，山茱萸 9 克，菟丝子 9 克，鹿角胶 9 克(烊化)，龟板胶 9 克(烊化)，制首乌 9 克，当归 9 克。水煎服。

若发育迟缓者，可加紫河车粉 3 克；若肝风内动、头及肢体颤抖者，加知母 9 克，炙鳖甲 9 克，地骨皮 9 克。

第十二节　过敏性紫癜

过敏性紫癜，又称许兰—亨诺氏病，是一种与毛细血管变态

sive small vasculitis, and manifested as skin purpura, gastrointestinal bleeding, and articular swelling and pain. The causative factors may be associated with infections, food, drug and pollen. This disease belongs to the category of "*ji nu*" (purpura) in TCM.

MAIN POINTS OF DIAGNOSIS

1. The clinical manifestations are characterised by abrupt onset, preceded by the history of upper respiratory tract infection accompanied with irregular fever and malaise.

2. Typical skin lesions or rashes usually appear around the ankles, on the lower limbs and buttocks, but rarely on the trunk and face. The rash initially appears as erythematous maculopapule which fades on pressure, but later, loses this feature and becomes purpura and ecchymosis in purple or brown colour, and eventually fades. Other patterns such as erythema multiforme and erythema nodosum may also occur.

3. Gastrointestinal symptoms may include abdominal colic, vomiting, blood in stools, and articular swelling, pain, tenderness or effusion which often involve the knees. Hematuria, albuminuria, moderate azotemia, hypertension and hypertensive encephalopathy may occur when the kidney is involved.

4. Laboratory examinations do not have much value. Thrombocyte, bleeding and coagulation times, clot retraction time, and capillary fragility test are normal. Elevated erythrocyte sedimetation rate and positive C-reactive protein may occur.

DIFFERENTIATION AND TREATMENT OF COMMON SYNDROMES

1. Affection by Exopathogenic Wind-heat

Main Symptoms and Signs: Sudden onset with purpura appearing on the limbs, especially on the legs and buttocks, as bright red papular eruption or erythema in different sizes and shapes, which may coalesce to form patches, symmetrical

反应有关的结缔组织病，以广泛的小血管炎为主，表现为皮肤紫癜，消化道出血和关节肿痛。其发生可能与感染、食物、药物、花粉等因素有关。本病属中医"肌衄"范畴。

【诊断要点】

1. 临床特点为急性发病。发病前有上呼吸道感染史，伴有不规则发热或不适。

2. 典型皮疹密集于踝关节周围、下肢和臀部，躯干和面部少见。皮疹开始为红斑样斑丘疹，压之退色，后变成压之不退色的紫癜和瘀斑，再变成紫色、棕色而消退。也可有多形性红斑和结节性红斑。

3. 病人可伴有腹绞痛、呕吐、大便带血，关节疼痛、水肿、压痛或积液，常为膝关节受累。肾受累时可出现血尿、蛋白尿、轻度的氮质血症、高血压和高血压脑病。

4. 实验室检查诊断价值不大。血小板、出凝血时间、瘀血块收缩时间均正常，毛细血管脆性试验正常。可有血沉增快和C反应蛋白增加。

【辨证论治】

1. 外感风热

主证：起病较急，紫癜发于四肢，尤以下肢和臀部为多，颜

spread, accompanied with itching, general discomfort, fever, loss of appetite, swelling and pain in the joints, nausea, vomiting, abdominal pain, hematochezia or hematuria, red tongue with thin fur, floating and rapid pulse, dark red and very clear superficial venule of the index finger.

Therapeutic Principle: Dispelling pathogenic wind, clearing away pathogenic heat and cooling blood to arrest bleeding.

Recipe: Modified Antiphlogistic Powder with Forsythia.

black schizonepta, *Herba Schizonaeptae*   6g
parched ledebouriella root, *Radix Ledebouriellae*   **6g**
arctium fuit, *Fructus Arctii*   9g
dried rehmannia root, *Radix Rehmanniae*   **12g**
moutan bark, *Cortex Moutan Radicis*   9g
red peony root, *Radix Paroniae Rubra*   9g
honeysuckle flower, *Flos Lonicerae*   9g
forsythia fruit, *Fructus Forsythiae*   12g
cicada slough, *Periostracum Cicadae*   9g

All the above drugs are to be decocted in water for oral administration.

For those with poor appetite, nausea and vomiting, add the following ingredients: red bean (*Semen Phaseoli*) 15g, coix seed (*Semen Coicis*) 15g, manshurian aristolochia stem (*Caulis Aristolochiae Manshuriensis*) 3g, plantain seed (*Semen Plantaginis*) 9g (wrapped in a piece of cloth before it is to be decocted). For those with articular swelling and pain, add the following ingredients: tetrandra root (*Radix Stephaniae Tetrandrae*) 9g, achyranthes root (*Radix Achyranthis Bidentatae*) 9g, stir-fried frankincense (*Resina Olibani*) 9g and myrrh (*Myrrha*) 9g. For those with hema tochezia, 9 grams of carbonized sanguisorba root (*Radix Sanguisorbae*) and 9 grams of sophora flower (*Flos Sophorae*) should be added. In case of hematuria, the following herbal medicines should be added: fresh rehmannia root (*Radix Rehman-*

色较鲜红，丘疹或红斑，大小形态不一，可融合成片，高出皮

面，对称分布，可伴有瘙痒、全身不适、发热、食欲不振、关节

肿痛、恶心、呕吐、腹痛、便血或尿血等，舌质红，苔薄，脉浮

数。指纹深红显露。

治则：疏风清热，凉血止血。

处方：连翘败毒散加减。

黑荆芥6克，炒防风6克，牛蒡子9克，生地12克，丹皮

9克，赤芍9克，银花9克，连翘12克，蝉蜕9克。水煎服。

若食欲不振，恶心呕吐者，加赤小豆15克，薏苡仁15克，

木通3克，车前子9克（布包煎）；关节肿痛者，加防己9克，牛

膝9克，制乳香9克，制没药9克；便血者，加地榆炭9克，槐

niae) 15g, fresh cogongrass rhizome (*Rhizoma Imperatae*) 30g, lotus node (*Nodus Nelumbinis Rhizomatis*) 9g, eclipta (*Herba Ecliptae*) 9g.

2. Bleeding due to Blood-heat

Main Symptoms and Signs: Usually abrupt onset with ecchymoses or petechiae which may coalesce to form big patches, bright red or dull purple in colour, commonly accompanied with high fever, excessive thirst, nasal hemorrhage, bleeding from the gum or hamaturia of bright-red colour, abdominal pain, hematochezia, deep-red tongue with yellow fur, slippery and rapid pulse, and dark red or dull purple superficial venule of the index finger.

Therapeutic Principle: Clearing away pathogenic heat and toxic material and removing blood-heat to stop bleeding.

Recipe: Modified Decoction of Rhinoceros Horn and Rehmannia.

rhinoceros horn powder, *Cornu Rhinocerotis* 1g (To be taken after being infused in the finished decoction)

rehmannia root, *Radix Rehmanniae*　9g

white peony root, *Radix Paroniae Alba*　9g

moutan bark, *Cortex Moutan Radicis*　9g

scutellaria root, *Radix Suctellariae*　9g

donkey-hide gelatin, *Colla Corii Asini*　9g, (To be melted in the finished decoction)

arnebia root, *Radix Arnebiae*　9g

powder of notoginseng, *Radix Notoginseng*　2g (To be taken after being infused in the finished decoction)

All the above drugs, except rhinoceros horn, donkey-hide gelatin and powder of notoginseng, are to be decocted in water for oral administration.

In case of tremendous noxious heat, choose from the following drugs: honeysuckle flower (*Flos Lonicerae*) 15g, forsythia fruit (*Fructus Forsythiae*) 12g, gyspsum (*Gypsum Fibrosum*) 30g,

花 9 克；尿血者，加鲜生地 15 克，鲜茅根 30 克，藕节炭 9 克，

旱莲草 9 克。

2．血热妄行

主证：发病多急骤，皮肤瘀点或瘀斑融合成片，颜色鲜红或

深紫，常伴有壮热、烦渴、鼻衄、齿衄或血尿，色鲜红，腹痛，

便血，舌质红绛，苔黄，脉滑数，指纹深红或紫暗。

治则：清热解毒，凉血止血。

处方：犀角地黄汤加减。

犀角粉 1 克(冲)，生地 9 克，白芍 9 克，丹皮 9 克，黄芩 9

克，阿胶 9 克(烊冲)，紫草 9 克，三七粉 2 克(冲)。水煎服。

若热毒较甚者，可选加金银花 15 克，连翘 12 克，生石膏30

anemarrhena rhizome (*Rhizoma Anemarrhenae*) 9g, scutellaria root (*Radix Scutellariae*) 9g, coptis root (*Radix Coptidis*) 3g, black capejasmine fruit (*Fructus Gardeniae*) 9g. For patients with severe bleeding from nose and gum, 30 grams of fresh cogongrass rhizome, (*Rhizoma Imperatae*) and 30 grams of fresh reed rhizome (*Rhizoma Phragmitis*) should be added.

3. Failure of the Spleen to Keep the Blood Flowing within the Vessels due to Spleen Deficiency

Main Symptoms and Signs: Recurrent purpura with pale, reddish ecchymoses for a long course, dim complexion, fatigue, dizziness, palpitation, vague abdominal pain, positive test of occult blood in stool, anorexia, loose stools, and spontaneous perspiration, pale reddish lips and tongue, and thready and soft pulse, pale reddish superficial venule of the index finger.

Therapeutic Principle: Invigorating the Spleen-*qi* to arrest bleeding.

Recipe: Modified Decoction for Invigorating the Spleen and Nourishing the Heart.

dangshen, *Radix Codonopsis Pilosulae*   12g

prepared astragalus root, *Radix Astragali Praeparata*   15g

Chinese angelica root, *Radix Angelicae Sinensis*   9g

parched white peony root, *Radix Paeoniae Alba*   9g

parched white atractylodes rhizome, *Rhizoma Atractylodis Macrocephalae*   9g

prepared rehmannia root, *Radix Rehmanniae Praeparata* 15g

eclipta, *Herba Ecliptae*   9g

All the above drugs are to be decocted in water for oral administration.

9 grams of carbonized biota tops (*Cacumen Biotae*) and 30 grams of fresh cogongrass rhizome (*Rhizoma Imperatae*) should be added in case of bleeding from the nose and gum; for those with hematuria, add 9 grams of donkey-hide gelatin (*Colla Corii Asini*) (To be taken after being melted in the boiling finished

克，知母 9 克，黄芩 9 克，黄连 3 克，黑山栀 9 克；鼻衄、齿衄

重者，加鲜茅根 30 克，鲜芦根 30 克。

3．脾不摄血

主证：紫癜反复发作，瘀点、瘀斑色较淡，病程较长，面色

不华，神疲乏力，头晕心悸，腹痛隐隐，大便潜血试验阳性，纳

呆，便溏，自汗，唇舌淡红，脉细软，指纹淡红。

治则：补气摄血。

处方：归脾汤加减。

党参 12 克，炙黄芪 15 克，当归 9 克，炒白芍 9 克，炒白术

9 克，熟地 15 克，旱莲草 9 克。水煎服。

若鼻衄、齿衄者，加侧柏炭 9 克，鲜茅根 30 克；血尿者，加

decoction), 9 grams of carbonized black plum (*Fructus Mume*) and 9 grams of carbonized hair (*Crinis Carbonisatus*); in case of hematochezia, add 0.5 gram of Yunnan White Drug-Powder (*Pulvis Medicinalis*), 6 grams of roasted aucklandia root (*Radix Aucklandiae*) and 9 grams of carbonized sanguisorba root (*Radix Sanguisorbae*).

Section 13

Juvenile Rheumatoid Disease

Juvenile rheumatoid disease is one of the common connective tissue diseases in children characterized by chronic arthritis, or synovitis with involvement of viscera. The pathogenesis is unknown, but may be associated with autoimmunity, infection and genetic factors. This disease belongs to the category of "*bi zheng*" (arthralgia-syndrome) in TCM.

MAIN POINTS OF DIAGNOSIS

1. Clinical manifestations of the disease vary greatly. Systemic type at its acute stage, also called allergic subsepsis, is characterized by persistent high fever of remittent fever type, tendency to recur, accompanied with rash, arthralgia, abdominal pain and myalgia. The polyarthritis type of the disease is symmetrical and involves over 5 joints marked by swelling, pain, stiffness or morning stiffness of joints, fusiform fingers and limited motion. The pausiarticular type only involves less than four large joints, and is often asymmetrical, and besides swelling and pain of joints, it is often accompanied with spondyloarthropathy and iridocyclitis.

2. Physical examinations may reveal swelling and tenderuess in joints and hepatosplenomegaly, lymphadenectasis and signs indicating involvement of the heart and kidney.

3. Laboratory examinations may show obvious leukocytosis, elevated erythrocyte sedimentation rate, anemia, increased

胶阿9克(烊冲)，乌梅炭9克，血余炭9克；便血者，酌加云南白药0.5克，煨木香6克，地榆炭9克。

第十三节　幼年类风湿病

幼年类风湿病是小儿时期常见的一种结缔组织病，以慢性关节炎或滑膜炎为主要特点，并可伴有内脏器官受累。其发病可能与自体免疫、感染和遗传因素有关。本病属中医"痹症"范畴。

【诊断要点】

1．临床表现有很大差异。全身型急性期，也称变应性亚败血症，表现为持续高热，呈驰张热型，易复发，伴皮疹、关节痛、腹痛和肌痛；多关节炎型呈对称性，5个以上的关节受累，有关节肿痛、僵硬或晨僵，梭状指，活动受限；少关节炎型往往不对称，累及大关节少于4个，除关节肿痛外，易伴有脊柱关节病和虹膜睫状体炎。

2．体格检查可发现关节肿胀、压痛，或有肝、脾、淋巴结肿大及心肾受累的体征。

3．实验室检查急性全身型多有白细胞明显升高，血沉快，贫

C-reaction protein in acute stage of systemic type, and positive rheumatoid facotor (RF) and antinuclear antibody (ANA) may be carried out in arthritis type.

4. X-ray examination on bone and joint may reveal pathogenic changes manifested as osteoporosis, arthrostenosis, etc.

DIFFERENTIATION AND TREATMENT OF COMMON SYNDROMES

1. Arthralgia-Syndrome of Heat Type

Main Symptoms and Signs: Pain, swelling, redness and heat in joints. The severe pain is averse to being touched with one or more joints, involved. There is limited motion of the joints relieved by cold. This type can be further divided into two types.

(1) Arthralgia-Syndrome due to Interior Heat Caused by *Yin*-Deficiency

Main Symptoms and Signs: In addition to the above symptoms and signs, tidal fever in afternoon, dysphoria with feverish sensation in the chest, palms and soles, muscular atrophy, dryness of the mouth and throat, dry stools, scanty urine, red tongue with little fur, and thready and rapid pulse.

Therapeutic Principle: Nourishing *yin*, clearing away pathogenic heat, dredging the channels and collaterals to relieve pain.

Recipe: Modified Dr. Ding's Decoction for Removing Pathogenic Heat from the Channels

swallowwort root, *Radix Cynanchi Atrati*   15g
wolfberry bark, *Cortex Lycii Radicis*   9g
dried rehmannia root, *Radix Rehmanniae*   12g
white peony root, *Radix Paeoniae Alba*   12g
dendrobium, *Herba Dendrobii*   15g
large-leaf gentian root, *Radix Gentianae Macrophyllae*   9g
clematis root, *Radix Clematis*   9g
luffa, *Retinervus Luffae Fructus*   15g
honeysuckle stem, *Ramulus Lonicereae*   18g

血,C-反应蛋白增加。关节炎型可有类风湿因子和抗核抗体阳性，

4．X线检查可见关节的改变，如骨质疏松、关节腔变窄等。

【辨证论治】

1．热痹

主证：关节红肿热痛，痛不可近，累及一个或多个关节，关节屈伸不利，遇冷则舒。本证可分为以下两型：

（1）阴虚内热

主证：除具有以上热痹症状外，尚有午后潮热、五心烦热、肌肉萎缩、口干咽燥、大便干结、小便短少，舌红少苔，脉细数。

治则：滋阴清热，通络止痛。

处方：丁氏清络饮加减。

白薇15克，地骨皮9克，生地12克，白芍12克，石斛15

earthworm, *Lumbricus*   9g

All the above drugs are to be decocted in water for oral administration.

(2) Arthralgia-Syndrome due to Excessive Damp-heat in the Interior

Main Symptoms and Signs: In addition to arthralgia syndrome of heat type, there are more severe joint swelling, pain and heavy sensation but less or vague burning sensation, accompanied with fever or recessive fever, nausea, poor appetite, loose stool, red tongue with yellow, and greasy fur and slippery and rapid pulse.

Therapeutic Principle: Clearing away pathogenic heat and dampness.

Recipe: Flavoured Two Wonderful Drugs Powder.

atractylodes rhizome, *Rhizoma Atractylodis*   9g

phellodendron bark, *Cortex Phellodendri*   6g

coix seed, *Semen Coicis*   18g

forsythia fruit, *Fructus Forsythiae*   9g

tale, *Talcum*   12g

honeysuckle stem, *Ramulus Lonicerae*   24g

silkworm excrement, *Excrementa Bombycum*   9g

erythrina bark, *Cortex Erythrinae*   9g

chaenomeles fruit, *Fructus Chaenomelis*   6g

oriental wormwood, *Herba Artemisiae Capillaris*   24g

poria, *Poria*   9g

All the above drugs are to be decocted in water for oral administration.

2. Arthralgia-syndrome of Cold Type

Main Symptoms and Signs: Joint stiffness and severe pain without redness and burning sensation on the diseased part, relieved by warmth and aggravated by cold, cold body and limbs, aversion to wind, thin and white fur on the tongue, and deep and slow pulse.

Therapeutic Principle: Warming the channels, dispersing

克，秦艽9克，威灵仙9克，丝瓜络15克，金银花藤18克，地龙9克。水煎服。

（2）湿热内盛

主证：除有热痹症状外，尚有关节肿胀较甚，疼痛重着，但灼热感较轻或不明显，伴发热或身热不扬，恶心或泛泛欲吐，纳呆，便溏，舌质红，苔黄腻，脉滑数。

治则：清热利湿。

处方：二妙散加味。

苍术9克，黄柏6克，薏苡仁18克，连翘9克，滑石12克，金银花藤24克，蚕砂9克，海桐皮9克，木瓜6克，茵陈24克，茯苓9克。水煎服。

2. 寒痹

主证：关节拘紧痛甚，患处不红不热，得热痛减，遇寒加重，形寒肢冷，怕风，舌苔薄白，脉沉迟。

pathogenic cold and wind and removing dampness.

Recipe: Modified Arthralgia-relieving Decoction by Relaxing Muscles and Tendons.

astragalus root, *Radix Astragali seu Hedysari*   15g
cinnamon twig, *Ramulus Cinnamomi*   6g
prepared aconite root, *Radix Aconiti Praeparata*   6g
Chinese angelica root, *Radix Angelicae Sinensis*   9g
red peony root, *Radix Paeoniae Rubra*   9g
notopterygium root, *Rhizoma seu Radix Notopterytii*   6g
chuanxiong rhizome, *Rhizoma Ligustici Chuanxiong*   6g
prepared frankincense, *Resina Olibanii Praeparata*   6g
prepared myrrh, *Myrrha Praepa rata*   6g
poria, *Poria*   9g
coix seed, *Semen Coicis*   15g

All the above drugs are to be decocted in water for oral administration.

3. Arthralgia-syndrome of *Qi*-blood Deficiency

Main Symptoms and Signs: Pale or sallow complexion, hyperhidrosis, fatigue, disinclination to talk, poor appetite, abnormal stools, swelling and deformity of joint, pale tongue with thin and white fur.

Therapeutic Principle: Replenishing *qi* , nourishing blood, and removing pathogenic dampness to dredge the channels and collaterals.

Recipe: Modified Eight Precious Ingredients Decoction.
dangshen, *Radix Codonopsis Pilosulae*   9g
poria, *Poria*   9g
parched white atractylodes rhizome, *Rhizoma Atractylodis Macrocephalae*   9g
Chinese angelica root, *Radix Angelicae Sinensis*   9g
red peony root, *Radix Peaoniae Rubra*   9g
chuanxiong rhizome, *Rhizoma Ligustici Chuanxiong*   6g
prepared rehmannia root, *Radix Rehmanniae Praeparata*   9g

治则：温经散寒，祛风除湿。

处方：舒筋除痹汤加减。

黄芪15克，桂枝6克，附子6克，当归9克，赤芍9克，

羌活6克，川芎6克，制乳香6克，制没药6克，茯苓9克，薏

苡仁15克，水煎服。

3．气血两虚

主证：面色㿠白或萎黄，多汗，少气懒言，纳呆，大便不

调，关节肿胀变形，舌质淡，苔薄白。

治则：补气养血，化湿通络。

处方：八珍汤加减。

党参9克，茯苓9克，炒白术9克，当归9克，赤芍9克，

astragalus root, *Radix Astragali seu Hedysari*   24g
desertliving cistanche, *Herba Cistanchis*   12g
white mustard seed, *Semen Sinapis Albae*   9g
licorice root, *Radis Glycyrrhizae*   3g
chaenomeles fruit, *Fructus Chaenomelis*   9g

All the above drugs are to be decocted in water for oral administration.

Section 14

Epilepsy

Epilepsy is defined as paroxysmal and temporary distur- bance of brain characterized by loss of consciousness and muscle tic or abnormal sensation, emotion and behavior. In TCM, this disease is categorized as *"xian zheng"* (epilepsy syn- drome) and *"dian xian"* (epilepsy).

MAIN POINTS OF DIAGNOSIS

1. The histories of family, epileptic attack and encephalo- pathia should be inquired carefully.

2. Clinical manifestations of the disease vary greatly. There may be grand mal, petit mal, rolandic mal and infan- tile spasms. The grand mal is characterized by sudden loss of consciousness, general totanic spasm with apnea, cyanosis and foam in the mouth, which usually last for 1—5 minu- tes. The patients may then fall into sleep and become consci- ous a few hours later. The petit mal is characterized by sudden, short loss of consciousness without aurae and muscle tic, accom- panied with interruptions of speech and action which usual- ly persist for 2—10 seconds. The patient usually comes to cons- ciousness rapidly.

3. Electroencephalogram examination and tomography may be useful for the diagnosis of epilepsy.

DIFFERENTIATION AND TREATMENT OF

川芎6克，熟地9克，黄芪24克，肉苁蓉12克，白芥子9克，甘草3克，木瓜9克。水煎服。

第十四节 癫 痫

癫痫是指阵发性的暂时性、脑功能失调，发作时表现为意识障碍、肌肉抽搐，或感觉、情感、行为异常。本病属中医"痫证"、"癫痫"范畴。

【诊断要点】

1. 详细询问家族史、癫痫发作史和脑部病变史。

2. 临床表现多种多样，如大发作、小发作、运动型发作和婴儿痉挛症等。大发作的特点是突然意识丧失、全身强直性痉挛，可伴有呼吸暂停、青紫、口吐白沫，一般持续1～5分钟，发作后嗜睡，数小时后意识清醒。小发作只有突然发生短暂的意识丧失，无先兆，伴有语言中断、活动停止，无肌肉抽搐，持续2～10秒钟，发作后意识很快恢复。

3. 脑电图检查、脑电子计算机X线断层摄影(CT)检查对癫痫的诊断有帮助。

COMMON SYNDROMES

1. Epilepsy Induced by Terror

Main Symptoms and Signs: Sudden panic resulting in confusion and loss of self-control, sometimes fright and sometimes alarm and restlessness, crying with fear during sleep, tendency to remain in the mother's arms, alternative flush and pallow on the face, red tongue with white fur, taut and rapid rapid or taut and slippery pulse.

Therapeutic Principle: Tranquilizing the mind and resolving phlegm to arrest epilepsy.

Recipe: Modified Polygala Bolus.

polygala root, *Radix Polygalae*　　9g

dangshen, *Radix Codonopsis Pilosulae*　　15g

poria, *Poria*　　9g

grassleaved sweetflag rhizome, *Rhizoma Acori Graminei*　　9g

dragon's teeth, *Dens Draconis*　　15g (To be decocted prior to others)

curcuma root, *Radix Curcumae*　　9g

arisaema with bile, *Arisaema cum Bile*　　9g

wild jujuba seed, *Semen Ziziphi Spinosae*　　15g

arborvitae seed, *Semen Biotae*　　9g

cicada slough, *Periostracum Cicadae*　　9g

lucid asparagus, *Radix Asparagi*　　9g

All the above drugs are to be decocted in water for oral administration.

2. Epilepsy due to Accumulation of Phlegm

Main Symptoms and Signs: Convulsion of extremities during a fit of epilepsy, unconsciousness or vertigo, headache and abdominal pain, accompanied with stridor produced by phlegm in the throat, salivation, yellow face, thick fur of the tongue, and slippery and rapid pulse.

Therapeutic Principle: Removing phlegm and inducing resuscitation.

Recipe: Modified Phlegm-removing Decoction.

【辨证论治】

1. 惊痫

主证：突然惊恐意乱，不能自主，时而恐怖，时而惊惕不安，睡中惊叫，喜投母怀，面色乍红乍白，舌质红，苔白，脉弦数或弦滑。

治则：镇心安神，化痰定痫。

处方：远志丸加减。

远志9克，党参15克，朱茯苓9克，石菖蒲9克，龙齿15克（先煎），郁金9克，胆南星9克，酸枣仁15克，柏子仁9克，蝉蜕9克，天门冬9克。水煎服。

2. 痰痫

主证：发作时四肢抽搐，昏仆或眩晕，头痛，腹痛，伴喉间痰鸣、口吐涎沫，面色黄，舌苔厚、脉滑数。

治则：涤痰开窍。

处方：涤痰汤加减。

pinellia tuber, *Rhizoma Pinelliae*   6g

tangerine peel, *Pericarpium Citri Reticulatae*   6g

poria, *Poria*   9g

bamboo shavings, *Caulis Bambusae in taenis*   6g

bitter orange, *Fructus Aurantii*   9g

gastrodia tuber, *Rhizoma Gastrodiae*   9g

arisaema with bile, *Arisaema cum Bile*   9g

grassleaved sweetflag rhizome, *Rhizoma Acori Graminei*
    9g

scorpion, *Scorpio*   6g

licorice root, *Radix Glycyrrhizae*   3g

All the above drugs are to be decocted in water for oral administration.

3. Epilepsy due to Blood Stasis

Main Symptoms and Signs: With a history of birth injury or tramuma often manifested as paroxysmal localized headache, occasional vomiting, paroxysmal convulsion of the whole body or half body or local region upon attack, dark purple tongue with ecchymoses, thready and unsmooth pulses and dark purple superficial venule of the index finger.

Therapeutic Principle: Promoting blood circulation to remove blood stasis, waking up the patient from unconscious ness and arresting epilepsy.

Recipe: Modified Decoction for Activating Blood Circulation.

chuanxiong rhizome, *Rhizoma Ligustici Chuanxiong*   6g

red peony root, *Radix Paeoniae Rubra*   9g

peach kernel, *Semen Persicae*   9g

safflower, *Flos Carthami*   9g

bulb and root of Chinese green onion, *Bulbus et Radix Allii
    Fistulosi* 3 pieces

fresh ginger, *Rhizoma Zingiberis*   9g

Chinese-date, *Fructus Ziziphi Jujubae*   7 pieces

red sage root, *Radix Salviae Miltiorrhizae*   12g

半夏6克，陈皮6克，茯苓9克，竹茹6克，枳实9克，天麻9克，胆南星9克，石菖蒲9克，全蝎6克，甘草3克。水煎服。

3. 瘀血痫

主证：有产伤或外伤史，常表现为发作性头痛，痛有定处，有时呕吐，发作时全身、半身或局部抽搐，舌质紫暗或有瘀点，脉细涩，指纹紫滞。

治则：活血化瘀，通窍定痫。

处方：通窍活血汤加味。

川芎6克，赤芍9克，桃仁9克，红花9克，老葱根3枚，

musk, *Moschus*, 0.15g (Ground into powder to be taken after being infused in the finished decoction)

All the above drugs except musk are to be decocted in water for oral administration.

In case of deficiency of *qi*, add 30 grams of astragalus root (*Radix Astragali seu Hedysari*) and 12 grams of dangshen (*Radix Codonopsis Pilosulae*) into the above mentioned recipe.

Section 15

Acute Toxic Encephalopathy

Acute toxic encephalopathy is characterized by the abrupt appearance of symptoms and signs of the central nervous system in the course some of primary diseases. The pathogenesis is unknown. The onset of the disease may be associated with immunoreaction to infection and its toxin rather than pathogenic organism invading the brain tissue directly. This disease, in TCM, belongs to the category of "*jing feng*" (infantile convulsion).

MAIN POINTS OF DIAGNOSIS

1. This disease may occur at any age, but usually in infants from 1 to 3 years old. The symptoms of brain damage often follow the primary disorders within a few days or 1—2 weeks after their attack.

2. The clinical manifestations are various. The onset is usually abrupt with high fever, headache, vomiting, restlessness or lethargy, convulsion, coma, bulging of anterior fontanelle, platycoria, and delayed reaction to light, often accompanied with holotonia, decerebrate rigidity or opisthotonos, and unilateral or bilateral paralysis . Some patients may have the symptoms of meningeal irritation, increased or reduced tendon reflex, and also have cerebellar symptoms, such as ataxia, nystagmus and kinetic tremor.

3. Laboratory examinations show that cerebrospinal fluid

姜生 9 克，红枣 7 枚，丹参 12 克，麝香 0.15 克（研末冲服）。水
煎服。

若气虚者，加黄芪 30 克，党参 12 克。

第十五节　急性中毒性脑病

急性中毒性脑病是指在某种原发病的过程中突然出现的中枢
神经系统症状和体征。发病原因不明，可能与个体对感染及其毒
素的免疫反应有关，而非病原体直接侵入脑组织。本 病 属 中 医
"惊风"范畴。

【诊断要点】

1. 可发生于任何年龄，但多见于 1～3 岁小儿。大脑损害
症状多在原发病后几天或 1～2 周内出现。

2. 临床表现多种多样。突然发病，高热，头痛，呕吐，烦
躁或嗜睡，惊厥，昏迷，前囟膨隆，瞳孔扩大，对光反应迟钝，
常伴有全身性肌痉挛，去大脑强直或角弓反张，一侧 或 双 侧 瘫
痪，也可有脑膜刺激症状，腱反射增强或减弱。也可有小脑受累
症状，如运动失调、眼球震颤或动作性震颤。

3. 实验室检查脑脊液外观无色透明，除压力高外，其他一

is clear. All are normal except that the pressure is high and sometimes there is a slight increase of protein in cerebrospinal fluid.

4. Arteriolar spasm, blood stasis of the small vein and retinal edema or papilledema can be observed by fundus examination.

DIFFERENTIATION AND TREATMENT OF COMMON SYNDROMES

1. Intense Heat in Both *Qi* and *Ying* Systems

Main Symptoms and Signs: Often seen in the stage of cerebral edema of toxic encephalopathy, in the course of the primary disease, with abrupt high fever, headache, vomiting, restlessness, delirium, drowsiness, convulsions of the limbs, stiffness of the extremities and neck, involuntary staring, lockjaw, and unconsciousness, deep-red tongue with yellow and dry fur, either taut and rapid or slippery and rapid pulse.

Therapeutic Principle: Clearing away pathogenic heat from the *qi* and *ying* systems, arresting convulsions and inducing resuscitation.

Recipe: Modified Antipyretic and Antitoxic Decoction.
honeysuckle flower, *Flos Lonicerae*   18g
forsythia fruit, *Fructus Forsythiae*   9g
coptis root, *Radix Coptidis*   6g
gypsum, *Gypsum Fibrosum*   30g
anemarrhena rhizome, *Rhizoma Anemarrhenae*   9g
moutan bark, *Cortex Moutan Radicis*   9g
curcuma root, *Radix Curcumae*   9g
grassleaved sweetflag rhizome, *Rhizoma Acori Graminei*
    9g
rhinoceros horn, *Cornu Rhinocerotis*   3g (Ground into
    fine powder to be taken after being infused in the
    finished decoction)
antelope's horn powder, *Pulvis Cornus Saigae*   3g (infused)
lotus plumule, *Plumula Nelumbinis*   3g

般正常。有时脑脊液蛋白轻度增加。

4．眼底检查可见小动脉痉挛及小静脉瘀血，也可出现视网膜或视神经乳头水肿。

【辨证论治】

1．气营两燔

主证：常见于中毒性脑病水肿期。在原发病的过程中，突然出现高热、头痛、呕吐、烦躁、谵语，嗜睡、四肢抽搐、肢体强直、颈项强直、目上视、牙关紧闭、神识不清、舌质红绛，苔黄燥，脉弦数或滑数。

治则：清气凉营，熄风开窍。

处方：清瘟败毒饮加减。

金银花18克，连翘9克，黄连6克，生石膏30克，知母9克，丹皮9克，郁金9克，石菖蒲9克，犀角3克(冲)，羚羊角

All the above drugs are to be decocted in water for oral administration.

Drugs of cool or cold nature should be used very cautiously when there is pathogenic dampness with thick and greasy tongue coating. Instead, the following drugs should be added: agastache (*Herba Agastachis*) 9g, eupatorium (*Herba Eupatorii*) 9g, coix seed (*Semen Coicis*) 15g, round cardamon seed (*Semen Amomi Cardamomi*) 6g.

2. Deficiency of Both *Qi* and *Yin*

Main Symptoms and Signs: Often seen in the late stage of toxic encephalopathy with residual low fever, pale and occasional flush of zygomaticofacial region, vexation and insomnia, sluggish look, occasional convulsion, rigidity and paralysis of limbs or dysphagia, blindness, deafness, aphasia, emaciation, spontaneous perspiration, night sweat, deep-red tongue with thin white fur or without fur, thready, weak and rapid pulse.

Therapeutic Principle: Replenishing *qi*, nourishing *yin*, arresting convulsion and inducing resuscitation.

Recipe: Modified Great Pearl for Wind Syndrome.

dried rehmannia root, *Radix Rehmanniae*   9g

prepared rehmannia root, *Radix Rehmanniae Praeparata* 9g

white peony root, *Radix Paeoniae Alba*   12g

dangshen, *Radix Codonopsis Pilosulae*   9g

ophiopogon root, *Radix Ophiopogonis*   12g

white atractylodes rhizome, *Rhizoma Atractylodis Macrocephalae*   9g

Chinese angelica root, *Radix Angelicae Sinensis*   9g

tortoise plastron, *Plastrum Testudinis*   9g

fresh-water turtle shell, *Carapax Trionycis*   15g

astragalus root, *Radix Astragali seu Hedysari*   15g

grassleaved sweetflag rhizome, *Rhizoma Acori Graminei* 9g

All the above drugs are to be decocted in water for oral

粉3克(冲)，莲子心3克。水煎服。

若夹有湿浊、舌苔厚腻者，寒凉药应慎用，加藿香9克，佩兰9克，薏苡仁15克，白蔻仁6克。

2. 气阴两虚

主证：常见于中毒性脑病后期，低热留滞，面色㿠白，时有颧赤，心烦少寐，神情呆滞，时有抽动，肢体强直瘫痪，或吞咽不利，目盲，耳聋，失语，形体消瘦，自汗，盗汗，舌质红绛，苔薄白或无苔，脉细弱而数。

治则：益气养阴，熄风开窍。

处方：大定风珠加减。

生地9克，熟地9克，白芍12克，党参9克，麦冬12克，白术9克，当归9克，龟板9克，鳖甲15克，黄芪15克，石菖

administration.

3. Deficiency of the Liver and Kidney

Main Symptoms and Signs: Often seen in the convalescence of toxic encephalopathy with rigidity and spasm of limbs and occasional convulsions or mental disturbance, aphasia or slurred speech, blindness, deafness, red tongue with little fur, and feeble and rapid pulse.

Therapeutic Principle: Nourishing the liver and kidney; promoting blood circulation, dredging the channels and collaterals, and removing phlegm and inducing resuscitation.

Recipe: Modified prescriptions of Duqi Pill of Seven Ingredients and Decoction Invigorating *Yang* for Recuperation.

prepared rehmannia root, *Radix Rehmanniae Praeparata* 9g

dogwood fruit, *Fructus Corni*   9g

wolfberry fruit, *Fructus Lycii*   9g

Chinese angelica root, *Radix Angelicae Sinensis*   9g

poria, *Poria*   12g

earthworm, *Lumbricus*   6g

grassleaved sweetflag rhizome, *Rhizoma Acori Graminei* 9g

chuanxiong rhizome, *Rhizoma Ligustici Chuanxiong*   6g

safflower, *Flos Carthami*   6g

All the above drugs are to be decocted in water for oral administration.

In case of rigidity and spastic paralysis of limbs, add 9 grams of black-tail snake (*Zaocys*), 9 grams of batryticated silkworm (*Bambyx Batryticatus*) and 6 grams of scorpion (*Scorpio*); for those with flaccid paralysis of limbs and emaciation, add 18 grams of astragalus root (*Radix astragali seu Hedysari*), 9 grams of white atractylodes rhizome (*Rhizoma Atractylodis Macrocephalae*) and 9 grams of chaenomeles fruit (*Fructus Chaenomelis*); for those with blindness and deafness, 9 grams of glossy privet fruit (*Fructus Ligustri Lucidi*), 9 grams of dendrobium (*Herba Dendrobii*)

蒲 9 克。水煎服。

3．肝肾亏虚

主证：常见于中毒性脑病恢复期，肢体僵直，拘挛，时或抽搐，或有神志障碍，失语或语言不清，目盲，耳聋，舌红少苔，脉虚数。

治则：滋补肝肾，活血通络，化痰开窍。

处方：七味都气丸合补阳还五汤加减。

熟地 9 克，山萸肉 9 克，枸杞 9 克，当归 9 克，茯苓 12 克，地龙 6 克，石菖蒲 9 克，川芎 6 克，红花 6 克。水煎服。

若肢体强直、硬瘫者，加乌梢蛇 9 克，僵蚕 9 克，全蝎 6

and 9 grams of sweetgum fruit (*Fructus Liquidambaris*) should be used; and for those with intellectual disturbance, add 12 grams of bitter caramon (*Fructus Alpiniae Oxyphyllae*), 15 grams of parched wild jujuba seed (*Semen Ziziphi Apinosae*) and 9 grams of polygala root, (*Radix Polygalae*).

Section 16
Infectious Polyradiculitis

Infectious polyradiculitis, also called Guillain-Barré syndrome, is an inflammatory disease of nerve roots characterized by symmetric flaccid paralysis of limbs. It is often caused by the general viral and bacterial infections or intoxication. This disease belongs to the category of "*wei zheng*" (flaccidity syndrome) in TCM.

MAIN POINTS OF DIAGNOSIS

1. There may be histories of prodromal infection about 2 weeks before the appearance of nervous symptoms, such as upper respiratory tract infection, rubella, mumps, diarrhea, etc.

2. The early symptoms include irritating pain and paresthesia of the nerve roots. This gradually results in general sensational damage, including loss of the senses of pain, touch, temperature, locality and vibration. When the involvement of distal limbs—hands and feet occurs, it is often manifested as a "glove and stocking anesthesia." Paralysis of cranial nerve and paralysis of respiratory muscles may be present, the latter can produce dyspnea or respiratory failure in severe cases. These often appear with symptoms of vegetative nerve functional disturbance, such as hyperhidrosis or hypohidrosis, cold extremities, flush, transient retention or incontinence of urine, constipation or diarrhea. Loss or diminution of tendon reflexes, weakness and muscular atrophy are usually present in the course of the disease.

克；肢体软瘫、肌肉消瘦者，加黄芪 18 克，白术 9 克，木瓜 9 克；目盲、耳聋者，加女贞子 9 克，石斛 9 克，路路通 9 克；智力障碍者，加益智仁 12 克，炒酸枣仁 15 克，远志 9 克。

第十六节　感染性多发性神经根炎

感染性多发性神经根炎，亦称格林—巴利综合征，是以对称性、驰缓性肢体麻痹为特点的神经根的炎性疾病。多由全身性病毒感染、细菌感染或中毒后引起。本病属中医"痿证"范畴。

【诊断要点】

1. 神经系统症状出现前约 2 周有前驱感染史，如上呼吸道感染、风疹、腮腺炎或腹泻等。

2. 早期症状是神经根刺激性疼痛、麻木，逐渐发展成所有感觉损伤，如痛觉、触觉、温度觉、位置觉和振动觉缺失。手足末端受累即呈手套、袜套样感觉缺失。重者有颅神经和呼吸肌麻痹，后者引起呼吸困难和呼吸衰竭。常有植物神经功能障碍症状，如多汗或少汗、肢体发凉、脸红、一过性尿潴留或失禁、便秘或腹泻。病程中常伴有腱反射消失或减弱、虚弱和肌肉萎缩。

3. Laboratory examinations reveal elevated leukocyte and erythrocyte sedimentation rate. Cerebrospinal fluid (CSF) changes are of value in making diagnosis. The protein in CSF becomes elevated but white cell connt in CSF is normal 1—2 weeks after the onset of clinical manifestation. This feature is called "isolation phenomenon of cell-protein" and can persist for several months till convalescence.

DIFFERENTIATION AND TREATMENT OF COMMON SYNDROMES

1. Obstruction of the Channels and Collaterals by Damp-heat

Main Symptoms and Signs: Flaccid paralysis of extremities, especially symmetrical paralysis of lower limbs, accompanied with heavy sensation of the body, oppressed feeling in the chest, dysphoria with smothery sensation, difficult diarrhea, scanty yellow urine, red tip and margin of the tongue with yellow and greasy fur, soft or soft and rapid pulse.

Therapeutic Principle: Removing pathogenic heat and dampness.

Recipe: Three Wonderful Drugs Powder with additional herbs.

atractylodes rhizome, *Rhizoma Atractylodis* 9g
phellodendron bark, *Cortex Phellodendri* 9g
achyranthes root, *Radix Achyranthis Bidentatae* 9g
coix seed, *Semen Coicis* 15g
seven-lobed yam, *Rhizoma Diosoreae Septemlobae* 9g
large-leaf gentian root, *Radix Gentianae Macrophyllae* 9g

All the above drugs are to be decocted in water for oral administration.

In the presence of impairment of *yin* by damp-heat, manifested as feverish sensation in the feet, and dry tongue, the following drugs should be added: rehmannia root (*Radix Rehmanniae*) 9g, scrophularia root (*Radix Scrophulariae*) 9g, and dendrobium (*Herba Dendrobii*) 9g.

3．实验室检查可见血液白细胞升高，血沉增快。脑脊液改变对诊断有帮助，在病程1～2周后脑脊液蛋白高而细胞数正常，称蛋白细胞分离现象，此现象可持续几个月至恢复期。

【辨证论治】

1．湿热阻络

主证：肢体瘫痪，肌肉松弛，尤以下肢对称性瘫痪为常见，伴有身体困重、胸闷烦热、大便不爽、尿少色黄，舌尖边红，苔黄腻，脉濡或濡数。

治则：清热利湿。

处方：三妙散加味。

苍术9克，黄柏9克，牛膝9克，苡仁15克，草薢9克，秦艽9克。水煎服。

若湿热伤阴，两足热甚，舌干者，加生地9克，玄参9克，石斛9克。

2. Deficiency of the Liver-*yin* and Kidney-*yin*

Main Symptoms and Signs: Long-standing malady with muscular atrophy, deformity of the limbs, aching and weakness of the back and loins, red tongue without fur, and thready and rapid pulse.

Therapeutic Principle: Nourishing and invigorating the liver-*yin* and kidney-*yin*.

Recipe: Modified *Huqian* Bolus.

phellodendron bark, *Cortex Phellodendri*   9g

tortoise plastron, *Palstrum Testudinis*   9g

anemarrhena rhizome, *Rhizoma Anemarrhenae*   6g

prepared rehmannia root, *Radix Rehmanniae Praeparata*   9g

tangerine peel, *Pericarpium Citrii Reticulatae*   6g

white peony root, *Radix Paeoniae Alba*   9g

cynomorium, *Herba Cynomorii*   9g

dried ginger, *Rhizoma Zizigiberis*   3g

antler glue, *Colla Cornu Cervi*   9g (melted alone)

dodder seed, *Semen Cuscutae*   12g

mulberry fruit, *Fructus Mori*   9g

All the above drugs are to be decocted in water for oral administration.

3. Deficiency of Both *Qi* and Blood

Main Symptoms and Signs:Pale complexion, lassitude, disinclination to talk due to deficiency of *qi*, abnormal stool, flaccidity of the limbs, no warm feeling of the face, pale tongue with thin and white fur, and slow and weak pulse.

Therapeutic Principle: Invigorating *qi* and nourishing blood.

Recipe: Modified Decoction of Eight Precious Ingredients.

dangshen, *Radix Codonopsis Pilosulae*   9g

astragalus root, *Radix Astragali seu Hedysari*   12g

parched white atractylodes rhizome, *Rhizoma Artactylodis Macrocephalae*   9g

poria, *Poria*   12g

2. 肝肾阴虚

主证：久病不愈，肌肉萎缩，肢体变形，腰脊酸软，舌红无苔，脉细数。

治则：补益肝肾。

处方：虎潜丸加减。

黄柏9克，龟板9克，知母6克，熟地9克，陈皮6克，白芍9克，锁阳9克，干姜3克，鹿角胶9克(烊化)，菟丝子12克，桑椹子9克。水煎服。

3. 气血两虚

主证：面色㿠白，精神不振，少气懒言，大便不调，肢体痿软，面无热感，舌质淡，舌苔薄白，脉迟无力。

治则：补气养血。

处方：八珍汤加味。

党参9克，黄芪12克，炒白术9克，茯苓12克，当归9

Chinese angelica root, *Radix Angelicae Sinensis*   9g

red peony root, *Radix Paeoniae Rubra*   9g

white peony root, *Radix Paeoniae Alba*   9g

chuanxiong rhizome, *Rhizoma Ligustrici Chuanxiong*   6g

prepared rehmannia root, *Radix Rehmanniae Praeparata* 9g

cinnamon twig, *Ramulus Cinnamomi*   6g

achyranthes root, *Radix Achyranthis Bidentatae*   9g

licorice root, *Radix Glycyrrhizae*   3g

chaenomeles fruit, *Fructus Chaenomelis*   9g

All the above drugs are to be decocted in water for oral administration.

In case of deficiency of the spleen-*yang*, marked by cold limbs and aversion to cold, the following drugs should be added: prepared aconite root (*Radix Aconiti Praeparata*) 9g, dodder seed (*Semen Cuscutae*) 9g, desertlving cistanche (*Herba Cistanchis*) 9g and epimedium (*Herba Epimedii*) 9g.

Section 17

Chickenpox

Chickenpox (or varicella) is a common infectious disease caused by herpes virus. It is characterized by the appearance of pimples, herpeses and crusts on the skin and mucous membranes and often accompanied with mild constitutional symptoms. In TCM, this disease belongs to the categories of *"shui dou"*, *"shui hua"*, *"shui chuang"* (chickenpox).

MAIN POINTS OF DIAGNOSIS

1. There may be a history of contact with the patients with varicella. The incubation period ranges from 11 to 21 days.

2. The premonitory symptoms precede the characteristic rash by 1–2 days with slight fever, anorexia and malaise. The spreading of the rash is on the trunk and scalp;

克，赤芍 9 克，白芍 9 克，川芎 6 克，熟地 9 克，桂枝 6 克，牛

膝 9 克，甘草 3 克，木瓜 9 克。水煎服。

若脾阳不足、畏寒肢冷者，加附子 9 克，菟丝子 9 克，肉苁

蓉 9 克，淫羊藿 9 克。

第十七节　水痘

水痘是由于疱疹病毒引起的一种常见传染病，以皮肤、粘膜

出现丘疹、疱疹和痂疹为特点，且常伴有轻度的全身症状。本病

属中医"水花"、"水疮"、"水痘"范畴。

【诊断要点】

1. 多有接触史，潜伏期 11～21 天。

2. 前驱期 1～2 天，很快出现皮疹，伴有发热、厌食、倦

怠等。皮疹的分布是以躯干和头部为主，口咽结膜也可发疹，皮

and the mucous membranes of mouth and pharynx may also be involved. The rash is characterized by papules or scarlatiniform or morbiliform rash at the initial stage, and immediately developes into clear, often oval, ''tear-drop'' vesicles on an erythematous base in different sizes, not umbilicate but easy to break. Then it becomes scabbed. When the scabs come off in 1 to 3 weeks, no cicatrices are left. Characteristically, at the crisis of the disease, papules, vesicles and crusts are present at the same time.

3. Cerebritis after varicella and fulminant purpura may occur in a few of severe cases, sometimes with bullous eruptions.

4. Laboratory examinations show normal white cell count or mild leukocytosis, and thrombocytopenia in the patients with purpura. Virus giant cell may be present in the scraping from the floors of fresh vesicles, and the virus may be isolated in a histiocyte culture.

DIFFERENTIATION AND TREATMENT OF COMMON SYNDROMES

1. Wind-heat Mixed with Dampness

Main Symptoms and Signs: Fever, mild cough, running nose, poor appetite, sparse and round chickenpoxes with ruddy base, lucid liquid contents and itching sensation, thin and white fur of the tongue, floating and rapid pulse, and purplish red superficial venule of the index finger.

Therapeutic Principle: Dispelling wind, clearing away heat, removing toxic substances and expelling dampness.

Recipe: Modified Powder of Lonicera and Forsythia.

honeysuckle flower, *Flos Lonicerae*   15g

forsythia fruit, *Fructus Forsythiae*   15g

pueraria root, *Radix Puerariae*   15g

poria, *Poria*   12g

arctium fruit, *Fructus Arctii*   9g

tale, *Talcum*   12g

cicada slough, *Periostracum Cidadae*   9g

疹的特点初为丘疹或猩红热麻疹样皮疹。很快变为基底红润的大小不一的泪滴样痘疹，一般不凹陷，易破溃，然后结痂，1～3周痂脱落不留斑痕。在本病的极期，丘疹、痘疹、痂疹同时存在。

3. 少数严重病例可发生水痘后脑炎、暴发性紫癜，也可有大疱性皮疹。

4. 实验室检查可见血液白细胞计数正常或轻度升高，有紫癜者血小板减少。新鲜疱疹刮片可有病毒巨细胞，组织细胞培养可分离出病毒。

【辨证论治】

1. 风热夹湿

主证：发热，轻微咳嗽，流涕，纳减，痘疹根盘红润，稀疏澈园，泡浆清净明亮，内含水液，并有瘙痒，苔薄白，脉浮数，指纹红紫。

治则：疏风清热，解毒祛湿。

处方：银翘散加减。

银花 15 克，连翘 15 克，葛根 15 克，茯苓 12 克，牛蒡子 9

spirodela, *Herba Spirodelae*   6g

seven-lobed yam, *Rhizoma Dioscoreae Septemlobae*   9g

All the above drugs are to be decocted in water for oral administration.

2. Intense Damp-heat in the Interior

Main Symptoms and Signs: High fever, severe thirst, dry mouth and teeth, red lips and face, lassitude, densely spreading chickenpoxes in dark purple colour with turbid and opaque liquid contents, in severe cases vesicles on the mucous membrane of the mouth, swelling and pain of the gum, dry stools, scanty dark urine, yellow, dry and thick fur of the tongue, full and rapid pulse or slippery and rapid pulse, and purple superficial venule of the index finger.

Therapeutic Principle: Removing pathogenic heat, cooling blood, removing toxic substances and dampness

Recipe: Supplemented Antiphlogistic Decoction and Modified Decoction for Clearing Away Stomach-heat and Toxic Substances.

honeysuckle flower, *Flos Lonicerae*   15g

forsythia fruit, *Fructus Forsythiae*   9g

arctium fruit, *Fructus Arctii*   9g

red peony root, *Radix Paeoniae Rubra*   9g

scutellaria root, *Radix Scutellariae*   9g

moutan bark, *Cortex Moutan Radicis*   9g

gypsum, *Gypsum Fibrosum* 24g (To be decocted prior to others)

dried rehmannia root, *Radix Rehmanniae*   9g

anemarrhena rhizome, *Rhizoma Anemarrhenae*   9g

arnebia root, *Radix Arnebiae*   6g

umbellate pore-fungus, *Polyporus Umbellatus*   9g

poria, *Poria*   9g

coix seed, *Semen Coicis*   12g

All the above drugs are to be decocted in water for oral administration.

克，滑石 12 克，蝉蜕 9 克，浮萍 6 克，萆薢 9 克。水煎服。

2. 湿热内盛

主证：高热，烦渴，口齿干燥，唇红面赤，神萎不振，痘疹稠

密，疹色紫暗，痘浆混浊不透亮，甚则口腔也见疱疹，并有齿龈

肿痛，大便干结，小便短赤，苔黄燥而厚，脉洪数或滑数，指纹

紫。

治则：清热凉血，解毒渗湿。

处方：加味消毒饮合清胃解毒汤加减。

金银花 15 克，连翘 9 克，牛蒡子 9 克，赤芍 9 克，黄芩 9

克，丹皮 9 克，生石膏 24 克（先煎），生地 9 克，知母 9 克，紫

草 6 克，猪苓 9 克，茯苓 9 克，苡仁 12 克。水煎服。

In case of fulminant purpura, add 1 gram of powder of rhinoceros horn (*Pulvis Cornus Rhinocerotis*) and 1.5 grams of powder of antelope's horn (*Pulvis Cornus Saigae*). The above two powders should be taken after being infused in the hot finished decoction.

Section 18

Epidemic Parotitis

Epidemic parotitis (or mumps) is defined as an acute, general and non-suppurative disease caused by mumps virus. Its characteristics are swelling and pain of the parotid gland. In TCM, this disease is categorized as "*za sai*" (mumps).

MAIN POINTS OF DIAGNOSIS

1. There is a history of contact with mumps patients. The incubation period ranges from 14—24 days.

2. The prodromal symptoms and signs may be manifested as fever, malaise, muscular aching pain, loss of appetite and headache.

3. The onset of illness is usually characterized by swelling in one or both parotid glands with pain and tenderness which is easily elicited by intake of sour foods. And redness and swelling are commonly noted on the orifice of the Stensen's duct without purulent excretion. The submandibular and sublingual glands may be involved. The course of disease can persist for 1—2 weeks.

4. A few cases may be present with meningitis, some with pancreatitis, nephritis and myocarditis. Elder children may have orchitis or ovaritis as a complication.

5. Laboratory examinations show normal white blood cell count, but elevated lymphocyte in count of classification, elevated serum and urine amylases in acute phase. The serum special complement fixation test may show four-fold higher titer

若为暴发性紫癜，加犀角粉1克，羚羊角粉1.5克（冲服）。

第十八节　流行性腮腺炎

流行性腮腺炎是流行性腮腺炎病毒引起的以腮腺炎为主的急性全身性非化脓性疾病，主要特点为腮腺肿胀和疼痛。中医称之为"痄腮"。

【诊断要点】

1. 有腮腺炎接触史，潜伏期14～24天。

2. 前驱期可有发热、倦怠、肌肉酸痛、食欲下降、头痛等症状。

3. 腮腺肿胀多为一侧或两侧，伴有疼痛、压痛，服酸性食物疼痛更明显。颊内腮腺管口红肿，无脓性分泌物。也可累及颌下腺及舌下腺。病程1～2周。

4. 少数病人可发生脑膜炎，年长儿可并发睾丸或卵巢炎，有的病人伴有胰腺炎、肾炎或心肌炎。

5. 实验室检查血液白细胞总数正常，但分类淋巴细胞偏高。急性期血清淀粉酶、尿淀粉酶可升高，恢复期血清补体结合

in convalescence.

DIFFERENTIATION AND TREATMENT OF COMMON SYNDROMES

1. Virulent Pathogen on Exterior

Main Symptoms and Signs: Aversion to cold, fever, headache, mild cough, aching pain of the parotid region, difficulty in chewing followed by swelling and pain at one or both sides of the parotid glands without definite margins, pale tongue with thin and white fur, and floating and rapid pulse.

Therapeutic Principle: Dispelling pathogenic wind and clearing away pathogenic heat, removing obstruction of other virulent pathogens and promoting subsidence of swelling.

Recipe: Modified Powder of Lonicera and Forsythia.

honeysuckle flower, *Flos Lonicerae*   15g
forsythia fruit, *Fructus Forsythiae*   9g
isatis root, *Radix Isatidis*   9g
prunella spike, *Spica Prunellae*   9g
platycodon root, *Radix Platycodi*   9g
peppermint, *Herba Menthae*   6g (To be decocted later than others)
arctium fruit, *Fructus Arctii*   6g
scutellaria root, *Radix Scutellariae*   9g
licorice root, *Radix Glycyrrhizae*   3g

All the above drugs are to be decocted in water for oral administration.

2. Accumulation of Toxic Heat

Main Symptoms and Signs: High fever, headache, restlessness, thirst, poor appetite or vomiting, general lassitude, swelling of the parotid glands with burning pain, red and swollen throat, difficulty in chewing and swallowing, dry stools, scanty dark urine, red tongue with thin, greasy and yellow fur, and slippery and rapid pulse.

Therapeutic Principle: Removing pathogenic heat and toxic substances, softening and resolving hard mass to induce

试验呈 4 倍升高。

【辨证论治】

1. 瘟毒在表

主证：畏寒，发热，头痛，轻咳，耳下腮部酸痛，咀嚼不便，继之一侧或两侧腮部肿胀疼痛，边缘不清，舌淡红，苔薄白，脉浮数。

治则：疏风清热，散结消肿。

处方：银翘散加减。

银花 15 克，连翘 9 克，板蓝根 9 克，夏枯草 9 克，桔梗 9 克，薄荷 6 克（后下），牛蒡子 6 克，黄芩 9 克，甘草 3 克。水煎服。

2. 热毒蕴结

主证：高热头痛，烦躁口渴，食欲不振，或伴呕吐，精神倦怠，腮部漫肿，灼热疼痛，咽喉红肿，吞咽、咀嚼不便，大便干结，小便短赤，舌质红，苔薄腻而黄，脉滑数。

治则：清热解毒，软坚消肿。

subsidence of swelling.

Recipe: Modified Universal Relief Decoction for Disinfection.

scutellaria root, *Radix Scutellariae*   9g

scrophularia root, *Radix Scrophulariae*   9g

arctium fruit, *Fructus Arctii*   9g

isatis root, *Radix Isatidis*   15g

batryticated silkworm, *Bombyx Batryticatus*   9g

platycodon root, *Radix Platycodi*   9g

peppermint, *Herba Menthae*   6g (To be decocted later than others)

prunella spike, *Spica Prunellae*   15g

dandelion herb, *Herba Taraxaci*   9g

All the above drugs are to be decocted in water for oral administration.

In case of intense heat, the following ingredients should be added: gypsum (*Gypsum Fibrosum*) 24g, isatis leaf (*Folium Isatidis*) 15g, moutan bark (*Cortex Moutan Radicis*) 9g, anemarrhena rhizome (*Rhizoma Anemarrhenae*) 9g, wild chrysanthemum flower (*Flos Chrysanthemi Indici*) 9g.   In case of hard and painful swelling of the parotid glands, add the following: oyster shell (*Concha ostreae*) 15g, japanese sea tangle (*Thallus Laminariae*) 9g, sargassum (*Sargassum*) 9g. For patients with swollen and painful testis, add the following drugs: bitter orange (*Fructus Aurantii*) 9g, litchi seed (*Semen Litchi*) 9g, gentian root, (*Radix Gentianae*) 9g, corydalis tuber (*Rhizoma Corydalis*) 9g, bupleurum root (*Radix Bupleuri*) 9g. For complication of meningitis, add batryticated silkworm (*Bobmyx Batryticatus*) 9g, scorpion (*Scorpio*) 9g, uncaria stem with hooks (*Ramulus Uncariae cum Uncis*) 12g, earthworm (*Lumbricus*) 9g.   In addition to the above drugs, add 1 gram of Purple Snowy Powder or one pill of Treasured Bolus which is to be taken after being infused in the finished decoction. In case of constipation, add 6 grams of rhubarb (*Radix et Rhizoma Rhei*) which is to be decocted later than other drugs.

处方：普济消毒饮加减。

黄芩9克，玄参9克，牛蒡子9克，板蓝根15克，僵蚕9

克，桔梗9克，薄荷6克（后下），夏枯草15克，蒲公英9克。水

煎服。

若热重者，加生石膏24克，大青叶15克，丹皮9克，知母

9克，野菊花9克；腮肿明显硬痛者，加牡蛎15克，昆布9克，

海藻9克；并发睾丸肿痛者，加枳壳9克，荔枝核9克，龙胆草

9克，延胡索9克，柴胡9克；并发脑膜炎者，加僵蚕9克，全

For individuals with frequent vomiting, add one gram of *Yu Shu* Powder which is to be taken after being infused in the finished decoction.

蝎9克，钩藤12克，地龙9克，并加用紫雪丹1克或至宝丹1丸冲服；大便秘结者，加大黄6克（后下）；呕吐频繁者，加玉枢丹1克冲服。

EDITOR S NOTES

The chief authors of the book are Zhang Enqin and Zhang Jidong. The TCM part of Chapter One (internal medicine) was written by Zhang Jidong and Zhang Enqin, and the Western medicine part by Liu Zhigang. The TCM part of Chapter Two (obstetrics and gynecology) was written by Jin Weixin and Lian Fang, and the Western medicine part by Sun Shusan. In Chapter Three (pediatrics), the TCM part was written by Guo Xiaoyue and the Western medicine part by Wang Jizhou. All the manuscripts were revised and partially re-written by Zhang Enqin, Zhang Jidong and Dang Yi.

The chief translator of the whole book is Zuo Lianjun, who concretely bore responsibility for the English version of internal medicine, the Western part of which was equally contributed to by Liu Zhigang, Zuo Lianjun and Zhang Enqin. The TCM part of obstetrics and gynecology was translated by Zhang Yuxi, Gao Yan and Zhang Enqin; Gao Yan and Zhang Enqin also shared the work together with Sun Shusan for the translation of its Western part. The English version of the TCM part in pediatrics was provided with by Wang Ziwei, Zhang Yuxi, Gao Yan and Zhang Enqin; Gao Yan and Zhang Enqin also assisted Wang Jizhou in translating its Western part.

All the Chinese manuscripts were checked and approved by Wei Jiwu, with obstetrics and gynecology by Lu Tongjie, and pediatrics by Zhang Qiwen.

The English versions were read and revised mainly by Li Yulin, Zhang Enqin and Wen Hongrui, with some contents being retranslated. Moreover, the translation of internal medicine part was checked by Peng Wancheng; the translation of obstetrics and gynecology was examined by Xiao Gong and Zou Ling; pediatrics part by Yu Wenping and Dong Xuemei. All the translated manuscripts were in the end revised and approved by Li Yulin, Zhang Enqin, Wen Hongrui, Wang Jizhou, Zuo Lianjun, Yin Hongan and Nie Qingxi.

编 写 说 明

本册主要由张恩勤和张继东编写。其中，内科中医部分由张继东和张恩勤撰稿，西医部分由刘治刚撰稿；妇科中医部分由金维新和连方撰稿，西医部分由孙树三撰稿；儿科中医部分由郭孝月撰稿，西医部分由王济周撰稿。最后，全书由张恩勤、张继东和党毅修定，部分重写。

左连君担任本册主译。其中，内科中医部分由左连君翻译，西医部分由刘治刚、左连君和张恩勤翻译；妇科中医部分由张玉玺、高燕和张恩勤翻译，西医部分由高燕、孙树三和张恩勤翻译；儿科中医部分由王紫薇、张玉玺、高艳和张恩勤翻译，西医部分由王济周、高燕和张恩勤翻译。

本册全部中文稿由隗继武主审，妇科部分曾经吕同杰审阅，儿科部分曾经张奇文审阅。

李玉麟、张恩勤和温洪瑞担任本册英文主审并改译部分内容。此外，英文稿内科部分尚经彭万程审校，妇科部分曾经肖珙、邹玲审校，儿科曾经于文平和董雪梅审校。最后，全部英文译稿由李玉麟、张恩勤、温洪瑞、王济周、左连君、尹洪安和聂庆喜审校。

PUBLISHED ALONG WITH THE LIBRARY ARE:

- Rare Chinese Materia Medica
- Highly Efficacious Chinese Patent Medicines

《英汉对照实用中医文库》配套书

- 中国名贵药材
- 中国名优中成药

PUBLISHING HOUSE OF SHANGHAI COLLEGE OF TRADITIONAL
CHINESE MEDICINE
530 Lingling Road, Shanghai, China

Chinic of Traditional Chinese Medicine (I) in A Practical English-Chinese
Library of TCM
Editor-in-Chief Dr. Zhang Enqin

ISBN 7 - 81010 - 129 - 3/ R·128

Printed in Shanghai No. 3 Printing Works.

英汉对照实用中医文库
中医临床各科(上册)
主编 张恩勤
上海中医药大学出版社出版发行
(上海零陵路 530 号 邮政编码 200032)
新华书店上海发行所经销
江苏句容市排印厂印刷
开本 850×1168 1/32 印张 14.625 插页 6 字数 367 千字
1990 年 5 月第 1 版 2001 年 10 月第 7 次印刷
印数 15 501—17 500
ISBN 7 - 81010 - 129 - 3/R · 128
定价: 18.90 元